Simply Happy

ELECTRIC
PRESSURE COOKING

Sandy Clifton

Simply Happy Foodie LLC

In loving memory of my Nana

Watching you cook, standing only as tall as your apron strings

I was inspired

To mom

A true foodie with a loving heart

I miss you

Contents

Home Cooki... Secrets ...

KIRKLAND

We may live without friends,
we may live without books,
but civilized man cannot live
without cooks!

... DAWN

1/3 - 3/4 C. Brown Sugar
1/2 C. Flour
1/2 C. Rolled Oats
3/4 tsp Cinnamon
3/4 tsp Nutmeg
3/4 tsp. Clove
1/3 C. Butter, softened

OPTIONAL:
1 C. soaked Raisins
1 C. Walnuts

APPLES

2 c. diced o...
1/2 c. ch. onion
...ch. garlic, ch
1/2 c. butter
1/2 c. toast crumbs
4 c. toast crumbs...
1 tblspn. Sage
2 tsp salt
1/2 " Pepper

Crisp (apple, cherry...)
1/2 c. white sugar, 1 c...
1/2 c. whole wheat fl...
1/2 c. margarine
2 tsp. lemon extra...
— combine a...
Put fruit in grea...
" few tblspns. ju...
cover with above m...
*use cinnamon with...

... MUFFINS
... Boiling water
... milk or assorted milk
... 1 C. wheat germ
1 T. vanilla
1 t. cinnamon
options:
carrots
raisins
walnuts
Banana
apple

LAKE-VUE GARDEN...

Recipe from the
kitchen of Mom

COWBOY COOKIE
Kissin sweetie out
Cookin out

1 C. Brown Sugar
1 C. eggs
2 C. oatmeal
1 tsp. vanilla
1 6oz. pkg. Chips

2 C. flour
1 tsp. Soda
1/2 tsp. Salt
1/2 tsp. baking powder
1 C. Shortening

Salmon Ked...
15 2 oz. B.B. Red S...
Cooked eggs (...
cooked rice
shredded cheddar che...
bouillon cube - crumble...
(water)
Cayenne pepper...
parsley
Slices
sprigs
... Slice
as...

Mushroom~2...
Olive oil (or...
4 tbs. flour...
1 small onion, mixed
1 lb. fresh mushrooms
sliced or thick
1/4 tsp. garlic, salt
1/8 tsp. pepper
... sour cream
... clove chopped garlic

Kiss me cake
yields 24
... cut
} Put through
} food chopper, alter-
nately
mix w/above:
... flour

COCONUT...

1 can Eas...
1 8 1/2 #...
7 oz. co...

...chicken
...16 rolls.
375-20 min.
2 pkg. Pillsbury
crescent rolls
1 pkg. seasoned
stuffing mix
... butter. Add 1 c...
... stuffing mix ...
... and pepper to taste.
... Use 1 large tb...
... in 1 c. end of roll.
Dip in melted
butter and then into crush...
stuffing crumbs.
Sauce - 1 c. broth
(chicken)
1 can creamed/
chicken soup...
mix and ...
heat...
rolls.

(...n Hilliard)

1/4 # margerine NOT BUTTER
10 oz. pecans - chop fine

3/4 square paraffin wax

20 oz. chocolate chips

...milk and margerine well. Slowly add the rest of ingredients
...well mixed. Form into balls ...t aside for about an
...In a double boiler or ... ...lt chocolate and add
...ck paraffin (shaved)... ...paraffin until thin
...h to dip candy (u... ...n waxed paper to
...den. Decorate ...

...chopped garlic
...f fresh herbs, rosemary...
...oregano (more or less to taste)

...45
1 pkg...
chopp...
...oves cru...

... c. chopped green
... c. shredded...
...ly grape jell...
baking mix...
... + half w...

INTRODUCTION

Growing up around some really great cooks, I always wanted to make delicious meals like they did. My mom, Nana, and my friend/boss Ruth were the three cooks who influenced me the most as a young foodie.

I was raised on comfort foods, a lot from the South. However, one thing that was always fun (and funny) in our house was the weird foods.

My mom made such strange concoctions as peanut butter soup, which I just couldn't eat. She brought home pickled pigs feet, Limburger cheese, and sausages that I could not pronounce! We tried many foods!

But those feel-good comfort foods, with a few healthy options sprinkled in, is what I'm about these days. Especially if they can be made more simply. That's where the electric pressure cooker comes in!

I used a stove top pressure cooker when I was younger, and could not believe it when I found my first electric pressure cooker. That was a game changer for me.

These modern day "multi-cookers" with their sauté function, timers, and safety features are exploding in popularity. And no wonder, as they are so easy to use, and that one-pot aspect is awesome!

Many people have told me that the electric pressure cooker has rekindled their passion for cooking! It sure rekindled mine!

A few years ago, after getting my first electric pressure cooker, I started making my old favorite recipes from my youth. Nana's Beef Barley Vegetable Soup, Cranberry Sauce, and even Porcupine Meatballs!

I reworked many recipes to work in "The Pot" as I call it, and have created lots of new recipes as well. I even started a recipe blog, and three years later ended up with more than enough recipes for a cookbook!

This cookbook is all about making delicious recipes in your electric pressure cooker. Nothing too strange, (except maybe Dill Pickle Soup!) a great variety, and lots of flavor. From delicious dinners, easy side dishes, tasty desserts, to hot sauce and yogurt! There is something for practically everyone in this collection of my tried and true electric pressure cooker recipes.

From beginners to more advanced pressure cooker cooks, this cookbook will be a great addition to your kitchen library!

Besides being a wife and a mom to the best boys (and fur babies), I was a photographer for over 25 years, and a graphic designer. I've also been a dishwasher, waitress, a cook, and a retail sales manager. Cooking has always been in there!

Cooking is about more than just cooking. Does that make sense? How many of us were fed with love, and have wonderful memories built around food? It doesn't matter if you are using a modern day appliance or a camp fire. If you can feed your family a successful meal, it is a win for you, but becomes a memory for those you feed. Soon they will be asking you to make their favorite dish again and again! I think that is more than just liking how it tastes. YOU made it for them, and that is special!

Thank you for purchasing my cookbook! I hope this is the first of many more to come. I have lots of ideas! Visit me for more easy and delicious recipes at: www.SimplyHappyFoodie.com

Common Pressure Cooking Terminology

There are some unique terms and acronyms in pressure cooking. Here are some common ones.

6-6-6, 5-5-5, etc. Times for making hard cooked "boiled" eggs. 6 minutes under pressure, 6 minutes of natural pressure release, then 6 minutes in an ice water bath. Or 5-5-5 is 5 minutes, etc.

ANTI-BLOCK SHIELD Removable perforated metal cover that is over the steam release valve (on the underside of the lid). This helps "shield" the valve (Pin) from getting debris in it that could clog it during the building of and releasing of the pressure.

BURN MESSAGE If the contents of the pot are too thick, with not enough thin liquid to bring the pot to pressure, often the food will burn on the inside bottom of the pot. Also, there could be scorched food on the bottom of the pot, often due to not deglazing the pot before setting it to the pressure function.

CONDENSATION COLLECTOR/CUP A plastic 'cup' that attaches to the outside back of the Instant Pot. Designed to catch liquid that drips into the channel that the lid sits in, as well as condensation coming off of the valve and steam release knob housing area.

CONTROLLED QUICK RELEASE A controlled quick release means you release the steam in short bursts, then longer bursts, until you can be sure none of the sauce/liquid spews out of the vent with the steam from the intense pressure. Then fully open the vent and let it go.

DEGLAZE The method of getting the browned food bits off of the bottom of the pot after browning meat. Usually after browning the meat it is best to use broth or water, onion, etc to deglaze by sautéing it while scraping the bottom of the pot with a wooden spoon, etc.

EPC Electric Pressure Cooker

HP High Pressure (all models except the Lux line have both High and Low Pressure).

INNER LINER The actual cooking pot (stainless steel or ceramic coated), that goes into the pressure cooker base. This is where the liquids and other ingredients are placed and cooked in.

IP Instant Pot (Instant Pot® is a brand name of electric pressure cooker)

KEEP WARM The mode that the pot will automatically switch to when the cooking cycle has ended (unless disabled). In the IP brand, the actual warming doesn't begin until the temperature of the contents drops to 140° (F). The display will show L0 00, then as the time goes by it will count up in minutes, L0 01, L0 02, L0 03, etc., to show how long the pot has been Naturally Releasing Pressure.

LP Low Pressure.

NR / NPR Natural Release / Natural Pressure Release. When the cooking cycle ends, don't do anything to the pot. The steam will slowly dissipate on its own as the pot cools. Often this is attached to a time, such as a 15 minute NPR. The unit will show L0 00 after the cooking timer has elapsed, then it will begin counting UP in minutes, (i.e. L0 01, L0 02, etc.), to show how long it has been Naturally Releasing Pressure. The KEEP WARM light will be lit, indicating it has switched to that mode.

PC Pressure Cooker

PIN Also known as the Float Valve. A silver (or red on the 8 quart) metal pin in the lid that pops up when the pot is at pressure, and also locks the lid for safety. Conversely, the pin drops and unlocks when all of the pressure is out of the pot, making it safe to open the lid. NEVER try to force open the lid if the pin is up or locking it. Either manually release the pressure first by turning the steam release knob to Venting, or just wait for the pot to naturally release the pressure, and for the pin to drop.

PIP COOKING A method of cooking food that you don't want watered down (such as a quiche or cheesecake). So you put it in a separate cooking dish and set it atop the trivet/rack within the inner liner. Water goes directly in the inner pot, then the trivet/rack, then the dish of food sits on the trivet (never directly on the bottom of the inner liner). Resume pressure cooking as normal. PIP method usually requires a longer cook time than if the food was cooked directly in the inner liner.

QR / QPR Quick Release / Quick Pressure Release. When the cooking cycle ends, immediately turn the steam release knob to the Venting position to release the pressure as quickly as possible. Use for foods with a quicker cook time, such as veggies. Never QR a full pot of soup, most meats, or starchy foods. However, with pastas you need to QR, but don't do it all at once. Instead, do it in small bursts so the starch and liquid won't spew out of the Steam Release Knob and all over your kitchen!

SAUTÉ MODE This is the setting that is used to brown meat, sauté onions, etc. This function can also be used to warm up the liquid in the pot as the dish is being prepared, as the hot liquid will allow the pot to come to pressure faster (only for select recipes).

SEAL / SILICONE RING The "gasket" that provides the seal so the pot can come to pressure. A silicone sealing ring that is seated in the underside of the pressure cooker lid.

SEALING The pot is coming to or is at pressure, and is "sealed" so no steam escapes. Also the position on the lid that you turn the Steam Release Knob to so the pot can come to pressure.

SLING A long (approx. 28" x 3" wide) strip of (folded, for strength) aluminum foil (used to remove pans when using the Pot-In-Pot (PIP) method of cooking, such as a cheesecake). The sling ends, much like the stork carrying the baby bundle, becomes the handles.

STEAM RELEASE KNOB The wobbly knob that has holes in the top that the steam passes through as the pot is building pressure (turned to Sealing), and as the pot is releasing pressure (turned to Venting). On the ULTRA Instant Pot® model, there is a separate button on the lid to push to release the steam, but it still passes through the wobbly knob.

TRIVET / RACK The metal rack (often with collapsible handles) that sits on the bottom of the inner liner to keep food off of the bottom of the pot and out of the liquid. Also used in PIP cooking to set the dish on.

VENTING The process of steam leaving the pressure cooker through the Steam Release Knob. The position that you turn the Steam Release Knob to so that the steam can be released through the Steam Vent.

WATER TEST An initial test run of a Pressure Cooker using only water, to confirm it works properly. It also helps new users start to get comfortable with their pot.

YOGURT BUTTON A button that activates the boil, and Incubation functions in the yogurt making process (not all pressure cooker models have this).

The "Burn" Warning

Even though it is a safety feature, getting the dreaded "BURN" warning message on your electric pressure cooker is not fun. Here's what that warning message is all about.

The Instant Pot® brand of electric pressure cooker has a safety function called the BURN warning. It lets you know the food in the pot has scorched on the bottom, or is in danger of burning. Other brands may have a similar feature.

Why? It all comes down to what I call "thin liquid." Pressure cooking works by liquid boiling and making steam, which builds up inside the pot where it can't escape, and pressure is built. When there is full pressure, the cook time that you set will start to count down until it reaches zero and the cook time will have finished.

But what if the pressure never builds and you get a BURN warning? That happens because what you are trying to pressure cook is too thick, without enough thin liquid (water, broth, etc.) to create the necessary steam to build the pressure.

It will just sit there, with your food on the hottest part of the pot, the heating element, and it will burn if you don't catch it in time.

So what can you do to avoid the dreaded "BURN" warning?

Make sure the recipe you are cooking has enough thin liquid to create the necessary steam. Most tested recipes will have this factored in, however, some ingredients vary, so it's good to stay with your pot until it comes to pressure and the pin in the lid pops up.

After browning meat, be sure to deglaze the pot by scraping up all browned bits (called fond) from the bottom of the pot before adding the rest of the ingredients. Use a bit of water, broth, etc. to help loosen it, if needed.

For some recipes, you can keep the sauté setting on while you add the remaining ingredients (stirring occasionally so nothing gets stuck on the bottom of the pot), and then closing the lid, sealing it, and canceling the sauté setting. Then you can press the Pressure Cook or Manual button and input the cook time, and the pot will come to pressure a little faster as the ingredients are hot. That helps avoid the "BURN" warning in some situations (I do this with chili).

Another way to avoid the "BURN" warning is by layering your ingredients in the pot. Many of my recipes are layered to keep foods that are susceptible to scorching off of the bottom of the pot. For example, tomatoes, tomato sauce, cream based soups, etc. Then I don't stir them. This keeps the thinner liquid on the bottom, and by not stirring it you are not thickening the liquid. It works very well!

What do you do if you do get the BURN warning?

First, check to see if the pot has come to pressure. It is rare to have a pot that reaches full pressure also burn. But if that happens, you will need to clear the warning before moving on. If the pin in the lid has popped up, you will not be able to open it until you depressurize it. Turn the steam release knob to Venting and let out the pressure.

Then open the lid and stick a wooden spoon down in there and scrape the bottom of the pot. Add a little hot water or hot broth to increase the amount of thin liquid. About 1/4-1/2 cup to start. Then close the lid, seal it, and reset the cook time and start it again.

It's the same method for a pot that has not reached pressure, but has no "BURN" warning. Just open it up and do the same thing.

I always tell people to *stay with your pressure cooker until it has reached pressure*.

Don't just set it and walk away. That way you can get in there and save your food from being ruined. You can walk away after the pot has reached pressure and the timer starts to count down.

Sometimes you will need to cook the food using the Pot-In-Pot method. Cakes, bread pudding, lasagna, cheesecakes, etc. all need to be cooked Pot-In-Pot.

Pot-In-Pot Cooking

Also called PIP. The pressure cooker needs thin liquid, such as water or broth, to make steam that builds up and creates the pressure needed to pressure cook the food.

Pot-In-Pot is a method of cooking food that you don't want watered down (such as a quiche, lasagna or cheesecake). Or for foods that are too thick to build pressure (not enough thin liquid).

Soups do well, but a pot of bread pudding will absorb the liquid and there won't be any left to build steam and pressure. Then you will get the dreaded "BURN" message. Nobody wants that!

So you put the food in a separate cooking dish (preferably stainless, or an oven safe pan) and set it on the trivet/rack within the inner liner, where it is suspended above the water (*See Photo*).

The water goes directly into the inner pot, then the trivet/rack is set in the pot, then the pan of food sits on the trivet (never directly on the bottom of the inner liner). Cover it or not, depends on what's cooking.

Resume pressure cooking as normal. The PIP method usually requires a longer cook time than if the food was cooked directly in the inner liner.

Breakfast
eggs and more

Egg Loaf

Prep Time: 10 mins. | Cook Time: 6 mins. | Total Time: 30 mins.

Ingredients

1 1/2 cups Water (for the pressure cooker) Use 2 cups for an 8+ qt. size

8 - 10 Eggs (if using more eggs, increase cook time by 2 to 5 minutes)

Tools

6" or 7" Metal Pan or Oven Safe Dish* (See Note)

Metal Trivet/Rack with Handles (or without, but you will need oven or silicone mitts)

Instructions

1. Add the water to the inner liner pot.

2. Spray the oven safe dish with nonstick cooking spray.

3. Crack the eggs into the oven safe dish.

4. Set the dish on the trivet/rack, grasp the handles, and carefully lower it into the pressure cooker's inner liner pot.

5. Close the lid and set the steam release knob to the Sealing position.

6. Press the Pressure Cook/Manual button, then the +/- button to select 6 minutes if using a 7" pan* (7 minutes if using 6" pan). High Pressure.

7. When the cooking cycle has finished, let the pot sit undisturbed for 5 minute natural release. Then turn the knob to Venting to release the remaining pressure.

8. When the pin in the lid drops down, open the lid. If the eggs didn't fully cook in the time given, just put the lid back on and let them finish cooking in the residual heat. Or cook a few more minutes.

9. Use oven mitts (I like the silicone ones) to grasp the handles and carefully lift the pan out of the pressure cooker.

10. Invert the pan onto a cutting board to remove the egg loaf, and let the egg loaf cool.

11. Chop the egg loaf up to desired size and use in egg salad, potato salad, or other recipes!

Recipe Note
Cooking time may be longer with thicker glass dishes, and with smaller diameter dishes, as the egg loaf will be thicker.

Boiled Eggs

Prep Time: 5 mins. | **Cook Time: 5 hrs.** | **Total Time: 18 mins.**

Ingredients

1-2 cups Water, for the pressure cooker (use 2 cups for the 8 quart)

1 or more Eggs

Large bowl filled with ice cubes and water, for the ice bath

A set of tongs is very useful to get hot eggs out of the pressure cooker

Instructions

2-8-5 Method

1. Add 1 to 2 cups of water to the pot, and set the trivet/rack in the pot.

2. Place the eggs on the rack. It is okay to stack the eggs on top of each other.

3. Place the lid on the pressure cooker and lock in place. Turn the steam release knob to the Sealing position.

4. Press the Pressure Cook/Manual button. Then the +/- button to choose 2 minutes.

5. After the cook time ends, let the pot sit undisturbed and Naturally Release pressure for 8 minutes. Then manually release remaining pressure by turning the steam release knob to the Venting position.

6. After the pin in the lid drops down, immediately remove eggs to the bowl of ice water, using tongs. Let them sit in the water for at least 5 minutes before removing.

5-5-5 Method

7. Add 1 to 2 cups of water to the pot, and set the trivet/rack in the pot.

8. Place the eggs on the rack. It is okay to stack the eggs on top of each other.

9. Place the lid on the pressure cooker and lock in place. Turn the steam release knob to the Sealing position.

10. Press the Pressure Cook/ Manual button. Then the +/- button to choose 5 minutes.

11. After the cook time ends, let the pot sit undisturbed and Naturally Release pressure for 5 minutes. Then manually release remaining pressure by turning the steam release knob to the Venting position.

12. After the pin in the lid drops down, immediately remove eggs to the bowl of ice water, using tongs. Let them sit in the water for at least 5 minutes before removing.

Steel Cut Oats

2 Servings | Prep Time: 2 mins. | Cook Time: 25 mins. | Total Time: 27 mins.

Ingredients

1/2 cup Steel Cut Oats*
Regular, not the Quick type.

1 1/4 cup Water

1 tsp Butter

Pinch of Salt

Optional - Any or All of These

1 tsp Vanilla

1/4 cup Raisins

1 Chopped Apple

1/2 tsp Cinnamon

Instructions

Cooking Directly in Inner Liner

1. Add all ingredients to the pot and stir.

2. Close the lid and set the steam release knob to the Sealing position.

3. Press the Pressure Cook/Manual button, then the +/- button to select 10 minutes.

4. After cooking cycle ends, let naturally release pressure for 10 minutes. Let sit for 12 minutes for a bit creamier result.

5. Top with your favorite toppings: berries, nuts, brown sugar, maple syrup, honey, milk, etc.

Pot-in-Pot Method

(For making a single serving, or when there's not enough liquid to bring the pot to pressure)

1. Add oatmeal, water, salt, and any other ingredients to an oven safe stainless steel or baking dish/bowl (I have a 1 quart size oven safe round baking dish that I use, and sometimes I use a 1 quart stainless steel bowl).

2. Add one cup of water to the Instant Pot's inner liner.

3. Place the trivet or rack that came with the pot in the inner liner (if you don't have that one, use a rack with short legs as the bowl may sit up too high).

4. Set the bowl of oats on the rack (You may need to use a sling to do this if your dish or rack doesn't have handles). Leave bowl uncovered.

5. Close the lid of the Instant Pot and set the steam release knob to the Sealing position.

6. Press the Manual/Pressure Cook button, then the +/- button to select 10 minutes.

7. After cook cycle ends, let naturally release pressure for 10 minutes. 12 minutes for a creamier result.

Recipe Notes

*This recipe is easy to double: 1 cup of dry steel cut oats to 2 1/2 cups of water, 2 tsp butter. Same cooking time as the recipe states. Once you test a batch out, you will have a good idea of what will work for you and the type of oats you are making.
Your results may vary due to the age of your oats, your altitude, and the model of pressure cooker you have.

French Toast Casserole

Ingredients

8 cups Bread*, lg cubed
(Brioche, French, etc, dry)
1/4 cup Chopped Pecans

Egg Custard

5 Eggs
2 1/2 Tbsp Sugar
1 1/2 cup Whole Milk
1 tsp Vanilla

1 tsp Cinnamon
1/4 tsp Orange Zest (optional)
1/8 tsp Salt

Topping

4 Tbsp Melted Unsalted Butter
2 1/2 Tbsp Brown Sugar
3/4 tsp Cinnamon
pinch of salt

Tools

- Metal Trivet/ Rack, for pan to sit on
- 7"x3" or 6"x3" metal cake pan
- Cooking Spray
- Foil

Instructions

1. Spray or butter a 1.5 to 2 quart oven safe dish. Set aside (I use a 7"x3" stainless pan).
2. Place the bread cubes and pecans in a mixing bowl. Toss to mix. Set aside.
3. In a separate bowl, whisk together eggs, sugar, milk, vanilla, cinnamon, orange zest, and salt. Whisk very well.
4. Pour the custard mixture over the bread and lightly mix to coat all of the bread cubes. Transfer to the prepared pan. Gently press on the bread to help it absorb the custard.

Make the Topping

5. Melt the butter in the microwave. Mix in the brown sugar cinnamon, and salt.
6. Drizzle over the bread evenly.
7. Cover the pan tightly with foil that is sprayed with cooking spray. Crimp the edges well.

Cook the French Toast Casserole

8. Put 1 1/2 cups of water into the inner liner of the pressure cooker 2 cups for the 8 qt).
9. Using the handles of the trivet/rack, carefully lower the pan into the pressure cooker pot. It will need to sit on the rack, not directly on the bottom of the pot.
10. Place the lid on the pot and set the Steam Release Knob to Sealing.
11. Press the Manual/ Pressure Cook button, then the +/- button to select 30 minutes. High Pressure.
12. When cook cycle ends, let pot naturally release pressure for 15 minutes. Then manually release any remaining pressure by turning the knob to Venting.
13. When the pin in the lid drops open the lid and carefully remove the pan, using the rack's handles.
14. Remove the foil. Turn on broiler to 400° F.
15. When broiler is hot, place the pan on the middle oven rack. Brown the top to your liking. Keep an eye on it!
16. Serve with warm maple syrup, and powdered sugar.

Recipe Note: *Be sure to use stale/ day old bread so it doesn't get mushy.

Breakfast Burritos

Ingredients

Egg Base

8 Eggs

1/2 cup Half and Half

1/2 tsp Coarse Salt (or 1/4 tsp table salt)

1/4 tsp Pepper

1/2 tsp Garlic Powder (optional)

Any Combination of These

2 Tbsp Chives, chopped

1/4 cup Onion, diced

1 cup Ham, cooked, cubed (or 3/4 cup sausage or bacon)

3/4 cup Cheese, shredded (I use sharp cheddar)

1/2 cup Red Bell Pepper*, diced

1 cup Potato**, diced

To Serve

Flour Tortillas (any size you like for burritos)

Your favorite garnishes

Tools

• Metal Trivet/ Rack, for pan to sit on

• 6" or 7" diameter cake pan for egg mixture

• Cooking Spray

• Foil

Instructions

1. Pour 1 1/2 cups of water into the inner liner pot of the pressure cooker.

2. Spray the egg pan you will be cooking the casserole in with cooking spray.

3. Add the eggs and half and half to a mixing bowl and whisk them really well.

4. Add the remaining ingredients and stir them in. Pour the mixture into the egg pan and cover it tightly with foil.

5. Set the pan on the trivet and lower into the pressure cooker. Place the lid on the pot and close the steam release knob by turning it to the Sealing position.

6. Press the Pressure Cook/Manual button, then the +/- button to select 30 minutes.

7. When the cook time is finished, do a Quick Release of the steam/pressure by turning the steam release knob to the Venting position. *If you used lots of extras in your egg mixture, let it sit for 5 minutes before releasing the pressure.*

8. Carefully remove the pan from the pot, and carefully remove the foil. You can either use a spatula to get the servings from the pan, or use a spoon to gently stir and break up the mixture for making the breakfast burritos.

9. Wrap some egg mixture in a flour tortilla, and wrap them in foil if not eating immediately. They keep in the fridge for 3-5 days, and you can freeze them for up to 2 months

Recipe Note
* Using bell peppers are delicious, but note that they release a little water, which you can drain out of the eggs when done.

Southwest Biscuit Egg Bake

Ingredients

6-7 Eggs

1/2 cup Milk

2 Tbsp Chives, Fresh or Dried, chopped

1/2 cup Salsa

1 Tbsp Canned Green Chiles, or more to taste

1/4 tsp Salt

Pinch of Pepper

1/4 tsp Garlic Powder

1/4 tsp Oregano

3 Refrigerated Buttermilk Biscuits (3 individual biscuits, not 3 cans) (use buttermilk)

1 cup Cheddar Cheese, shredded

Optional

1/2 cup Chopped Bacon or Crumbled Sausage

Garnish

Sour Cream, Salsa

Instructions

1. In a mixing bowl, beat together the eggs and milk.

2. Add the chives, salsa, green chiles, salt, pepper, garlic powder, and oregano. Whisk well to combine. Set aside.

3. Generously spray a 6 cup bundt pan*. Tear the biscuits into 4 pieces each and arrange on the bottom and a little ways up the sides, if you can. Don't flatten them.

4. Pour in half of the egg mixture, then sprinkle the cheese over the eggs/biscuits.

5. Pour in the remaining egg mixture and jiggle the pan a bit to get the mixture to settle in.

6. Spray a piece of foil and loosely cover the bundt pan. Just crimp it around the edges.

7. Put 1 1/2 cups of water into the inner liner of the pressure cooker.

8. Use a the trivet/rack with long handles to put the bundt pan into the pot.

9. Close the lid. Turn the Steam Release knob to Sealing. Select the Steam setting (High) and use the +/- to select 15 minutes.

10. When the cook cycle ends, let the pot sit undisturbed for 15 minute natural release.

11. Turning the Steam Release knob to Venting to manually release remaining pressure.

12. Carefully gather up the ends of the sling and lift the pan from the pot to a cooling rack.

13. Take off the foil and test for doneness. If it is very jiggly, cook it another 4 minutes.

14. Serve, garnished with a dollop of sour cream and top with salsa.

Egg Bites

Yield: 7 Bites | Prep Time: 15 mins. | Cook Time: 8 mins. | Total Time: 36 mins.

Ingredients

1 cup Water (for the pressure cooker)

4 Eggs

1/2 cup Cottage Cheese

1/4 cup Heavy Cream

2/3 cup Gruyère Cheese, shredded (or emmental, Jarlsberg, etc.)

1/8 tsp Pepper

2 Tbsp Chives, minced

1 tsp Hot Sauce (optional)

3 slices Cooked Thick Sliced Bacon, chopped (or 1/2 cup Cooked Crumbled Sausage)

Optional Add-Ins*- (only use 1/2 cup total)

1/2 cup Broccoli (cooked, chopped small)

1/2 cup Tomatoes, deseeded, diced

1/2 cup Roasted Red Bell Peppers, diced

1/2 cup Mushrooms, diced

Instructions

1. Spray the silicone egg bites mold with the cooking spray. Set aside. Pour 1 cup of water into the inner stainless liner of the pot.

2. Add the eggs, cottage cheese, heavy cream, Gruyère cheese, pepper, and chives to the blender and blend for 2 minutes on medium speed, or until the mixture is light and fully incorporated.

3. Fill the egg bite mold openings halfway with the egg mixture. Then add 3/4 of the chopped bacon or other add-ins and gently press them in. Continue filling with the egg mixture until gone, and top with remaining bacon, and press it in. Each opening can be filled right to the top.

4. Set the full egg bites mold on the trivet and carefully lift it in the pot. Loosely cover with foil.

5. Close the lid of the pot and set the steam release knob to the Sealing position.

6. Press the Pressure Cook/Manual button then press the +/- button to select 8 minutes.

7. When the cook cycle is finished, let the pot sit undisturbed for 8 minute natural release. Then turn the steam release knob to Venting to release the remaining pressure.

8. When the pin in the lid drops down , open the lid and use silicone mitts to grasp the trivet handles and carefully remove the egg bites mold. Remove the foil. Set aside to rest for about 4 minutes. They may be puffed up quite a bit, but they will go back down. They will come out of the mold easier if they cool a little.

9. Serve warm as is, or with any garnish you like. I like hot sauce and a bit of sour cream.

Tools You'll Need
Cooking Spray · 1 Egg Bites Silicone Mold · 6 or 8 qt Pressure Cooker Trivet/Rack w/long handles
Blender / Immersion Blender · Foil

No Boil Yogurt

6-8 Servings | Prep Time: 5 mins. | Cook Time: 8 hrs. | Total Time: 8 hrs. 5 mins.

Ingredients

52 oz ULTRA Pasteurized Milk*, divided

2 Tbsp Yogurt Starter (use fresh yogurt with live, active cultures)

1 14 oz can Sweetened Condensed Milk (optional)

1 cup Heavy Cream (optional)

2-3 tsp Vanilla (optional)

Instructions

1. Pour 1/4 of the milk into the inner liner (stainless pot).

2. Add 2 heaping Tablespoons of the yogurt starter (I like to use Greek). Whisk to incorporate completely.

3. Add sweetened condensed milk (if using), and whisk very well to completely dissolve and combine.

4. Add the heavy cream and vanilla (if using) and the remainder of the milk, and whisk well to combine.

5. Place a lid on the pot. You can use the IP lid (on venting), a glass lid, silicone, a dinner plate, etc., since no pressure will be building.

6. Press the **Yogurt** button, and set time, using the +/- button, for either 8 hours (default) or 9 hours (for a more tart flavor). Longer incubation time equals a tarter yogurt.

7. When incubation time is finished, cover the inner liner with a paper towel, with a lid over that, and put it in the fridge to chill. *Do not stir until chilled*, for best results.

8. Remove from fridge and stir. Yogurt should be nice and thick. If you want it even thicker, you will need to strain it.

9. To strain, place coffee filters in a strainer set over a bowl and pour the yogurt in the lined strainer (or use a yogurt strainer). Place in fridge and strain until desired thickness is achieved.

Recipe Note
*Be sure to use *Ultra Pasteurized* milk or it won't work!*

Soups & Stews
to warm your soul

Beef Barley Vegetable Soup

8 Servings | Prep Time: 20 mins. | Cook Time: 35 mins. | Total Time: 1 hr. 20 mins.

Ingredients

2 Tbsp Olive Oil (or vegetable oil)

1 lb Chuck Roast, or stew meat (cut in 1 1/2"-2" bite size chunks)

1 Yellow Onion, chopped

2 Carrots, chopped

1 cup Celery, chopped

3 Garlic Cloves, minced

1 -14.5 oz Can of Diced Tomatoes (w/juice) or 2 cups of fresh tomatoes, chopped

1 lb Potatoes, chopped (about 2 cups)

8 oz Cabbage, chopped (about 2 cups)

2 Bay Leaves,

4 Sprigs of Fresh Thyme (or 3/4 tsp dried)

1 1/2 tsp Salt

1 tsp Black Pepper

1/3 cup Pearl Barley, rinsed

3 cups Beef or Chicken Broth, low sodium

Instructions

1. Turn on the Sauté setting. When the pot is hot, add the oil.

2. Add the beef chunks and spread out in one layer on bottom of pot. Let cook for a couple of minutes to develop a crust.

3. Turn the beef over and brown on other side.

4. Add the onion, carrots, and celery. Stir and scrape up brown bits on the bottom of the pot.

5. Add the garlic, stir and cook for just a minute.

6. Add the tomatoes w/juice, potatoes, cabbage, bay leaves, thyme, salt, pepper, barley, and broth. Stir.

7. Put the lid on the pot and set the steam release knob to the Sealing position.

8. Cancel the Sauté setting. Press the Manual or Pressure Cook button and then the +/- button to select 20 minutes. (This is a pretty full pot so it will take several minutes to come to pressure)

9. When cooking cycle ends, let the pot naturally release pressure for 15 minutes. Manually release the remaining pressure by turning the steam release knob to Venting. Open the lid when the pin in the lid drops.

10. Stir the soup. Discard bay leaves.

11. Serve immediately.

Recipe Note
If you are Gluten-Free, leave out the barley.

Hamburger Soup

6 -8 Servings | Prep Time: 15 mins. | Cook Time: 15 mins. | Total Time: 55 mins.

Ingredients

1 lb Lean Ground Beef (90% lean)

1 Onion, diced

3 lg Carrots, chopped large (or a small bag of baby carrots)

4 med Potatoes, chopped large

3 cups Beef Broth

1 packet Onion Soup Mix

1 Bay Leaf

2 tsp Italian Seasoning

2 tsp Garlic Powder (or 3 cloves garlic, minced)

1 tsp Salt

1/2 tsp Pepper

1 Tbsp Worcestershire Sauce

1 (14 oz) can Diced Tomatoes (w/juice)

1 (6 oz) can Tomato Paste

3 cups Frozen Mixed Vegetables (with corn, green beans, etc.)

Instructions

1. Turn the pot on to Sauté setting. Add the ground beef and the onions. Cook, stirring occasionally, until the meat is cooked. Don't break up the meat completely, as some bigger chunks are nice in the soup.

2. Add the chopped carrots, potatoes, beef broth, onion soup mix, bay leaf, Italian seasoning, garlic powder, salt, pepper, and Worcestershire sauce. Stir.

3. Dump the can of diced tomatoes and tomato paste on top and **do not stir**.

4. Close the lid and set the steam release knob to the Sealing position.

5. Cancel the Sauté setting. Press the Pressure Cook/Manual button then the +/- button to select 7 minutes. High pressure. It will take several minutes to come to pressure.

6. When the cooking cycle is finished, let the pot sit undisturbed for 15 minute natural release. Then carefully, in short bursts at first, manually release the remaining pressure by turning the steam release knob to Venting.

7. Stir the soup well to incorporate the tomato paste.

8. Then stir in the frozen vegetables and let sit for a few minutes before serving. The veggies will cook in the heat of the hot soup.

9. Serve hot with some nice crusty bread!

Stuffed Pepper Soup

6 Servings | Prep Time: 15 mins. | Cook Time: 14 mins. | Total Time: 55 mins.

Ingredients

1 lb Lean Ground Beef or Turkey

1 Bay Leaf

1/3 cup Celery, diced

1 Onion, diced

4 cloves Garlic, minced

1 Tbsp Paprika (sweet)

1 tsp Italian Seasoning

1/4 tsp Thyme Leaves, dried

1/2 tsp Oregano

1 1/4 tsp Salt

1/2 tsp Pepper

3 Bell Peppers (2 green and 1 red), Chopped

4 cups Beef Broth, low sodium (use 5 if you like it soupier)

1 Tbsp Worcestershire Sauce

3/4 cup Long Grain White Rice, rinsed, uncooked

1 (14 oz) can Diced Tomatoes, with juice

1 (14 oz) can Tomato Sauce

Instructions

1. Before you start to cook, get all of your ingredients prepped first. Chop and measure everything.

2. Turn on the pot's Sauté function. When it is hot, add the ground beef and the bay leaf. Cook for 5 minutes, stirring occasionally.

3. Add the celery and onion, and cook for 3 minutes.

4. Add the garlic and spices and cook for 30 seconds.

5. Add the peppers, and stir.

6. Pour in the beef broth, Worcestershire, and the rice. Stir. Put a lid on for a few minutes to let the broth heat up (I use the glass lid, or the PC's lid on venting).

7. Add in the tomato sauce and diced tomatoes & their juice, but **do not stir**.

8. Close the lid and set the steam the release knob to Sealing.

9. Cancel the Sauté function and set the Pressure Cook/Manual setting. Use the +/- button to choose 4 minutes. High Pressure.

10. After the cook cycle has ended, let the pot sit undisturbed for 10 minute Natural Release. Then turn the steam release knob to Venting and release the remaining pressure.

11. When the pin in the lid drops down, carefully open the lid and stir the soup. Taste and adjust salt.

12. Serve immediately.

Albondigas Soup

Ingredients

MEATBALL MIXTURE
1 Egg
1 tsp Garlic Powder
1/4 tsp Onion Powder
1 tsp Kosher Salt
1/4 tsp Pepper
1/2 tsp Cumin
1/4 tsp Cayenne Pepper
2 tsp Oregano
1 lb Ground Beef, Turkey, Sausage, or a combination of any two
1 Tbsp Chopped Cilantro Leaves
3 Tbsp Fresh Spearmint Leaves, minced
1/2 cup Cooked Rice, al dente

SOUP
2 Tbsp Olive Oil
1 lg Onion, chopped
1/4 cup Celery, diced
4 cloves Garlic, minced fine
1 (14 oz can) Diced Tomatoes, w/juice
6 cups Chicken or Beef Broth, low sodium
1 cup Water
2 med Carrots, chopped
1 lg Potato, peeled & cubed
1 Bay Leaf
1 tsp Cumin
2 tsp Oregano
1/2 tsp Salt
1/2 tsp Pepper
1 sm Zucchini, diced
1 cup Corn Kernels (frozen is fine)
1 (15 oz) can Cut Green Beans, drained

GARNISH
Cilantro, Sour Cream, Avocado

Instructions

Make the Meatball Mixture

1. Whisk the egg in a mixing bowl, then add the garlic powder, onion powder, salt, pepper, cumin, cayenne pepper, and oregano. Mix well.
2. Add the meat, cilantro leaves, spearmint leaves, and rice. Mix together until well combined. Set aside.

Make the Soup

3. Turn on the Sauté setting. When hot, add the oil, then the onion and celery. Sauté until softened.
4. Add the garlic, stirring constantly, and cook about 20-30 seconds.
5. Add the can of diced tomatoes and stir.
6. Add the broth, water, carrots, potato, bay leaf, cumin, oregano, salt, and pepper. Bring to a simmer.
7. Using a 1 Tbsp scoop or spoon, scoop out one meatball at a time and gently add to the simmering soup. After all of the meatballs are in the soup, close the lid and seal it.
8. Turn off the Sauté setting. Then press the Pressure Cook/Manual button, then the +/- button to select 4 minutes. High Pressure.
9. When the cook cycle has finished, turn the steam release knob to Venting to Release the pressure. Watch it to be sure no broth spurts out with the steam. If it does, close the vent, release in bursts.
10. When the pin in the lid drops back down, open the lid and very carefully stir the soup.
11. Add the zucchini, corn, and green beans. Let the residual heat soften the vegetables before serving.

Chicken and Dumplings

Ingredients

2 tsp Olive Oil

1 Tbsp Butter

1 sm Onion, diced

1 Bay Leaf

1 cup Chopped Carrots (2 or 3 carrots)

1 cup Chopped Celery (2 ribs)

3 lg cloves Garlic, minced (1 Tbsp)

1 tsp Salt (more to taste)

1/2 tsp Pepper

1/4 tsp Poultry Seasoning

1/2 tsp Sage, dried

4 sprigs Thyme (2 tsp leaves or 1/2 tsp dried)

1 (4") sprig Rosemary (2 tsp leaves, minced, 1 tsp dried & crushed)

4 cups Chicken Broth, low sodium

1 lg Potato, chopped

1 1/2 lbs Chicken Thighs, and/or Breasts, cut in slightly larger than bite sized pieces

TO FINISH

1 cup Frozen Peas (or mixed vegetables)

1/2 cup Heavy Cream

QUICK DUMPLINGS

6 jumbo Canned Buttermilk Refrigerator Biscuits (16 oz pkg contains 8)

HOMEMADE DUMPLINGS

1 1/2 cups Flour

3/4 tsp Salt

2 tsp Baking Powder

3 Tbsp Shortening (such as Crisco)

3/4 cup Whole Milk (or buttermilk)

1/4 cup Chives, finely chopped (fresh or dried)

Instructions

Choose the Type of Dumplings You Want to Make, and Prepare Them:

Canned Dumplings

For the canned biscuits, roll each one flat and cut into 6 equal slices. Do this to all 6 and set aside in a bowl. You can also just cut them in fourths and not roll them flat.

Homemade Dumplings

1. Put all ingredients except milk in a bowl and use a pastry cutter or a fork to mix well and incorporate the shortening into the dry ingredients.

2. Stir the milk (and chives, if using) in and combine, until just moistened. Set aside.

Prepare the Chicken and Sauce

1. Turn the pressure cooker on to the Sauté setting. When the pot is hot, add the olive oil and the butter. Then add the onion and bay leaf. Stir.

2. Add the carrot, celery, and garlic. Cook for a few minutes, scraping the bottom of the pot to get up any brown bits (deglaze).

3. Add salt, pepper, poultry seasoning, sage, thyme, and rosemary. Cook for a few seconds.
4. Stir in chicken broth. Put a glass lid on the pot and let the contents warm up to a simmer.
5. Add the potato and chicken. Stir.

Add the Dumplings

6. **Homemade:** Drop heaping teaspoonfuls into the broth (not too large as they need to cook through, and they expand).
7. **Biscuits**: Add the sliced biscuits into the broth and gently stir to distribute them.
8. Cancel the Sauté function.
9. Place the lid on the pot and lock in place. Turn the steam release knob to the sealing position.
10. Press the Pressure Cook/Manual button, then the +/- button to select 7 minutes. High Pressure.
11. When the cook cycle is finished, do a *Controlled Quick Release* of the pressure. When the pin in the lid drops down, open the lid and stir in the frozen peas/ mixed vegetables.
12. Stir in the heavy cream (if using) and put the glass lid on to let it sit and heat through.
13. Taste and adjust salt, if needed, and serve hot.

White Chicken Chili

6-8 Servings | Prep Time: 10 mins. | Cook Time: 25 mins. | Total Time: 50 mins.

Ingredients

3 Tbsp Olive Oil

1 Yellow Onion, chopped

2 ribs Celery, diced

4 Chicken Breasts raw, cubed (or a rotisserie chicken, deboned & shredded)

4 cloves Garlic, pressed or minced

1 Tbsp Cumin

2 tsp Chili Powder

1 tsp Mexican Oregano (or regular)

2 tsp Coriander

1/2 tsp Black Pepper

1 tsp Kosher Salt

1 (7 oz) can Diced Green Chiles (w/juice)

1 (14.5 oz) can Diced Tomatoes (w/juice)

1 1/2 cups Salsa Verde

3 (14.5 oz) cans White Beans, drained

4 cups Chicken Broth(low sodium)

1/2 cup Cilantro, rinsed and chopped

1 Tbsp Fresh Lime Juice

To Finish

5 (6") White Corn Tortillas, sliced in strips (helps thicken & gives good flavor)

1 cup Sour Cream

Garnishes

Diced Jalapeño, Sour Cream, Avocado

Crushed Tortilla Chips, Shredded Cheese

Cilantro Leaves

Instructions

1. Turn pot on to Sauté. When hot, add the oil.
2. Add onion and celery and stir. Cook until starting to get translucent.
3. Add chicken and stir. Cook, stirring occasionally, until white. Don't cook until completely done. If using pre-cooked chicken, just add it and move forward.
4. Add the garlic and spices. Stir.
5. Add the can of chiles, diced tomatoes, salsa verde, and beans. Stir.
6. Add the chicken broth, cilantro, and lime juice. Stir.
7. Place the lid on the Instant Pot turn the steam release knob to the Sealing position.
8. Press the Cancel/Keep Warm button to turn off the sauté function.
9. Press the Manual/Pressure Cook button, then the +/- button to choose 10 minutes. High pressure.
10. When cook cycle ends, let the pot sit undisturbed to for 15 minute natural release.
11. Turn the steam release knob to Venting to manually release the remaining pressure, very carefully, and gradually (I use a wooden spoon and tap it slightly open, then closed a few times until I'm sure the soup won't spew out of the vent).
12. When the pin in the lid drops, open the lid. Stir, taste, and adjust salt, if desired.

To Finish

13. Slice up white corn tortillas and add to the chili. Stir and let them soak up the liquid and they will break apart and give the chili a nice masa corn flavor. Then stir in the sour cream.
14. Serve with your favorite garnishes.

Chicken Noodle Soup

8 Servings | Prep Time: 20 mins. | Cook Time: 35 mins. | Total Time: 1 hr. 35 mins.

Ingredients

2 Tbsp Olive Oil

1 Tbsp Butter

1 large Onion, chopped

2 Bay Leaves

5 - 7 cloves Garlic, pressed or minced

1 1/2 cups Celery, chopped

3 Carrots, chopped (about 1 1/2 cups)

1 Turnip, chopped (optional)

1 Parsnip, peeled and chopped (optional)

3 tsp Rubbed Sage, dry

4 sprigs Fresh Thyme, (or 1/2 tsp dried)

2 (4") sprigs Fresh Rosemary

1 - 2 tsp Kosher Salt (or more to taste)

1/2 tsp Pepper

7 cups Water, divided

2 Tbsp Soy Sauce

3 - 4 lb Whole Chicken (or bone-in parts)

8 oz Wide Egg Noodles uncooked (3 cups)

Instructions

1. Turn on the Sauté function. When pot is hot, add the oil and butter.
2. Add onions, and bay leaf. Cook until vegetables are tender, stirring occasionally.
3. Add the celery and carrots (also turnip and parsnip, if using), and 1 cup of the water. Stir and scrape the bottom of the pot.
4. Add the sage, thyme, rosemary, salt, and pepper. Stir.
5. Add the garlic and cook for 30 seconds, stirring constantly, then pour in 4 cups of the water and add the soy sauce. Stir.
6. Add the chicken to the pot breast side up. Then pour in another 2 cups of the water, but don't use all of it if it gets too full (You can add more at the end).
7. Place the lid on the pot and set the steam release knob to Sealing.
8. Cancel the Sauté function. Press the Pressure Cook/Manual button, then press the +/- button to select 25 minutes.
9. When the cook cycle ends, let the pot naturally release pressure for 10 minutes. Then manually release the remaining pressure in bursts, by turning the knob to Venting. This is a full pot, so do a controlled Quick Release.
10. When the pin in the lid drops down, open the lid and stir the soup. Very carefully take out the chicken with tongs and a large spoon and place it in a large bowl to cool down a little before you shred it. Remove bay leaves and discard.
11. Turn on the Sauté function again and add the noodles to the pot. Cook for 5-8 minutes, or until noodles are cooked to your liking.
12. Meanwhile, shred and debone the chicken. Set aside.
13. Cancel the Sauté function. Add the chicken back into the soup and stir. At this point you can add another cup of water if you want more broth. Taste and adjust salt, if needed.
14. Serve with some warm, crusty bread!

Taco Soup

Ingredients

1-2 lbs Ground Beef or Turkey use a little oil for browning turkey

1 packet Taco Seasoning Mix (or try my Easy Taco Seasoning recipe)

1 tsp Garlic Powder

1/2 tsp Onion Powder

1/2 tsp Oregano

1/2 tsp Salt

1/2 tsp Pepper

1 packet Ranch Dressing Mix (optional)

1 (10 oz) can Tomatoes w/Green Chiles

1 (7 oz) can Mild Diced Green Chiles, w/juice

4 cups Chicken Broth, low sodium

1 (14 oz) can Black Beans, rinsed & drained

1 (14 oz) can Garbanzo Beans, rinsed & drained

1 (14 oz) can Red Kidney or Pinto Beans, rinsed & drained

1 (14 oz) can Diced Tomatoes, with juice

TO FINISH

4 -5" Corn Tortillas, cut in thin strips (optional, but adds a nice masa flavor)

1 cup Frozen Corn (or 1 can of corn, drained)

GARNISHES

Sour Cream, Tortilla Chips

Cheddar or Monterey Jack Cheese,

Avocado, Red Onion, Jalapeño

Instructions

1. Turn the pressure cooker on to the Sauté setting. Add the meat (add a little oil if using turkey). Cook for a few minutes.

2. Add the taco seasoning, garlic powder, onion powder, oregano, salt, and pepper. Continue cooking, stirring occasionally, until meat is cooked.

3. Add the Ranch packet, if using, tomatoes w/green chiles, mild green chiles, and chicken broth. Stir, and place a glass lid on the pot to help the broth heat up faster. Once the broth is at a slow simmer, add all of the beans and stir well.

4. Add the can of diced tomatoes, but don't stir. Place the lid on the pot and lock in place. Turn the steam release knob to the Sealing position.

5. Cancel the Sauté setting, then press the Pressure Cook/Manual button, then the +/- button to choose 6 minutes. The pot will take several minutes to build up pressure.

6. When the cooking cycle has finished, let the pot sit undisturbed for 15 minutes. Then do a controlled release of the pressure by turning the knob towards the Venting position in short bursts. When you are sure that no soup will spew out with the steam, open fully.

7. When the pin in the lid drops down, you can open the lid facing away from you. Give the soup a stir, carefully as there could be some hot steam pockets in there.

8. Taste and adjust salt, if needed, then add the tortillas and the corn. Stir well and let sit for a few minutes, stirring occasionally to help dissolve some of the tortillas.

9. Serve with any of the garnishes you like!

Sweet Potato Quinoa Chicken Chili

10 Servings | Prep Time: 15 mins. | Cook Time: 13 mins. | Total Time: 40 mins.

Ingredients

2 Tbsp Olive Oil

1 lg Onion, chopped

1 Bay Leaf

1 rib Celery, chopped

4 cloves Garlic, minced

2 Tbsp Chili Powder

1 Tbsp Cumin

2 tsp Oregano

1 tsp Salt

1/2 tsp Pepper

1 tsp Smoked Paprika

1 (14 oz) can Diced Tomatoes, w/juice

2 cups Chicken Broth, low sodium

1 1/2 lbs Boneless/Skinless Chicken Thighs, frozen or fresh

2/3 cup Quinoa, rinsed very well

2 (15 oz) cans Black Beans, drained & rinsed

1 1/2-2 lbs Sweet Potato, (about 3 lg) peeled and cut in 1.5"-2" cubes

Instructions

1. Prepare all of the vegetables, measure out the broth, drain and rinse the beans, rinse the quinoa, and gather all of the ingredients together.

2. Turn on the Sauté setting. When hot, add the oil, onion, and bay leaf. Cook, stirring occasionally, for a few minutes.

3. Add the celery and stir. Cook for a couple of minutes.

4. Add the garlic and stir. Then add the chili powder, cumin, oregano, salt, pepper, smoked paprika, and diced tomatoes. Stir.

5. Add the chicken broth and the chicken thighs. If they are frozen, place a glass lid on the pot and let the contents heat up before proceeding. If fresh, move to the next step.

6. Add the quinoa and black beans. Stir.

7. Add the sweet potatoes on top and gently press them down into the mixture. They don't have to be covered, they will cook down.

8. Close the lid and set the steam release knob to the Sealing position.

9. Press the Pressure Cook/Manual button, then the +/- button to select 4 minutes. High Pressure.

10. When the cook cycle has finished, turn off the pot and let it sit undisturbed for 7 minute natural release. Then turn the steam release knob to Venting to release remaining pressure.

11. When the pin in the lid drops back down, open the lid. Discard the bay leaf.

12. Remove the chicken thighs to a plate and shred them using two forks. Then add them back to the pot. Gently stir the chili. The sweet potatoes will break down the more you stir the chili, thickening it.

13. Garnish with your favorite chili toppings, or serve as is.

Wild Rice Soup with Chicken

8 Servings | Prep Time: 25 mins. | Cook Time: 35 mins. | Total Time: 1 hr. 20 mins.

Ingredients

5 slices Bacon, chopped

1 med Onion, chopped

2 lg Carrots, chopped (2 cups)

3 ribs Celery, chopped (2 cups)

2 Tbsp Butter

1 Bay Leaf

1/2 tsp Thyme, dried

3 lg cloves Garlic, pressed or minced

4 cups Chicken Broth, low sodium

8 oz Mushrooms, sliced

1 sprig Rosemary, fresh

1 cup Wild Rice, rinsed

1 1/2 cups Heavy Cream, divided in half

2 tsp Kosher Salt (or 1 1/2 tsp table salt)

1/2 tsp Pepper

2 Chicken Breasts, uncut (skinless/boneless)

TO FINISH

1/4 cup Flour

3/4 cup Heavy Cream (from the divided heavy cream above)

Instructions

1. Turn the pot to Sauté. Add the bacon and cook, stirring occasionally, until mostly done. If you use a leaner bacon, leave the fat in. If there is more that 1 Tbsp of fat, spoon it out, leaving 1 Tbsp.

2. Add the onion, carrots, and celery. Stir and cook a couple of minutes.

3. Add the butter, bay leaf, and thyme. Cook for a couple of minutes.

4. Add the garlic and stir it in, cooking for 1 minute.

5. Add the broth, mushrooms, rosemary, and rice. Stir.

6. Add 3/4 cup of heavy cream, salt, and pepper, then stir (if you want to use milk, add after pressure cooking as it can curdle. Heavy cream or half and half tolerate pressure cooking).

7. Add the chicken breasts, and submerge them in the broth.

8. Put the lid on the pot and set the steam release knob to the Sealing position. Then cancel the Sauté setting. Press the Pressure Cook/Manual button, then press the +/- button to select 35 minutes. High pressure.

9. When the cooking cycle is finished, let the pot sit undisturbed for 15 minute Natural Release. Then release the remaining pressure, slowly, using a controlled Quick Release (Open the valve a little at a time to be sure no soup is going to spew out along with the steam).

10. When the pin in the lid drops down, open it up and carefully remove the chicken to a bowl.

11. Mix the flour and remaining 3/4 cup of heavy cream together very well. Stir into the hot soup.

12. Shred the chicken and add it back into the soup. Let sit for a few minutes to thicken.

13. Serve hot. Even better the next day!

Lemon Chicken Orzo Soup

6-8 Servings | Prep Time: 20 mins. | Cook Time: 13 mins. | Total Time: 43 mins.

Ingredients

2 Tbsp Olive Oil

1 Onion, chopped (~1 cup)

1-2 stalks Celery, chopped (about 1/2 cup)

2 Carrots, chopped (~1 cup)

3 cloves Garlic, minced

2 Chicken Thighs or Breasts, skinless/boneless (cut in larger than bite sized pieces)

1 sprig Fresh Rosemary (about 1 1/2 tsp chopped leaves)

1/2 tsp Kosher Salt (or 1/4 tsp table salt) or to taste

1/4 tsp Pepper

5 cups Chicken Broth, low sodium

1 tsp Lemon Zest

1/2 cup Orzo Pasta, uncooked

AFTER PRESSURE COOKING

1/4 cup Lemon Juice, fresh

2-3 cups Baby Spinach Leaves

GARNISH

Grated Parmesan Cheese

Lemon Wedges, Fresh Parsley

Instructions

1. Have the ingredients prepped before you start cooking the soup. Veggies chopped, etc.
2. Turn pot on to the sauté setting. When the pot is hot add the olive oil. Then add the onions and cook, stirring occasionally, until turning translucent.
3. Add the celery, carrots, and garlic and cook, stirring constantly, for about 20 seconds.
4. Add the chicken, rosemary, salt, pepper, broth, lemon zest, and orzo pasta. Stir.
5. Place the lid on and set the steam release knob to the Sealing position.
6. Press the Pressure Cook/Manual button, then the +/- button to select 3 minutes.
7. When the cook time is finished, do a Controlled Quick Release of the steam/pressure. Release the steam in short bursts, then longer bursts, until you are sure none of the soup spews out of the vent with the steam from the intense pressure. Then fully open the vent.
8. When the pin in the lid drops down, open it and add half of the lemon juice and the spinach leaves. Taste and adjust salt, if needed, and add the remaining lemon juice if you want. I tell people to use half in case they think it's too lemony. I like the full amount, but you may not.
9. Serve hot with some bread, lemon wedges, parmesan, or whatever you like.

Creamy Chicken Gnocchi Soup

8 Servings | Prep Time: 18 mins. | Cook Time: 17 mins. | Total Time: 55 mins.

Ingredients

6 slices Thick Bacon, chopped

2 Tbsps Butter

1 Onion, chopped

3 lg Carrots, chopped

1 Bay Leaf

2 ribs Celery, chopped

6 cloves Garlic, minced

1 - 5" sprig Fresh Rosemary

1 tsp Basil, dried

1/2 tsp Thyme, dried

1/4 tsp Poultry Seasoning

2 tsp Italian Seasoning

1/2 tsp Kosher Salt

1/2 tsp Pepper

4 cups Chicken Broth, low sodium

3 Chicken Breasts, boneless/skinless

16 oz Gnocchi (refrigerated, frozen, or from the dry pasta aisle)

1/2 cup Parmesan Cheese, grated

5 oz Baby Spinach, fresh

1 cup Heavy Cream

Instructions

1. Turn on the Sauté function and add the chopped bacon. Cook until mostly done.
2. Add the butter, onion, carrot, celery, and bay leaf. Cook, stirring occasionally, for 5 minutes or until onions are just starting to turn translucent.
3. Add the rosemary, basil, thyme, poultry seasoning, Italian seasoning, salt, pepper, and the garlic. Cook for 30 seconds, stirring frequently.
4. Add the chicken broth. Stir, then add in the chicken breasts.
5. Put the lid on and Set the steam release knob to the Sealing position. Cancel the sauté function.
6. Press the Pressure Cook/Manual button, and then the +/- button to select 9 minutes. High pressure. It will take several minutes to come to pressure.
7. When cooking cycle has ended, let the pot sit undisturbed for 10 minute natural release.
8. Turn the steam release knob to Venting (in short bursts until you are sure no soup spews out of the vent with the steam) to let remaining pressure out. When the pin in the lid drops down, open the lid.
9. Remove the chicken breasts to a bowl and discard the bay leaf.
10. Turn on the sauté function again. Add the gnocchi and stir. Place the glass lid, if you have one, on the pot. If you use the pressure cooker's lid, make sure it is turned to Venting.
11. Cook the gnocchi until it floats to the top. Just a few minutes.
12. Meanwhile, shred the chicken breasts.
13. Turn off the pot. Add the parmesan cheese and stir.
14. Add the chicken back in, and the spinach and heavy cream. Stir.
15. Serve hot.

Bone Broth

2-4 Quarts | Prep Time: 5 mins. | Cook Time: 4 hrs. | Total Time: 4 hrs. 35 mins.

Ingredients

Bones* (any kind, previously cooked)

Water** (enough to just cover bones)

2 tsp Kosher Salt

1 tsp Black Pepper

1 Large Yellow Onion, cut in quarters or eighths to fit in pot

5 cloves Garlic, smashed

2 Bay Leaves

OTHER OPTIONS

1-2 Tbsp Apple Cider Vinegar***

2 Carrots, cut in large pieces

1 Rib Celery, cut in large pieces

Herbs, whatever you like

2 inches Fresh Ginger, chopped

Instructions

1. Put all of the ingredients into the inner liner of your Instant Pot.

2. **Add enough water to just cover the bones.

3. Close the lid, set steam release knob to the Sealing position.

4. Press the Manual/Pressure Cook button, then the +/- button until you get to 240 minutes. That's 4 hours. If your pot only goes up to 120, just add another 120 after the first 120 minute cooking cycle ends.

5. After the cook cycle ends, let the pot naturally release pressure for at least 1 hour. You can let it NPR longer if you want, or very carefully do a manual pressure release after the hour.

6. Allow to cool, or if you can't wait, very carefully remove bones from the pot using a slotted spoon or a stainless steel spider.

7. Strain the remaining contents of the pot and put the bone broth into mason jars or other sealable containers. You might notice sediment on the bottom, and that's perfectly fine. If you want a clearer broth, strain again using a finer mesh or coffee filters (I never do this as I like the rich flavor the stuff has!).

Recipe Notes
*You will want to fill pot at least halfway with bones.
**Watch that you don't go over the manufacturer's recommendation for amount of liquid. I go below the max fill line. Please use caution!
***Not absolutely necessary, some say it helps break down the bones.

Ham Hock and Bean Soup

8 Servings | Prep Time: 15 mins. | Cook Time: 35 mins. | Total Time: 1 hr. 20 mins.

Ingredients

1 1/2 lbs Ham Hock (or a meaty ham bone) (I use one large ham hock)

1 lb Navy Beans* (dry, or soaked for 2 hours)

6 cups Broth or Water (low sodium) chicken or pork

1 lg Yellow Onion, chopped

3 Ribs Celery, chopped

3 Carrots, chopped (chop larger pieces if you want firmer veggies, as they will be soft)

4 Cloves Garlic, finely minced

2 Bay Leaves

3 sprigs Fresh Thyme (or 1/4 tsp dried)

1/3 cup Fresh Flat Leaf Parsley, chopped

1/2 tsp Kosher Salt

1/2 tsp Black Pepper

Instructions

1. Add all ingredients to the inner liner of the pot. Stir (Make sure the beans are fully submerged so you don't get any crunchy ones).

2. Put the lid on, and set the steam release knob to the Sealing position.

3. Press the Pressure Cook / Manual button, then the +/- button to choose 45 minutes.

4. When the cooking cycle ends, turn off the pot and let it naturally release pressure for 20 minutes.

5. Turn the steam release knob to Venting to release the remaining pressure manually, using short bursts at first to make sure the soup won't spew out of the steam release knob. When all steam is out of the pot, and the pin in the lid drops, open the lid and stir the soup.

6. Serve hot with some nice bread or rolls.

Recipe Notes
If you soak your beans for 2 hours use 40 minutes for this recipe.
If you don't soak your beans, use 45 minutes and add more time if you need to.
Old beans may need more cook time.

Zuppa Toscana

8-10 Servings | Prep Time: 20 mins. | Cook Time: 25 mins. | Total Time: 1 hr. 5 mins.

Ingredients

3 Strips of Thick Smoky Bacon, chopped

2 lbs Bulk Hot Italian Sausage (use 1/2 hot and 1/2 mild if you don't like much spice)

1 lg Onion, chopped

1 tsp Oregano, dried

5 Cloves of Garlic, pressed or minced

5 med Potatoes, halved & sliced 1/4" thick

6 cups Chicken Broth, low sodium

1 bunch of Kale chopped, ribs removed

1 1/2 cups Heavy Cream

Optional Substitute for the Kale

1 pkg Frozen Chopped Spinach (thawed) or fresh Baby Spinach

Instructions

1. Turn on the Sauté setting, and add the chopped bacon. Cook, stirring occasionally, until the bacon renders out most of its fat. Remove and set aside.

2. Add the sausage and brown it, stirring a few times. More brown means more flavor!

3. Spoon out all but 2 tsp of the fat (enough to cook the onions).

4. Add the onions and the oregano. Stir.

5. When the onions start to turn translucent, add the garlic and stir.

6. Pour in the broth, stirring, and make sure you scrape the bottom of the pot to get up any brown bits (deglaze).

7. Add the potatoes, and the bacon back in.

8. Check to make sure the contents don't go over the Max Fill line marked on the inner liner.

9. Cancel Sauté setting. Close the lid, set the steam release knob to Sealing.

10. Press the Manual/Pressure Cook button, then the +/- button to select 5 minutes (High Pressure). The pot will take several minutes to come to pressure.

11. After cooking cycle ends, allow a 10 minute NPR (Natural Pressure Release).

12. Do a controlled Quick Release for the rest of the steam, and when the pin in the lid drops, open the lid.

13. Add in the kale, (or thawed spinach, if using) and stir well. Cover and let heat through for 5 minutes or so to soften the kale. If using spinach, stir it in and proceed to the next step.

14. Stir in the heavy cream.

15. Serve!

Split Pea Soup

Ingredients

1 Tbsp Olive Oil

2 Tbsp Butter

1 Onion, diced

3 Stalks of Celery, diced

2 Bay Leaves

1/4 tsp Thyme Leaves, dried

3 Carrots, chopped

4 cloves Garlic, pressed or minced

1/4 tsp Pepper

6 cups Chicken or Vegetable Broth, low sodium (use only 5 cups for a thick soup, 7 cups for a thinner soup)

1 lb Green Split Peas, rinsed and sorted (unsoaked)

1 tsp Liquid Smoke (Optional, for vegetarian version)

1/2 tsp Kosher Salt (add last, after cooking, if needed) (1/4 tsp table salt)

Use any of these as your meat

(or a combination of them)

6 slices Bacon (Optional) chopped

2 small Ham Hocks (Optional) Not very meaty, but add a nice smoky flavor and richness.

1 Leftover Ham Bone (Optional) I like to use this with the diced ham

2 - 3 cups Diced Leftover Ham (Optional)

Instructions

1. Turn the pressure cooker to the Sauté function. When hot add the olive oil and butter.

2. Add the onion, celery, bay leaves, and thyme. Cook, stirring occasionally, until onion starts to turn translucent.

3. Add the carrots, garlic, bacon or ham, if using, and pepper. Cook for a minute.

4. Add the broth and ham bone or ham hocks, if using (Add liquid smoke, if using, for vegetarian version). Let come to a simmer.

5. Stir in the split peas.

6. Place the lid on the pot and lock it in place. Set the steam release knob to Sealing.

7. Cancel the sauté function. Press the Pressure Cook/Manual button, then the +/- button to choose 18 minutes. High pressure.

8. When the cook time is finished, let the pot sit undisturbed for 15 minute natural release. Then turn the steam release knob to Venting to release remaining pressure.

9. When the pin in the lid drops down, open the lid, remove the bay leaves and any bones.

10. Taste and add the salt if needed.

11. Serve hot. The soup will thicken quite a bit when it cools, that is normal.

Simple Potato Soup

Ingredients

6 slices Bacon, chopped

1 small Onion, diced

2 stalks Celery, diced

5 medium Potatoes, peeled & diced

5 cups Chicken Broth

1 tsp Salt (more to taste)

1/2 tsp Pepper

1/4 cup Flour

4 Tbsp Butter, softened

1 cup Heavy Cream

Instructions

1. Turn on the pot's sauté function and add the chopped bacon and onion. Cook until bacon is done and onions are translucent, stirring occasionally.

2. Add the celery. Stir, and scrape up any brown bits from the bottom of the pot.

3. Add the potatoes, broth, salt, and pepper. Put the lid on and lock in place. Set the steam release knob to the Sealing position.

4. Cancel the sauté setting. Press the Pressure Cook/Manual button. Then the +/- button to select 8 minutes.

5. When the cook cycle ends, let the pot sit undisturbed for 10 minute natural release. Then do a controlled quick release of the remaining steam/pressure (release steam in short bursts until you are sure no soup will spew out with the steam).

6. While the pot is naturally releasing, combine the softened butter and flour in a small dish, using a fork. If the butter isn't soft enough, warm it in the microwave for 10 seconds. Mix thoroughly until all lumps are gone.

7. When all of the pressure is out of the pot, carefully open the lid, and turn on the sauté setting. Let the soup come to a simmer (don't let it scorch on the bottom), then stir in the flour mixture and stir until thickened. Cancel the sauté setting and stir well.

8. You can use a potato masher to mash some of the potatoes to help it thicken a little more and give the soup more texture.

9. Then Add the heavy cream. Taste and adjust salt if desired.

10. Serve with some crusty bread.

Lentil Soup

8 Servings | Prep Time: 15 mins. | Cook Time: 13 mins. | Total Time: 40 mins.

Ingredients

- 1/2 lb Thick Sliced Smoky Bacon (about 6 slices cut in 1/2" pieces)
- 1 large Onion, diced
- 4 Carrots, diced
- 3 Stalks of Celery, diced
- 1 Bay Leaf
- 5 cloves Garlic, pressed or minced
- 1 (28 oz) can Crushed Tomatoes in Puree
- 1/4 tsp Oregano, dried
- 3/4 tsp Coriander Powder
- 3/4 tsp Cumin
- 1 tsp Sweet Paprika
- 1 tsp Smoked Paprika
- 1 tsp Kosher Salt
- 1/2 tsp Pepper
- 1 4 inch sprig Fresh Rosemary
- 3 sprigs Fresh Thyme, or 1/2 tsp dried
- 1 Tbsp Balsamic Vinegar
- 1 T Fresh Lemon Juice
- 5 cups Chicken Broth, low sodium
- 1 1/2 cups Brown Lentils, sorted & rinsed

Instructions

1. Before you cook, have all of your ingredients prepared; veggies chopped, cans opened, spices measured, etc. This will make the process a lot easier for you!

2. Turn on the pot's Sauté function and add the bacon. Cook bacon until done, but not crisp. Remove from pot and set aside on a paper towel. Discard all but 2 Tbsp of the fat.

3. Add onions, carrots, celery, and bay leaf. Cook until vegetables are just tender, stirring occasionally and scraping the bottom of the pan to get brown bits off the bottom.

4. Add the garlic and cook for 30 seconds, stirring constantly.

5. Add tomatoes, oregano, coriander, cumin, sweet paprika, smoked paprika, salt, pepper, rosemary, thyme, vinegar, lemon juice, and broth, and rinsed lentils. Stir.

6. Place the lid on the pot and set the Steam Release Knob to Sealing. Cancel Sauté function.

7. Press the Pressure Cook (or Manual) button. Set time to 4 minutes using the +/- button.

8. When cook cycle ends, let pot naturally release pressure for 13 minutes. Then manually release the remaining pressure by turning the knob to Venting.

9. When the pin in the lid drops, open the lid and carefully stir the soup. Taste and adjust salt, if needed.

10. Add the bacon back in and stir.

11. Serve as is, or garnish with sour cream, cilantro, or whatever you like!

Clam Chowder

Ingredients

3 (6.5 oz) cans Chopped Clams*
(reserve the clam juice)

Water (to add to clam juice)

5 slices Bacon, chopped

3 Tbsp Butter

1 Onion, diced

2 stalks Celery, diced

2 sprigs Fresh Thyme (or 1/4 tsp dried)

2 cloves Garlic, pressed or minced

1 1/4 tsp Kosher Salt (3/4 tsp table salt)

1/4 tsp Pepper

1 1/2 lbs Potatoes, 4 cups peeled/diced potatoes

1/2 tsp Sugar (optional)

1 1/3 cups Half and Half

1 1/2 Tbsp Potato or Corn Starch
(optional, for thickening)

Chopped Chives, for garnish

Instructions

1. Open the cans of clams and drain the clam juice into a 2 cup measuring cup. Add enough water to make 2 cups of liquid. Set the clams and juice/water aside.

2. Turn on the pressure cooker's Sauté function and add the chopped bacon. Cook, stirring occasionally, until fat has rendered out of it, but not crispy.

3. Add the butter, onion, celery, and thyme. Cook, stirring and scraping the bottom of the pot to get up all of the brown bits, until the onion starts turning translucent.

4. Add the garlic, salt, and pepper. Cook for 1 minute, stirring frequently.

5. Add the potatoes, sugar (if using) and clam juice/water mixture and stir.

6. Put the lid on the pot and lock in place. Turn the steam release knob to the Sealing position. Cancel the Sauté function.

7. Press the Pressure Cook/Manual button, then the +/- button to choose 4 minutes (High Pressure). When cook time ends, leave the pot undisturbed for 3 minutes, then do a controlled Quick Release.

8. When the pin in the lid has dropped down, open the lid and stir the chowder.

9. Use a potato masher to carefully mash some or all of the potatoes, as desired.

10. Turn the Sauté function back on, and use the Lowest setting (on the IP is called Less).

11. Add the clams and the half and half. Let them heat through, try not to boil it.

12. If you want it thicker, you can thicken it with potato or corn starch mixed with some of the half and half, mixed well, and stir it in. Or use potato flakes.

13. Turn off the pot and garnish with chopped chives, and serve with crackers, bread or rolls.

Sweet Potato Kale Soup

6 Servings | Prep Time: 15 mins. | Cook Time: 15 mins. | Total Time: 40 mins.

Ingredients

2 Tbsp Olive Oil

1 small Onion, diced

2 small Bay Leaves

2 medium Sweet Potatoes, peeled and cubed (1 1/2 lbs)

1/2 tsp Coriander Powder

1/2 tsp Cumin

1/8 tsp Cinnamon

1 tsp Turmeric

1 tsp Kosher Salt (or 3/4 tsp table salt)

1 (3-4") sprig Fresh Rosemary (don't use dried)

3 cloves Garlic, pressed or minced

1 (15 oz) can Diced Tomatoes, w/ juice

1 tsp Paprika, sweet

1 (14 oz) can Coconut Milk

1 1/2 cups Water

5 oz Kale, chopped (1/2 of a 10 oz bag)

Instructions

1. Turn on pressure cooker to the Sauté function. When hot add the oil.

2. Add the onion and bay leaves. Cook, stirring occasionally, until onion is turning translucent.

3. Add the sweet potatoes, coriander, cumin, cinnamon, turmeric, salt, rosemary, and garlic. Stir well and cook for about 1 minute.

4. Add the tomatoes and paprika. Cook, stirring, for 2 minutes.

5. Stir in the coconut milk, incorporating it well, and then add the water and stir.

6. Close the lid. Turn the steam release knob to Sealing.

7. Cancel the Sauté function and press Pressure Cook/Manual button, then the +/- button to choose 5 minutes. High Pressure.

8. When cooking cycle has ended, let the pot sit undisturbed for 10 minute Natural Release. Then turn the steam release knob to Venting to release remaining pressure.

9. When the pin in the lid drops down, open the lid carefully. Don't stir the soup yet.

10. Add the kale to the soup and very gently fold it into the soup (Do this gently so the sweet potatoes don't all break up. You do want some of them to as this naturally thickens it. Use your own judgement on this).

11. Let the soup sit for a couple of minutes so the kale can wilt. Then taste and adjust salt, if desired.

12. Serve nice and hot. Garnish with some extra coconut milk, or heavy cream.

Butternut Squash Soup

6-8 Servings | Prep Time: 25 mins. | Cook Time: 10 mins. | Total Time: 50 mins.

Ingredients

2 Tbsp Olive Oil

1 Large Yellow Onion, chopped

5 Garlic Cloves, chopped

1 1/2 inch Piece of Ginger, peeled, diced

2 Carrots, chopped

1 Apple, peeled, cored, chopped

3 lbs Butternut Squash, peeled, seeded, chopped in 3" chunks

1 tsp Salt

1/2 tsp Black Pepper

1 Sprig of Fresh Rosemary

2 Sprigs of Fresh Thyme

1/2 tsp Nutmeg

3 cups Vegetable Broth (or chicken)

Optional

1 tsp Orange Zest (cook with soup)

1/4 tsp Cayenne Pepper

Finish (add right after pureeing)

1/2 (13.5 oz) can Coconut Milk (or 1/2 cup of Heavy Cream)

Garnish

Coconut Milk Drizzle (or Heavy Cream)

Fresh Herbs of your choice

Instructions

1. Turn the Instant Pot to Sauté. When the display reads HOT, add the olive oil.

2. Add the onion and sauté for 5 minutes or until they turn slightly translucent.

3. Add garlic, and ginger. Let cook for a minute, stirring constantly.

4. Add carrots, apple, squash, salt, pepper, rosemary, thyme, and nutmeg. Stir well.

5. Add broth and optional orange zest and/or cayenne powder, if using, and stir.

6. Put the lid on the pot and set the steam release knob to the Sealing position.

7. Cancel the Sauté mode. Press the Manual (or Pressure Cook) button, then the +/- button to select 10 minutes.

8. When the cook cycle ends, leave the pot undisturbed for 15 minute natural release. Then manually release the remaining pressure. After the pin in the lid drops, open it.

9. Stir the soup and then use an immersion blender to puree to a creamy consistency (If you don't have an immersion blender you can transfer contents to a food processor or a blender. Puree the soup in batches as you can't put much hot food in either of those appliances. Be very careful when pureeing hot food).

10. Finish the soup by stirring in the coconut milk, or cream.

11. Taste and adjust salt if needed, then garnish as desired and serve.

Mushroom Soup

Ingredients

2 Tbsp Olive Oil

3 Tbsp Butter

2 Leeks, chopped (the white and light green parts)

1 small Onion, diced

5 cloves Garlic, pressed or finely minced

2 lbs Mushrooms, chopped (use a mix of portobello, shiitake, crimini)

1 1/2 tsp Kosher Salt (or 1 tsp table salt)

1/2 tsp Pepper

1 1/2 tsp Fresh Thyme Leaves

1/2 cup Cooking Sherry (or dry white wine)

6 cups Chicken Broth, low sodium (or a good mushroom broth)

TO FINISH

6 Tbsp Flour

1 cup Heavy Cream (more if needed)

Fresh Parsley, as garnish

Instructions

1. Before you begin cooking, have all of the veggies chopped, and all the ingredients ready.

2. Turn on the pot's Sauté setting. When it is hot, add the olive oil and butter. Then add the leeks and onion. Cook, stirring occasionally, until they are tender, translucent, and have a little bit of browning on them for best flavor.

3. Add the garlic, mushrooms, salt, pepper, and thyme leaves. Cook, stirring frequently, until mushrooms start releasing their liquid and turn a darker shade of brown.

4. Add the sherry or wine and stir, scraping the bottom of the pot to deglaze.

5. Pour in the broth and stir. Place the lid on the pressure cooker and set the steam release knob to the Sealing position.

6. Cancel the Sauté setting. Then press the Pressure Cook /Manual button, then the +/- button to select 5 minutes. The pot will take several minutes to come to pressure.

7. When the cook cycle ends, let the pot sit undisturbed for 15 minute Natural Release. Then turn the knob to the Venting position to do a Quick Release of the remaining pressure. Do this slowly at first to make sure no soup spews out with the steam!

8. When the pin in the lid drops down, turn the pot off and open it. Gently stir the soup.

9. Whisk together the flour and heavy cream.

10. Turn on the Sauté setting and let the soup come to a simmer. Whisk in the flour mixture and let it simmer for a few minutes to thicken. Then turn off the pot.

11. Use an immersion blender to blend some of the soup, but not all of it, unless you don't want any of the texture.

12. Serve garnished with a little cream and some fresh parsley

Broccoli Cheddar Soup

8 Servings | Prep Time: 15 mins. | Cook Time: 15 mins. | Total Time: 40 mins.

Ingredients

3 Tbsp Butter

2 tsp Olive Oil

1 small Onion, diced

1 large Carrot, shredded (about 1 cup)

1 small Potato (optional), peeled & diced

1/2 tsp Pepper

1 tsp Paprika

1 tsp Kosher Salt (or 3/4 tsp table salt)

1/4 tsp Nutmeg

2 cloves Garlic, pressed or minced

2 cups Chicken or Veggie Broth, low sodium

1 1/2 lbs Broccoli Florets, fresh or frozen (chopped, about 6-8 cups)

To Thicken

1/4 cup Flour + 1/4 cup Butter

To Finish

6 oz Cheddar Cheese, shredded (1 1/2 cups)

4 oz Monterey Jack Cheese, shredded (about 1 cup)

2 cups Half and Half

Instructions

1. Gather all ingredients, and prepare all of the vegetables, and shred the cheese. It's easier if you have it all ready to go.
2. Turn on the pot's Sauté setting. When hot, add the butter and olive oil. Then add the onion and cook for a few minutes.
3. Add the grated carrot and the potato (if using) and cook for a minute to soften.
4. Add the pepper, paprika, salt, nutmeg, and garlic. Cook for a minute, stirring.
5. Add the broth and stir.
6. Add the broccoli, but don't stir. Put the lid on and lock it in place. Set the steam release knob to the Sealing position.
7. Cancel the Sauté function. Then press the Pressure Cook/Manual button. Then the +/- button to select 5 minutes. High Pressure.
8. When the cooking cycle is finished, let the pot sit undisturbed for 5 minute Natural Release. Then slowly at first, in bursts, Quick Release the remaining pressure by turning the steam release knob to Venting. Turn off the pot.
9. Use a potato masher to mash up the veggies well. If you want a creamier consistency, use an immersion blender.
10. Mix the flour and butter together in a microwave safe dish and microwave for 15 seconds. Then mix very well until it is smooth.
11. Turn the Sauté setting on and mix in the flour/butter mixture. Stir until it starts to thicken.
12. Add the cheeses and stir in.
13. Cancel the Sauté function and add in the half and half. Stir well.
14. Taste and adjust salt, if necessary.
15. Serve with some nice bread or rolls.

Minestrone Soup

10 Servings | Prep Time: 30 mins. | Cook Time: 15 mins. | Total Time: 1 hr. 10 mins.

Ingredients

3 Tbsp Olive Oil

1 Yellow Onion, chopped

2 Bay Leaves

7 cloves Garlic, pressed or minced

2 lg Carrots, chopped

2 ribs Celery, chopped

2 tsp Oregano, dried

1 tsp Basil, dried

1 sprig Fresh Rosemary

1 tsp Kosher Salt

1/2 tsp Pepper

7 cups Chicken Broth (or vegetable)

1 Parmesan Rind (optional)

1 - 2 (15 oz) cans Red Kidney Beans, drained & rinsed

1 (15 oz) can Garbanzo Beans, drained

2 (15 oz) cans Diced Tomatoes, w/juice

1 (14 oz) can Crushed Tomatoes in Puree

1 (6 oz) can Tomato Paste

AFTER PRESSURE COOKING

1 sm Zucchini, sliced into half circles, not too thick

1 cup Pasta, dry (med. shells, small macaroni)

1 (14 oz) can Cut Green Beans, drained

1/2 cup Parmesan Cheese, grated

1/4 cup Fresh Basil Leaves, chopped

Instructions

1. Before you begin cooking, have all your ingredients ready. Chop the veggies, open the cans, rinse the beans, measure the spices. This will make the process go smoother.

2. Turn on the pot's Sauté setting. When hot, add the olive oil. Then add in the onion and bay leaves and cook, stirring occasionally, until onions start to turn translucent.

3. Add the garlic and cook for about 20 seconds, stirring constantly, or until it is fragrant.

4. Add the carrots, celery, oregano, basil, rosemary, salt, and pepper. Stir.

5. Pour in the chicken broth, parmesan rind, if using, kidney beans, and garbanzo beans. Stir.

6. Pour in diced tomatoes and crushed tomatoes. Do not stir.

7. Spoon the tomato paste on top. Gently press to submerge it, but do not stir (tomatoes burn easily, so this method helps prevent that).

8. Place the lid on the pot and set the steam release knob to the Sealing position.

9. Cancel the Sauté setting.

10. Press the Pressure Cook/Manual button, then the +/- button to select 5 minutes. High Pressure. The pot will take 10-15 minutes to come to pressure as it is full.

11. When the cook cycle ends, let the pot sit undisturbed for 15 minute Natural Release. Turn the knob to Venting to release the remaining pressure. Do this slowly at first to make sure no soup spews out with the steam!

12. When the pin in the lid drops down, open the lid and carefully stir the soup.

13. Turn the Sauté setting back on and add in the zucchini and pasta. Put a glass lid on, or a silicone lid to keep the heat in so it comes to a simmer faster. Take off the lid when it starts to simmer (there is a chance that it won't simmer, but the pasta will cook as it is very hot).

14. The zucchini and pasta will cook in 5 to 10 minutes, depending on the type of pasta, and how thinly you cut the zucchini.

15. Add the drained can of green beans and stir in the parmesan. Let them heat through.

16. Garnish with some fresh basil leaves, more parmesan, and serve hot with nice crusty bread.

Easy Tomato Soup

4-6 Servings | Prep Time: 5 mins. | Cook Time: 12 mins. | Total Time: 37 mins.

Ingredients

1 Tbsp Olive Oil

2 Tbsp Butter

1 Onion, chopped

4 Cloves of Garlic, pressed or minced

1/4 tsp Red Pepper Flakes (optional)

3 (15 oz) Cans of Diced or Crushed Tomatoes, with juice

4 cups Broth, chicken or vegetable

1 tsp Salt

1/2 tsp Pepper

1 tsp Italian Seasoning

1 Tbsp Fresh Basil, (chopped) or 1 tsp dried

To Finish-Optional

1/2 cup Grated Parmesan Cheese (or more to taste)

1/2 cup Heavy Cream

GARNISH

Croutons, Fresh Basil, Parmesan Cheese

Instructions

1. Press the Sauté button on the Instant Pot. When the display reads "Hot" add the oil and butter.

2. Add the onion and cook until translucent, about 7 minutes (let the onion brown a little for better flavor). Stir occasionally.

3. Add the garlic and red pepper flakes (if using). Cook 30 seconds, stirring constantly.

4. Add the tomatoes, broth, salt, pepper, Italian seasoning, and basil. Stir and close the lid of the pot and lock it into place. Set steam release knob to Sealing position.

5. Cancel the Sauté mode. Press the Manual/Pressure Cook button, then the +/- button to choose 5 minutes.

6. When the cook cycle ends, let the pot naturally release pressure for 15 minutes. Then turn the steam release knob to Venting and release the remaining pressure.

7. When the pin in the lid drops, open the lid and stir the soup.

8. Use an immersion blender to puree the soup to a creamy consistency. Or transfer to a blender and carefully blend the soup in batches. Please use caution!

9. Stir in the Parmesan cheese and let it melt into the soup.

10. Stir in the heavy cream. Taste and adjust salt, if desired.

11. Garnish as desired and serve.

Corn Chowder

6-8 Servings | Prep Time: 20 mins. | Cook Time: 20 mins. | Total Time: 55 mins.

Ingredients

6-8 ears Corn, (shucked & kernels removed or 5 cups of corn

7 slices Thick Cut Bacon, chopped

1 Onion, diced

3 Tbsp Butter

2 cloves Garlic, minced

1 tsp Kosher Salt

1/2 tsp Pepper

2 sprigs Fresh Thyme (or 1/2 tsp dried thyme leaves. Not ground)

3 med Potatoes, peeled and diced

4 cups Chicken Broth, low sodium

TO FINISH

3 cups Half and Half

6 Tbsp Flour

Reserved Cooked Bacon

Fresh Parsley (garnish) chopped

Instructions

1. Turn on the Sauté setting and add the bacon to the pot. Cook until done and remove to a plate and set it aside. Discard all but 2 Tbsp of the bacon fat.

2. Add the onion and butter to the pot and cook it until softened.

3. Add the garlic and cook for about 30 seconds, stirring frequently.

4. Add the corn, salt, pepper, thyme, and potatoes. Stir.

5. Add the broth and half of the cooked bacon. Cancel the sauté setting.

6. Close the lid and set the steam release knob to the Sealing position.

7. Press the Pressure Cook/Manual button, then the +/- button to select 5 minutes. High Pressure.

8. When the cook cycle has finished, turn off the pot and let it sit undisturbed for 15 minute natural release. Then turn the steam release knob to the Venting position to release the remaining pressure.

9. When the pin in the lid drops back down, open the lid.

10. Whisk the flour into the half and half until dissolved. Turn on the Sauté setting and when the soup starts to simmer, stir in the flour/half and half mixture. Stir until thickened.

11. Turn off the pot and add the remaining bacon. Taste and add more salt if needed.

12. Garnish with parsley and serve.

> **Recipe Note**
> I like to add extra frozen corn at the end, to bulk it up and have the crunch of the partially cooked corn. I do this even when using fresh or leftover corn!

Black Bean Soup

Ingredients

1/2 lb Bacon, chopped - Omit for vegetarian

1 Tbsp Olive Oil

1 large White Onion, diced

1 cup Celery, diced

2 large Carrots, diced

2 Pasilla Chile Peppers (they are mild) 1" dice (or 1 (7 oz) can diced green chiles)

6 Garlic Cloves (finely minced)

1 (15 oz) can Diced Tomatoes, w/juice

2 Bay Leaves

1 Tbsp Cumin

2 tsp Mexican Oregano (or regular)

1/2 tsp Thyme, dried

1/4-1/2 tsp Red Pepper Flakes

1 tsp Kosher Salt (or 3/4 tsp table salt)

1/4 tsp Pepper

6 cups Chicken or Vegetable Broth, low sodium

1 1/2 cups Dry Black Beans* (rinsed) or canned (3 (15 oz) cans)

1 Tbsp Fresh Lime Juice

Garnish (Any or all of these)

Fresh Cilantro, Sour Cream, Avocado

Hot Sauce, Corn Tortillas

Cooked Rice (pour soup on top of rice)

Instructions

1. Turn pot to Sauté and cook the bacon until done, but not crisp.

2. Add the olive oil and the onion. Cook, stirring occasionally, until softened.

3. Add celery, carrots, chile peppers, and garlic. Stir, cooking for a minute.

4. Stir in tomatoes, bay leaves, cumin, oregano, thyme, red pepper flakes, salt, and pepper.

5. Add broth, and black beans. Stir, then put the lid on the pressure cooker. Set the steam release knob to the Sealing position. Cancel the Sauté mode.

6. Press the pressure Cook/Manual button and then the +/- button to select 40 minutes High Pressure. *If you use canned beans, rinse them first, and reduce the cook time to 5 minutes, with a 15 minute natural release.

7. When the cook cycle has ended, let the pot naturally release pressure for 20 minutes. Then manually release the remaining pressure. Open the lid after the pin in the lid drops.

8. Stir the soup, and test the beans for doneness (old beans need more time, in which case just put the lid back on and set for 10 minutes more, and 15 natural release).

9. Taste and adjust salt if needed. Stir in the lime juice.

10. Garnish as desired and serve.

Moroccan Chickpea Stew

8 Servings | Prep Time: 15 mins. | Cook Time: 50 mins. | Total Time: 1 hr. 25 mins.

Ingredients

1/4 cup Olive Oil

1 Yellow Onion, cut in 1 inch dice

7 Cloves Garlic, pressed

1 tsp Cinnamon

1 1/2 tsp Cumin

2 tsp Sweet Paprika

1/8 tsp Cayenne Pepper

1 (14.5 oz) Can Diced Tomatoes

1 cup Chopped Carrots

3 (14.5 oz) Cans Chickpeas, (garbanzo beans) rinsed and drained

4 cups Vegetable or Chicken Broth, low sodium

1/2 tsp Black Pepper

1/2 tsp Kosher Salt

1 tsp Sugar

7 oz Baby Spinach

Instructions

1. Turn on the Sauté setting.
2. Add the onions and stir, cooking until translucent.
3. Add the garlic and stir, cooking for a minute, being careful not to burn it.
4. Add in the cinnamon, cumin, paprika, and cayenne pepper. Stir and cook for a minute.
5. Stir in the can of diced tomatoes, juice and all.
6. Add the carrots, chickpeas and broth. Stir.
7. Add the pepper, salt, and sugar, stir.
8. Place the lid on the pressure cooker and lock it in place, setting the steam release knob to Sealing.
9. Cancel the Sauté setting.
10. Press the Pressure Cook/Manual button and then the + or - button to choose 7 minutes. The pot may take 10 minutes or so to come to pressure.
11. When the cooking cycle ends, let the IP go into Natural Release phase by letting it sit undisturbed for 15 minutes.
12. Turn off the pot and release the remaining pressure. When the pin in the lid drops, open it.
13. Stir the stew and give it a taste. Adjust salt if desired.
14. Using a potato masher, mash up most of the stew, but leave some of the chickpeas whole. This gives the stew wonderful texture.
15. Add the baby spinach to the stew and gently stir it in. It will wilt nicely.
16. Serve immediately.

Recipe Notes
If you want to add some meat, adding a couple of small chicken thighs would be very delicious!

Side Dishes

rice, beans, veggies, etc.

Cornbread Stuffing

Ingredients

5-6 cups Prepared Cornbread Pieces

1/2 cup Butter

1 small Onion, diced

1 cup Celery, diced

2 tsp Rubbed Sage

1/2 tsp Poultry Seasoning

1 tsp Kosher Salt

1/4 tsp Pepper

1 clove Garlic, finely minced

1 1/2 - 2 cups Turkey Broth (or chicken)

1 1/2 cups Water, for the pressure cooker

OPTIONAL ADD-INS

1/2 cup Crumbled Cooked Sausage

1/2 cup Cooked Chestnuts, chopped

Chopped Mushrooms

Dried Cranberries

Walnuts or Pecans

Instructions

1. Break up the cornbread into a mixing bowl and set aside. This can be done ahead of time if you want it to dry out a bit first (fresh cornbread will yield a softer stuffing).

2. Turn on the pot's Sauté setting and add the butter, onions, celery, sage, poultry seasoning, salt, and pepper. Cook, stirring frequently, until vegetables soften.

3. Add the garlic and sauté with the vegetables for a couple of minutes.

4. Add the vegetable mixture and the turkey broth to the cornbread and combine.

5. Put the cornbread mixture into a sprayed 6 cup bundt pan, or a 7"x3" metal pan.

6. Cover the pan with foil and seal it well.

7. Rinse out the inner pot, dry it, and put it back in the pressure cooker.

8. Add the water and a trivet/rack to the inner pot in the pressure cooker.

9. Use a sling* (or a rack with long handles) to lower the pan into the pot. Fold over the ends of the sling to get them out of the way. Make sure they don't block the steam valve.

10. Close and lock the lid in place, and set the Steam Release Knob to Sealing.

11. Press the Pressure Cook/Manual button, then the +/- button to select 18 minutes. High Pressure.

12. When the cook cycle has ended, do a Quick Release of the steam by turning the steam Release Knob to Venting.

13. When all of the pressure is out and the pin in the lid drops, open it and remove the pan to a cooling rack.

14. Leave the foil in place and let it sit for 5 minutes, then remove foil and serve hot.

Mushroom Risotto with Peas

5 Servings | Prep Time: 10 mins. | Cook Time: 17 mins. | Total Time: 42 mins.

Ingredients

3 Tbsp Olive Oil

4 Tbsp Butter

1 sm Onion, diced

3 cloves Garlic, minced

1 1/2 cups Arborio Rice

12 oz Mushrooms, chopped

1/2 cup White Wine (or broth)

4 cups Chicken Broth, low sodium (or veggie)

1/2 tsp Kosher Salt

1/8 tsp Pepper

3/4 cup Grated Parmesan Cheese

1 cup Frozen Peas

Instructions

1. Have everything ready to go before you begin, for best results.
2. Turn on the sauté setting. When the pot is hot, add the olive oil and the butter.
3. Add the onions to the pot and cook, stirring occasionally, until they begin to turn translucent.
4. Add the garlic and stir. Cook about 20 seconds.
5. Add the rice and stir well, until all grains are coated with the oil/butter. Cook for about 4 minutes.
6. Add the mushrooms and the wine and stir, scraping the bottom of the pot to get up any browned bits (deglaze).
7. Next, pour in the broth and add the salt & pepper. Stir.
8. Place the lid on the pot and lock in place. Turn the steam release knob to the Sealing position. Cancel the Sauté setting.
9. Press the Pressure Cook or Manual button. Then press the +/- button to select 7 minutes. High pressure.
10. When the cook cycle is finished, let the pot sit undisturbed for 10 to 15 minutes, then turn the steam release knob to the Venting position to release any remaining pressure/steam.
11. When the pin in the lid drops down, open and stir the risotto and then add the peas and stir again.
12. Add the parmesan and stir. Then place a glass lid on the pot and let the residual heat warm the peas and melt the parmesan.
13. Give the mixture a final stir and serve hot.

French Onion Rice

Ingredients

2 cups Long Grain White Rice, uncooked, rinsed very well

1 (10.5 oz) can French Onion Soup

1 1/4 cups Beef Broth

1/4 cup Water

1 (4 oz) can Sliced Mushrooms, drained (optional)

1/2 med Sweet Onion, sliced thinly and cut into quarter moon shapes

1 Tbsp Dried or Fresh Parsley Flakes

1 lg clove Garlic, finely minced

4 Tbsp Melted Butter

1/4 tsp Kosher Salt

1/4 tsp Pepper

Instructions

1. Add all of the ingredients in the inner liner pot of the pressure cooker. Stir well.
2. Close the lid and set the steam release knob to the Sealing position.
3. Press the Pressure Cook/Manual button or dial.
4. Then press the +/- button or dial and select 3 minutes. High pressure.
5. The pot will take about 5 minutes to come to pressure.
6. When the cook time is finished, let the pot sit undisturbed for 9 minute Natural Release.
7. Turn the steam release knob to the Venting position to release the remaining pressure.
8. When the pin in the lid drops back down, open the lid carefully.
9. Fluff the rice with a fork, and gently stir.
10. Serve the rice hot, with extra parsley on top, if desired.

Recipe Note
Make in the 3 qt, 5 qt, 6 qt, or 8 qt pot.
You can add chicken to this if you want a one-pot meal. For an average sized 8 oz skinless/boneless breast, cut it in fourths. This will ensure it cooks without drying out. If the pieces are pretty thick, cut them just a little smaller, maybe in sixths and toss them in with the rice.

Lemon Rice

Ingredients

1 Lemon, zested and juiced

1 1/2 cups Long Grain White Rice, well rinsed

1 Tbsp Butter, unsalted

1/2 tsp Kosher Salt

1/4 tsp Turmeric Powder (optional, for pretty color)

1 1/2 cups Water

Garnish

1 Tbsp Fresh Parsley, chopped

Instructions

1. Wash the lemon. Zest it before you juice it. Add zest & juice to the inner liner of the pressure cooker.

2. Add the rice, butter, salt, turmeric, and water to the pot. Stir.

3. Close the lid and set the steam release knob to the Sealing position.

4. Press the Pressure Cook/Manual button or dial, then the +/- button to select 11 minutes. LOW Pressure*. The pot will take about 5 minutes to come to pressure.

5. When the cook cycle has finished, turn the steam release knob to the Venting position to Quick Release the steam/pressure.

6. When the pin in the lid drops back down, open the lid.

7. Fluff the rice with a fork and transfer to a serving dish. Garnish with parsley.

8. Serve immediately.

***You can also use the Rice Button with a Quick Release.
Or, if your pot doesn't have Low Pressure, set to High Pressure for 3 minutes and do a 9 minute natural release.**

Cilantro Lime Rice

Ingredients

2 cups Long Grain White Rice, well rinsed

2 cups Water

1 tsp Kosher Salt (or 3/4 tsp table salt)

1 clove Garlic, minced

1 Tbsp Butter (or 2 tsp olive oil)

Juice of 1/2 lg Lime (~ 2 1/2 Tbsp)

Zest of 1 Lime

1/4 cup Cilantro Leaves, finely chopped

Instructions

1. Rinse the rice until water runs clear.

2. Add rice to the pot, then add water, salt, garlic and dot the butter on top (or olive oil on top).

3. Place the lid on the pot and set the steam release knob to Sealing. Then press the Rice button, or use dial. The rice setting cooks on LOW pressure for 12 minutes (in case you don't have a Rice button, set this time/pressure). Then do a Quick Release of the pressure when done.

4. If your pot doesn't have LOW pressure, set for 3 minutes at HIGH pressure, then let it do a 10 minute natural release. Then release the remaining pressure manually.

5. Fluff the rice with a fork. Then add the lime juice, lime zest, and cilantro. Mix well. Taste and adjust seasoning.

6. Serve with beans, or on tacos, burritos, and in burrito bowls.

Recipe Note
*Serve with beans for a vegetarian meal.

Brown Rice Pilaf

4 Servings | Prep Time: 10 mins. | Cook Time: 21 mins. | Total Time: 51 mins.

Ingredients

3 Tbsp Butter, unsalted

1 sm Onion, diced

1 1/2 cups Long Grain Brown Rice (or Brown Basmati rice)

3 cloves Garlic, pressed or finely minced

1 tsp Fresh Rosemary, minced

1/4 tsp Thyme, dried

3/4 tsp Kosher Salt (or 1/3 tsp table salt)

1/4 tsp Pepper

1 3/4 cups Broth, low sodium chicken or vegetable

1/2 tsp Lemon Zest

1 tsp Lemon Juice, fresh

2 Tbsp Fresh Parsley, minced

2 Tbsp Shredded Carrot

Instructions

1. Turn the pot on to the Sauté setting. When the pot is hot, add the butter.

2. Add the onion and cook, stirring occasionally, until it turns translucent.

3. Stir in the rice and cook, stirring constantly, until all of the rice is coated in the butter.

4. Add the garlic and cook, stirring constantly, until fragrant (careful not to burn it).

5. Add the rosemary, thyme, salt, and pepper and stir.

6. Pour in the broth and stir.

7. Place the lid on the pot and lock in place. Turn the steam release knob to the Sealing position.

8. Press the Pressure Cook or Manual button, then the +/- button to select 21 minutes. High pressure.

9. When the cook time has finished, let the pot sit undisturbed for 10 minute natural release. Then turn the steam release knob to Venting to release the remaining pressure.

10. Give the pilaf a good stir, and test for doneness. If the rice isn't soft enough, put the lid back on for a few minutes.

11. Add the lemon zest & juice, parsley and carrot. Stir. Taste and adjust salt, if needed.

12. Serve immediately.

Collard Greens

7-9 Servings | Prep Time: 10 mins. | Cook Time: 1 hr. 5 mins. | Total Time: 1 hr. 15 mins.

Ingredients

1 Tbsp Olive Oil

1 large Onion, chopped

1 tsp Seasoned Salt

1/4 tsp Red Pepper Flakes

1/2 tsp Kosher Salt

4 Garlic Cloves, minced

32 oz Chicken Broth, low sodium

1 Ham Hock (about 1 1/2 lbs)

1 lb Collard Greens, washed, and chopped (or 1 or 2 (10 oz) bags of pre-washed and chopped)

Instructions

Recipe Note
This is a Two Step Recipe, but don't worry, it's still faster than on the stove, and the results are excellent!

Step 1

1. Set the Instant Pot to the Sauté setting. When hot add the oil and the onion and cook it, stirring occasionally, until tender.

2. Add the seasoned salt, red pepper flakes, salt, and garlic. Cook 30 seconds, stirring.

3. Stir in the chicken broth and set the ham hock in the broth.

4. Turn off the Sauté mode and put the lid on the pot. Set the Steam Release Knob to Sealing. Press the Pressure Cook/Manual button then the +/- button to select 35 minutes.

5. When the cooking cycle has finished wait 10 minutes turn the knob to Venting to release the pressure. When the pin in the lid drops, open the lid.

6. Try to break up the ham hock a little using 2 forks. It might still be tough, so don't try too hard as it will be hot! It's okay if you can't or don't want to. Just flip it over!

Step Two

7. Add the collard greens to the pot and use a spoon to push them down into the liquid.

8. Make sure the silicone ring is in place, then put the lid back on and set to Sealing.

9. Press Manual (or Pressure Cook) and use the +/- button to choose 25 minutes.

10. When cook cycle is done, let the pot naturally release pressure for 10 minutes. Then manually release the remaining steam until the pin in the lid drops.

11. Open the lid and remove the ham hock to a bowl. Use 2 forks to separate the fat and bones from the meat. Discard the fat. Shred the meat and add it into the collard greens.

12. Serve them hot with a side of cornbread to sop up the pot likker (pot liquor)!

Braised Cabbage and Apples

Ingredients

4 slices Thick Cut Bacon, chopped

1 small Onion, thinly sliced

4 Whole Cloves

1 head Cabbage, shredded

2 med Apples, peeled, cored, thinly sliced

1/2 cup Apple Cider Vinegar

1/2 cup Apple Cider

1-2 Tbsp Sugar (more or less to taste)

1/2 tsp Kosher Salt (more or less to taste)

1/4 tsp Pepper (more or less to taste)

Instructions

1. Before you begin cooking, have all of the vegetables chopped, and the other ingredients ready to go.

2. Turn on the Sauté setting and add the chopped bacon. Cook until crisp. Remove to a paper towel and set aside.

3. Add the sliced onion to the bacon drippings and cook, stirring occasionally, until turning translucent.

4. Add the cloves, shredded cabbage, apples, vinegar, and apple cider. Stir well.

5. Place the lid on the pot and set the steam release knob to the Sealing position.

6. Cancel the Sauté setting. Then press the Pressure Cook or Manual button, then the +/- button to select 3 minutes (4 if you like softer cabbage). The pot will take several minutes to come to pressure.

7. When the cook cycle has ended, turn the knob to the Venting position to do a Quick Release of the remaining pressure. When the pin in the lid drops down, open the lid and stir the cabbage.

8. Remove the cloves.

9. Add the salt and pepper, and 1 Tablespoon of the sugar and stir well. Taste and adjust any of these to suit your taste.

10. Top with the reserved bacon and serve hot.

Green Beans, Potatoes and Bacon

6-8 Servings | Prep Time: 15 mins. | Cook Time: 15 mins. | Total Time: 45 mins.

Ingredients

1 - 1 1/2 lbs Fresh Green Beans, ends trimmed, cut in half

1 1/2 lbs New Potatoes (red or white. Leave small ones whole, cut in half / quarter large ones)

2/3 lb Thick Sliced Bacon, chopped

1 Sweet Onion, (Vidalia or Walla Walla) cut in half and sliced

2 cloves Garlic, minced

1/2 tsp Salt

1/2 tsp Pepper

1 (14.5 oz) can Chicken Broth, low sodium

Instructions

1. Prepare the green beans by cutting off the ends and cutting the beans in half. Set aside.

2. If the potatoes are pretty small, leave them whole. If they are larger, either quarter or cut them in half. Set aside.

3. Turn on the Sauté feature of your pot. Add the chopped bacon and the sliced onion. Cook, stirring occasionally, until onions soften and bacon is looking mostly done.

4. Add the garlic and cook for a minute, stirring.

5. Add the salt, pepper, chicken broth, and stir, scraping the bottom of the pot to get up any browned bits (deglaze).

6. Add the potatoes and green beans. Stir.

7. Place the lid on and set the steam release knob to the Sealing position.

8. Turn off the Sauté setting, then press the Pressure Cook/Manual button. Then use the +/- button to select 5 minutes. High Pressure.

9. When the cook time is finished, do a Quick Release of the pressure by turning the steam release knob to the Venting position.

10. Watch it as the broth may spew out with the steam. If this happens, turn the knob back to Sealing. Then release steam in bursts until you are sure only steam will be coming out.

11. Serve with some of the "pot likker" (liquid from the pot) so you can enjoy all of that flavor. Corn bread is very good to sop up that likker with!

Creamy Bacon Brussels Sprouts

4-6 Servings | Prep Time: 10 mins. | Cook Time: 2 mins. | Total Time: 30 mins.

Ingredients

1 lb Brussels Sprouts

3/4 cup Chicken Broth (or veggie) low sodium

2 cloves Garlic, pressed

1 Tbsp Butter

1/4 tsp Pepper

4 oz Cream Cheese (1/2 of an 8 oz block)

4 slices Thick Bacon, cooked, chopped

1/3-1/2 cup Parmesan Cheese, grated

Instructions

1. Trim the ends of the Brussels sprouts and rinse them in hot water. Then add them to the inner liner pot of the pressure cooker.

2. Add the chicken broth, garlic, butter, pepper, and cream cheese.

3. Close the lid and set the steam release knob to the Sealing position.

4. Press the Pressure Cook/Manual button, then the +/- button to select 2 minutes (3 minutes for a softer result). The pot will take a few minutes to come to pressure.

5. When the cooking cycle has finished, Turn the steam release knob to the Venting position to do a Quick Release of the steam/pressure.

6. When the pin in the lid drops down, open the lid and stir the Brussels sprouts until the cream cheese is smooth.

7. Add the parmesan and stir well.

8. Add the bacon and mix it in.

9. Serve hot!

Recipe Notes
This recipe can be doubled.
1. Don't double the broth, just increase by 1/4 cup. Then, after cooking, you can add a little if it is too thick.
2. Keep cook time the same.

Refried Beans

6 Servings | Prep Time: 10 mins. | Cook Time: 45 mins. | Total Time: 1 hr. 25 mins.

Ingredients

1 lb Beans, dry (rinsed, sorted) Kidney, Pinto, or Black Beans

1 Large Onion, finely chopped

1 Tbsp Bacon Fat, Lard, or Olive Oil

3-4 cloves Garlic, minced

1 tsp Kosher Salt

1/2 tsp Black Pepper

2 tsp Chili Powder

1 1/2 tsp Cumin

1/2 tsp Mexican Oregano (or regular)

2 Bay Leaves

4 1/4 cups Chicken Broth (or Vegetable or Water)

1-2 Jalapeño, seeded and chopped

1 Chipotle Pepper in Adobo (optional)

Instructions

1. Rinse, drain, and sort the beans. Put them in the inner liner of the Instant Pot.

2. Add the chopped onion, fat/oil, jalapeño, garlic, spices, and bay leaves, and chipotle pepper (if using). Stir.

3. Add the broth/water.

4. Put the lid on the IP and set the steam release knob to the   Sealing position.

5. Press the Pressure Cook / Manual button, then the +/- button to select 45 minutes (High Pressure).

6. When cook cycle ends, let the pot sit and naturally release the pressure for 20 minutes, or longer if you want.

7. Manually release the remaining pressure by turning the steam release knob to Venting, and when the pin in the lid drops, carefully open the lid.

8. Stir the beans. It will look a little thin at first, but will thicken as it cools. You can scoop out some of the liquid before pureeing for even thicker results.

9. Use an immersion blender (or food processor) to blend up the beans (Careful doing this with hot beans). Or use a potato masher if you like more texture. It thickens up as it cools.

Cuban Black Beans

Ingredients

1 lb Black Beans, unsoaked, rinsed

1 lg Yellow Onion, whole

2 Jalapeños, deseeded

10 cloves Garlic, leave whole

2 Bell Peppers, 1 green, 1 red, whole

1 tsp Oregano

1/2 tsp Cumin

4" Cinnamon Stick (optional)

2 Bay Leaves

4 cups Chicken Broth, low sodium (or veggie)

To Finish

2 tsp Kosher Salt (or more to taste)

1 Tbsp Sugar

2 Tbsp Red Wine Vinegar

1/3 cup Olive Oil

Instructions

1. Peel the onion, but leave it whole. Cut the jalapeños in half and scrape out the seeds. Peel the garlic and leave the cloves whole. Cut the tops off of the bell peppers and shake out the seeds. Leave them uncut.

2. Add the beans, onion, jalapeños, garlic, bell peppers, oregano, cumin, cinnamon stick, bay leaves, and chicken broth to the inner liner pot of the pressure cooker. Make sure the beans are submerged.

3. Close the lid and set the steam release knob to the Sealing position.

4. Press the Pressure Cook/Manual button, then the +/- button to select 40 minutes. High Pressure.

5. When the cook cycle has finished, turn off the pot and let it sit undisturbed for 15 minute natural release. Then turn the steam release knob to Venting to release the remaining pressure. When the pin in the lid drops back down, open the lid.

6. Remove the cinnamon stick, and bay leaves. Discard.

7. Spoon out the onion, jalapeños, garlic and bell peppers. Put them into a blender, along with about 1/3 cup of the beans and 1/4 cup of the liquid from the pot.

8. Blend until smooth. Pour mixture into the pot and stir.

9. Add the salt, sugar, vinegar, and olive oil. Stir.

10. Serve hot, over rice or alone.

Smoky Sweet Baked Beans

Prep Time: 15 mins. | **Cook Time: 40 mins.** | **Total Time: 1 hr. 10 mins.**

Ingredients

1 lb Navy Beans, soaked overnight, or Quick Soaked*

7 cups Water, for soaking the beans

6 slices Thick Cut Bacon, cut in 1" pieces

1 lg Yellow Onion, chopped

4 cloves Garlic, minced

1/2 tsp Kosher Salt

1/4 tsp Pepper

2 cups Water

1/4 cup Pure Maple Syrup

1/4 cup Ketchup

1/2 cup Molasses

1/2 cup Smoky BBQ Sauce

1 Tbsp Prepared Yellow Mustard

1 tsp Balsamic Vinegar (or apple cider vinegar)

1 tsp Liquid Smoke

1/3 cup Brown Sugar

---

*Quick Soak Method
if you didn't soak the beans overnight:

Pressure cook the beans in 4 cups of water, on High Pressure, for 2 minutes. Then turn the pressure cooker off and let the beans naturally release for 30 minutes. Drain, set aside, and continue with the recipe as directed.

Instructions

1. Soak beans in a bowl with 7 cups of water overnight. Then drain and rinse them. Set aside (You can also make this recipe from Quick Soaked beans. See Note. Sort, rinse, & set aside).

2. Turn the pot on to the Sauté function. Add the bacon. Cook until mostly done.

3. Add onions to the bacon and cook, stirring occasionally, until onion starts turning translucent.

4. Add the garlic and cook for 1 minute, or until fragrant, stirring frequently.

5. Add salt, pepper, water, syrup, ketchup, molasses, BBQ sauce, mustard, vinegar, liquid smoke, and stir well. Bring to a simmer and scrape the bottom of the pot to get up any browned bits.

6. Add beans and brown sugar. Stir, and place the lid on the pot and lock in place. Set the steam release knob to Sealing.

7. Cancel the Sauté function. Press the Pressure Cook/Manual button and use the +/- button to select 40 minutes.

8. Let naturally release the pressure for 15 minutes after cooking cycle ends. Then release remaining pressure.

9. When the pin in the lid drops down, open the lid and give the beans a stir. Sample a few of the beans to check for tenderness. If they are too firm, place the lid back on and set the time for another 10 minutes, and a 15 minute natural release.

10. When they are done cooking, if they are too soupy for your taste, turn on the Sauté function and stir them frequently as they cook down. Turn off the pot. They thicken a little more as they cool.

11. You can set the pot to the Keep Warm setting if you aren't serving them right away. Put a lid on them.

Easy Potato Salad

8 Servings | Prep Time: 15 mins. | Cook Time: 4 mins. | Total Time: 19 mins.

Ingredients

1 Cup Water (for the pot)

8 med Potatoes (bite-sized cubes, peeling optional)

5-6 Eggs (use 4 for less "eggy")

Dressing

1 1/4 Cup Mayonnaise

1 Tbsp Yellow Mustard

1 1/2 Tbsp Dill Pickle Juice

1/2 tsp Kosher Salt (more to taste)

1/2 tsp Pepper

1 sm Sweet Onion (finely chopped)

Optional to Load it Up!

1/2 cup Cooked Chopped Bacon

1 cup Shredded Cheddar Cheese

1/4 - 1/2 cup Sour Cream (reduce mayo)

1/2 cup Green Onions, sliced

Instructions

1. Prepare a bowl of ice water for the eggs. Set Aside. Pour 1 cup water in the pressure cooker.

2. Add cubed potatoes to a mesh colander or basket that is safe to cook in, and can hold all of the potatoes. Set the whole eggs directly on top of the potatoes as they will cook together.

3. Set the basket in the pot and close the lid. Turn the steam release knob to Sealing.

4. Press the Pressure Cook/Manual button, then the +/- button to select 4 minutes. High Pressure.

5. While the potatoes cook, put all of the dressing ingredients, including the onion, in a bowl and whisk together. Taste and adjust seasonings to your liking (I like mine a bit salty, as there are a lot of potatoes to season. Start with recommended amount).

6. When the cook cycle is done, turn the pot off and turn the steam release knob to Venting to Quick Release the pressure. Once the pressure is out and the pin drops, open the lid.

7. Take out the eggs using tongs, and put them in the bowl of ice water. Then carefully take out the basket of potatoes. I take out the basket using pot holders.

8. To cool the potatoes faster, spread them out on a baking sheet in a single layer and stir them a few times. That helps a lot.

9. Peel the eggs and chop them to the size you want.

10. Put the cooled potatoes into a large bowl, pour the dressing on and stir. Add the chopped eggs and fold them in.

11. Refrigerate salad for a couple of hours, if you can wait that long, and serve!

Baked Potatoes

Ingredients

1 1/2 - 2 cups Cold Water

1 - 8 Potatoes, scrubbed

Optional (to crisp skin after pressure cooking)

Olive Oil / Vegetable Oil

Salt

TOPPINGS

Butter, Cheese

Sour Cream, Chives

Bacon, Chili

Instructions

1. Place the metal trivet into the inner liner pot of the pressure cooker. Then pour the water in. Use 1 cup for a 3 qt, 1 1/2 cups for a 6 qt pot, 2 cups for an 8 qt.

2. After scrubbing the potatoes, pierce the skin a few times with a knife or a fork. Then place them in the pot on the trivet. It's okay to stack them.

3. Close the lid and set the steam release knob to the Sealing position. Then press the +/- button to select the time in minutes:

   Small Potatoes (approx. 4 oz): 10 minutes
   Medium Potatoes (approx. 6 oz): 15 minutes
   Large Potatoes (approx. 9 oz): 20 minutes
   Ex-Large Potatoes (approx. 12 oz): 25 minutes

4. When the cook cycle has ended, let the pot sit undisturbed for 10 minute natural release. Turn the steam release knob to Venting to release remaining pressure.

5. When the pin in the lid drops down, open the lid and check the potato for doneness. Pierce the potato with a knife. If the knife doesn't slide through easily, the potato needs a few more minutes cook time. Close the lid and set the time for a few more minutes.

Crisp the Potato Skin (optional step)

6. When the potatoes are done, you can crisp up the skin by rubbing a little vegetable oil on them, sprinkle with salt, and baking in a 400° oven for about 5-10 minutes.

7. Slit the cooked potato lengthwise and open it so the toppings fit.

8. Top the baked potato with butter, cheese, sour cream, bacon, chives, or anything you like! Serve hot.

Cheesy Scalloped Potatoes

6-8 Servings | Prep Time: 15 mins. | Cook Time: 6 mins. | Total Time: 41 mins.

Ingredients

2 lbs Potatoes, sliced 1/4" thick

5 oz Smoked Cooked Ham (thin sliced and cubed)

1/2 tsp Kosher Salt

1/4 tsp Pepper

1/4 tsp Onion Powder

1/2 tsp Garlic Powder

1/4 tsp Nutmeg (optional)

1/2 tsp Fresh Thyme Leaves (optional)

1 cup Broth (low sodium chicken or vegetable)

Add After Pressure Cooking

2 1/2 cups Monterey Jack Cheese, shredded, divided

1/4 cup Heavy Cream (or half and half)

Instructions

1. Peel the potatoes and slice them 1/4" thick (no thinner as they will be too soft. No thicker or they may not cook completely). Add them to the pressure cooker pot.

2. Stack a few slices of the ham on top of each other and cut them into strips, then into squares. Add to the pot.

3. Sprinkle in the salt, pepper, onion powder, garlic powder, and thyme leaves, if using.

4. Pour in the cup of broth.

5. Put the lid on the pot and set the steam release knob to the Sealing position. Then press the Pressure Cook/Manual button, then the +/- button to select 1 minute.

6. When the cooking cycle has ended do a Quick Release of the pressure by turning the steam release knob to Venting. When the pin in the lid drops down, open the lid.

7. Using a large slotted spoon, carefully remove the potatoes to the 8"x8" baking dish, leaving behind the broth/liquid in the pot.

8. Adjust oven rack to about 6" from broiler element. Then turn on the broiler to 400°.

9. Turn on the pot's Sauté setting (**Low heat**).

10. Add 1 1/2 cups of the cheese*, the heavy cream, and the nutmeg to the liquid left in the pot. Stir until melted and creamy, then turn off the pot

11. Spoon or Pour the mixture evenly over the potatoes/ham (the pot will be hot, so if you choose to lift it out to pour the cheese mixture out, use pot holders and caution!

12. Sprinkle the remaining cup of cheese over the potatoes and set the baking dish under the broiler for 5-10 minutes, or until the cheese is browned to your liking. Keep an eye on it!

13. Serve hot.

Creamy Mashed Potatoes

Prep Time: 10 mins. | Cook Time: 5 mins. | Total Time: 22 mins.

Ingredients

5 lbs Potatoes*, quartered

Water to just cover potatoes
(~6-8 cups)

2 1/2 tsp Salt (divided)

2 cloves Garlic (optional)

1/2 tsp Pepper

1/2 cup Butter

1/2 cup Sour Cream

1/2 cup Half and Half

Instructions

1. Cut potatoes in fourths. Add potatoes, water, 1 tsp salt, and garlic (if using), to the pot.

2. Close the lid and set the steam release knob to the Sealing position.

3. Press the Pressure Cook/Manual button, and then the +/- button to select 10 minutes. High Pressure.

4. When the cook cycle is finished, turn the steam release knob to the Venting position to quick release the pressure.

5. When the pin in the lid drops down, open the pot and drain the potatoes. Then return them to the pot.

6. Add the remaining 1 1/2 teaspoons of salt, pepper, butter, sour cream, and half and half to the potatoes.

7. Use a potato masher to mash up the potatoes to your desired consistency.

8. Serve hot or keep on Warm in the pot or a slow cooker.

Recipe Notes

1. Try using red potatoes. They have a nice flavor, and a bit of a heavier consistency. Use gold or russet for a fluffier texture.

2. The garlic is optional, but adds a lot of flavor. Use more than 2 cloves if you want a stronger garlic flavor.

*You can cut this recipe in half. Keep the cook time the same.

Baby Potatoes

4 Servings | **Prep Time: 5 mins.** | **Cook Time: 15 mins.** | **Total Time: 25 mins.**

Ingredients

1 cup Water

1 lb Baby Potatoes
(red or gold)

1 Tbsp Olive Oil

4 Tbsp Butter

1/2 tsp Garlic Powder

1/2 (1 oz) pkg Zesty
Italian Dressing Mix

Instructions

1. Add the water to the inner liner pot of the pressure cooker. Set a steamer basket in the pot.

2. Gently scrub and rinse potatoes. Place them in the steamer basket.

3. Place the lid on the pot and set the steam release knob to the Sealing position.

4. Press the Pressure Cook/Manual button, then the +/- button to select 12 minutes. High pressure. The pot will take a few minutes to come to pressure.

5. When the cook time is finished, turn the steam release knob to the Venting position to do a Quick Release of the pressure/steam.

6. When the pin in the lid drops down, open and carefully remove the steamer basket of potatoes.

7. Empty the inner pot and dry it. Then put it back in the main housing and turn on the Sauté setting.

8. When hot, add the olive oil and butter, then add the cooked potatoes. Let them sit a minute before stirring. Try to get them a little browned on all sides.

9. Sprinkle the Italian dressing mix and garlic powder over the potatoes. Gently stir to coat all of the potatoes. Cook just a few seconds more to let the seasoning bloom.

10. Turn off the Sauté setting and remove potatoes to a serving bowl. Drizzle with any butter/oil left in the pot.

11. Serve immediately.

Potatoes with Herb Butter

4-5 Servings | Prep Time: 10 mins. | Cook Time: 7 mins. | Total Time: 23 mins.

Ingredients

3 lbs Gold or Red Potatoes, cut in half (about 3" size, not Baby)

1/2 cup Butter, sliced

1/2 tsp Dried Basil

1/2 tsp Rosemary, dried, or 1 tsp fresh

1/2 tsp Onion Powder

1/4 tsp Pepper

3/4 tsp Kosher Salt (or 1/2 tsp table salt)

4 cloves Garlic, pressed or minced

1/2 cup Water (or broth)

1/3 cup Grated Parmesan Cheese

1 Tbsp Parsley

Instructions

1. Turn on the Sauté setting of the pot. When hot add the butter slices. Stir until melted.

2. Add the basil, rosemary, onion powder, pepper, salt, & garlic. Stir well while cooking about 20 seconds. Don't let the garlic burn.

3. Add the potatoes and toss in the butter until coated.

4. Pour in the water/broth. Then cancel the sauté setting.

5. Place the lid on the pot and set the steam release knob to the Sealing position.

6. Press the Pressure Cook/Manual button. Then press the +/- button to select 7 minutes (if your potatoes are larger, increase the time or quarter the potatoes).

7. When the cook time is finished, turn the steam release knob to the Venting position to do a Quick Release of the pressure.

8. When the pin in the lid drops down, open the lid and gently stir the potatoes.

9. If you want to crisp your potatoes, remove them from the pot (saving the buttery sauce) and place on a baking sheet. Put under the broiler for a few minutes, turning once. Watch them so they don't burn.

10. Garnish with parmesan, parsley, and the reserved buttery sauce from the pot.

Mashed Cauliflower

Ingredients

1 cup Water (for the pressure cooker)

1 large head Cauliflower, chopped

3/4 tsp Coarse Salt (or 1/2 tsp table salt, or to taste)

1/4 tsp Pepper

1 Tbsp Butter (or more to taste)

1/4 cup Parmesan Cheese, grated

Optional (use any or all!)

Roasted Garlic Cloves, to taste

1/4 cup Sour Cream

1/2 cup Bacon (cooked & chopped)

More Parmesan to taste

1/4 cup Chives, finely chopped

Instructions

1. Pour the water into the inner liner pot of the pressure cooker. Place a steamer basket or trivet in the pot. If using a steamer basket, use one that can hold the entire amount of cauliflower, otherwise, cut the cauliflower slightly larger and put it directly on the trivet.

2. Add the chopped cauliflower and place the lid on and set the steam release knob to the Sealing position.

3. Press the Pressure Cook/Manual button, then the +/- button to select 4 minutes. When the cook time is finished, turn off the pot and do a quick release of the pressure/steam.

4. Remove the cauliflower to a mixing bowl and mash it with a potato masher. Some people like to use an immersion blender, or hand mixer. Whatever you want to use is fine.

5. Add the salt, pepper, and butter. Mix well.

6. Add the parmesan and mix well.

7. Add any other extras you like, mix them in, and serve immediately.

Cinnamon Glazed Carrots

Ingredients

1 or 2 lb bag Baby Carrots*
(see note)

1/2 cup Orange Juice

1 tsp Cinnamon

2 Tbsp Butter

Add After Pressure Cooking

3/4 cup Brown Sugar, lightly
packed

1/4 cup Honey

3 tsp Corn Starch

3 tsp Water

Instructions

1. Add the carrots, orange juice, cinnamon, and butter to a 3 qt or 6 qt pressure cooker pot (double the recipe if using an 8 qt, or just double all ingredients except for the carrots, if you want).

2. Close the lid and set the steam release knob to the Sealing position.

3. Press the Pressure Cook (or Manual) button, then the +/- button to select 2 minutes (3 minutes for softer carrots). If you have very thin or thick carrots, adjust accordingly.

4. When the cook cycle is finished, turn the pot off and turn the steam release knob to the Venting position to do a Quick Release of the steam/pressure.

5. When the pin in the lid drops down, open the lid and use a slotted spoon to remove the carrots to a bowl.

6. Turn on the Sauté setting and add the brown sugar and the honey. Stir well to combine. Let the mixture cook for a few minutes and reduce a little.

7. Mix the corn starch and water together and add to the simmering mixture. Stir constantly until mixture thickens, then turn off the pot.

8. Add the carrots back in and stir to coat them all.

9. Serve directly from the pot, or transfer to a serving dish.

> **Recipe Note**
> *If you only want to make only 1 lb of carrots, that will work, but you'll need to keep the other ingredient amounts as written so the pot has enough liquid to come to pressure.

German Red Cabbage

Ingredients

4 Tbsp Butter

1 Bay Leaf

1 Onion, sliced

1 (2 lb) Head Red Cabbage, shredded thinly

1/2 tsp Kosher Salt (or 1/4 tsp table salt)

1/8 tsp Pepper

1/2 tsp Allspice

1/3 cup Balsamic Vinegar (or Apple Cider Vinegar)

1 Tbsp Sugar (or more to taste)

2 Granny Smith Apples, peeled, cored and diced

Instructions

1. Have all of the vegetables prepared and ready to go before you start cooking.

2. Turn on the Sauté setting. When the pot is hot, add the butter, bay leaf, and the onion. Cook, stirring occasionally, until just starting to soften.

3. Add the cabbage and stir. Cook for a few minutes, stirring occasionally and breaking up any clumps of cabbage that stuck together.

4. Add the salt, pepper, allspice, and bay leaf. Stir well.

5. Add the balsamic vinegar and sugar. Stir

6. Add the apples, stir them in.

7. Cancel the Sauté setting. Then press the Pressure Cook/Manual button, then press the +/- button to select 5 minutes. High pressure.

8. When the cook time has finished, do a Quick Release of the pressure by turning the steam release knob to the Venting position. Turn off the pot.

9. When the pin in the lid drops back down, open the lid. Stir the cabbage.

10. Serve hot with pork, sausages, or any main dish you like.

Lemon Asparagus

4 Servings | Prep Time: 5 mins. | Cook Time: 1 min. | Total Time: 11 mins.

Ingredients

1 bunch Fresh Asparagus, ~ 10 oz

1/2 cup Water

4 Tbsp Butter

1 clove Garlic, minced

1/4 tsp Salt

2-4 tsp Fresh Lemon Juice (optional)

1/4 cup Grated Parmesan Cheese

Instructions

1. Make sure your asparagus fit in the pot. Trim the ends to make them fit.

2. Add the water and butter to the pot. Also add garlic, if using.

3. Press the Pressure Cook/Manual button, then press the +/- button to select 1 minute. Select 0 minutes for thinner asparagus*, or for crisper results (see recipe note).

4. When the butter is melted and the water is hot, add the asparagus, laying half in the pot, and the other half cross-ways over the first layer. You don't need a steamer rack, but use one if you like. It is optional.

5. Close the lid and set the steam release knob to the Sealing position. The pot will take a few minutes to come to pressure.

6. As soon as the cooking cycle is finished, turn the steam release knob to the Venting position. When the pin in the lid drops back down, open the lid.

7. Use tongs to gently take the asparagus out of the pot onto a plate.

8. Add the salt and lemon juice to the liquid in the pot. Taste and adjust salt and/or lemon juice as needed.

9. Stir in the parmesan and then spoon the mixture over the asparagus.

10. Serve immediately.

> **Recipe Note**
> *If your asparagus is really thin, or you like it a little crisper, try using Low pressure to help avoid overcooking it.

Buttered Cabbage

4-6 Servings | Prep Time: 5 mins. | Cook Time: 5 mins. | Total Time: 10 mins.

Ingredients

3/4 cup Low Sodium Chicken Broth (use 1/2 cup for small head of cabbage)

6 Tbsp Unsalted Butter

1 head Green Cabbage, chopped into 1"-2" pieces

1/2 tsp Salt (or more/less to taste)

1/2 tsp Pepper (or more/less to taste)

Instructions

1. Add the broth and butter to the pot.

2. Add the chopped cabbage.

3. Close the lid and set the steam release knob to the Sealing position.

4. Press the Pressure Cook/Manual button, then the +/- button to select 5 minutes. High Pressure. The pot will take several minutes to come to pressure.

5. When the cook cycle has finished, turn off the pot and let it sit undisturbed for 3 minute natural release. Then turn the steam release knob to the Venting position to release the remaining pressure.

6. When the pin in the lid drops back down, open the lid.

7. Add the salt and pepper. Stir and serve!

Milk and Honey Corn on the Cob

6-8 Servings | Prep Time: 10 mins. | Cook Time: 5 mins. | Total Time: 30 mins.

Ingredients

4 cups Water

2 cups Whole Milk

1 stick Salted Butter (1/2 cup)

2 tsp Salt (omit if using Creole seasoning)

1/3 cup Honey

2-3 Tbsp Creole or Cajun Seasoning (optional)

6-8 ears Corn, shucked

Instructions

1. Place the inner liner in the pot. Pour the water and milk into the pot.

2. Turn on the Sauté setting (to start warming the liquid).

3. Slice the butter into several pieces and add them to the pot.

4. Whisk in the salt.

5. When the liquid is warm, whisk in the honey and stir until it dissolves.

6. Stir in the Creole seasoning, if using.

7. Cover the pot and let the liquid start to simmer.

8. Carefully add the corn to the pot.

9. Close the lid and set the steam release knob to the Sealing position.

10. Press the Pressure Cook/Manual button, then the +/- button to select 4 minutes. High Pressure. The pot will take several minutes to come to pressure.

11. When the cook cycle has finished, turn off the pot and let it sit undisturbed for 5 minute natural release. This will help the foam subside a bit.

12. Turn the steam release knob to the Venting position and do a Controlled Quick Release of the steam/pressure.

13. When the pin in the lid drops back down, open the lid.

14. Serve the corn from the pot using tongs.

15. Garnish as desired.

Candied Yams

6 Servings | Prep Time: 10 mins. | Cook Time: 20 mins. | Total Time: 30 mins.

Ingredients

1 1/2cups Water, for pressure cooker

3 lbs Yams or Sweet Potatoes, Fresh (about 4 medium, weighing about 12 oz ea.)

5 Tbsp Butter, softened, divided

1/2 to 3/4 cup Brown Sugar

3/4 tsp Vanilla

sm Pinch of Cloves

1/2 tsp Cinnamon

1/2 tsp Nutmeg

1 1/2 cups Mini Marshmallows

GARNISH

Toasted Pecans

Instructions

1. Add the water and a rack/trivet to the inner liner of the pressure cooker.

2. Scrub the Yams and use a fork to pierce a few holes in them. Set them in the pot on the rack/trivet.

3. Close the lid, lock it in place, and set the Steam Release Knob to the Sealing position.

4. Press the Pressure Cook/or Manual button, and use the +/- button to select 22 minutes (If your yams are small, reduce time to 16 minutes, large - 27 minutes).

5. While the yams are cooking, in a mixing bowl cream together 4 Tbsp of the softened butter, brown sugar, vanilla, cloves, cinnamon, and nutmeg. Set aside.

6. Get a pie plate or similar sized baking dish. Set aside.

7. When cook cycle ends, let the pot sit undisturbed for 15 minute natural release. Turn off the pot. Turn the Steam Release Knob to Venting and release the pressure.

8. When the pin in the lid drops, open it and carefully remove yams to the baking dish.

9. Heat Broiler to 350° (F) with the rack in the middle position.

10. Use a fork to scrape away the skins. Then use fork to mash the yams.

11. Add the butter mixture and combine well with the yams.

12. Dot with bits of the remaining butter. Spread the marshmallows out on the top in an even layer.

13. Put under the broiler (middle rack) for 5-10 minutes, or until marshmallows brown to your liking. Keep an eye on it!

To Reheat If Made Ahead*

14. Bake at 350° (F) for 15-25 minutes, or until heated through, then add remaining Tbsp of butter and the marshmallows and continue cooking until marshmallows brown.

15. Garnish with toasted pecans (just a few minutes in a dry skillet to toast them. You can do that ahead of time). Serve immediately.

Recipe Note
*These can be made ahead and heated in the oven before serving.

Stuffing / Dressing

Ingredients

12 oz Dry Cubed Seasoned Stuffing
(1 bag or box)

1/2 cup Butter

1 med Sweet Onion, diced

1 cup Celery, diced

1 tsp Rubbed Sage, dried

1/2 tsp Kosher Salt (or 1/4 tsp table salt)

1/4 tsp Pepper

2 cloves Garlic, pressed or finely minced

1 1/2 cups Turkey Broth (use 2 cups for a

more moist result)

1 1/2 cups Water, for pressure cooker

OPTIONAL (any combination of these)

1/2 cup Dried Cranberries

Raisins

1/2 cup Walnuts or Pecans, chopped

1/2 cup Apple, diced

1/2 cup Mushrooms, chopped

1/2 cup Bacon, cooked, chopped

Instructions

1. Pour stuffing cubes into a large mixing bowl. Mix in any of the optional ingredients you choose to use (pictured is dried cranberries and walnuts). Set aside.

2. (This step can also be done on the stove, using a skillet. I prefer doing it all in one pot) Set pot to Sauté function (Less/Low heat).

3. Add butter, onion, and celery. Cook, stirring frequently, until vegetables soften.

4. Add sage, salt, pepper, and garlic. Cook until fragrant, stirring constantly (about 30 seconds).

5. Add broth and stir. Let mixture just come to a simmer, then Cancel the sauté mode.

6. Using pot holders, remove the inner liner with the broth mixture from the pressure cooker and pour the mixture carefully over the stuffing cubes.

7. Toss together the stuffing cubes and broth mixture until well combined.

8. Rinse out the inner liner, dry it, and set it back in the pressure cooker base. Add 1 1/2 cups of water to the inner liner pot.

9. Transfer stuffing to a sprayed 2 quart stainless or aluminum cooking pan (metal works better than glass in this case). I use my 7"x3" Pan in my 6 qt.

10. Gently pat the stuffing into the pan. Don't pack it in there too tightly. Spray a piece of foil and cover the pan tightly, crimping the edges.

11. Set the pan on a trivet/rack with handles and put them into the pot. Close the lid and lock into position. Set the Steam Release Knob to the Sealing position.

12. Press the Pressure Cook/Manual button. Then the +/- button to choose 20 minutes.

13. After the cook cycle ends, let the pot sit and naturally release pressure for 5 minutes. Then manually release the remaining pressure, by turning the Steam Release Knob to Venting

14. When all of the pressure is out of the pot and the pin in the lid drops, open the lid and use pot holders to very carefully lift the rack and pan out of the pot.

15. Set on a cooling rack and keep covered until you are ready to serve. Or, turn on your broiler to 375° (F) and set the pan under it for a few minutes to brown the top.

Pasta
spaghetti, goulash and more

Lasagna

6 Servings | Prep Time: 25 mins. | Cook Time: 24 mins. | Total Time: 1 hr. 4 mins.

Ingredients

Meat Mixture

1/2 lb Lean Ground Beef

1/2 lb Ground Italian Sausage

(or can use all beef or sausage)

1/2 tsp Kosher Salt (1/4 tsp table salt)

1/4 tsp Pepper

1/2 tsp Onion Powder

1/2 tsp Garlic Powder

1/2 tsp Italian Seasoning

Cheese Mixture

1 cup Ricotta Cheese (or Cottage Cheese)

1 Egg

1/2 cup Mozzarella Cheese, shredded

1/2 cup Parmesan Cheese, grated

1 1/2 tsp Garlic Powder

1 1/4 tsp Onion Powder

1 1/4 tsp Italian Seasoning

1/2 tsp Oregano

1/2 tsp Salt (if your pasta sauce is salty, decrease to 1/4 tsp)

1/2 tsp Pepper

1/4 cup Chopped Fresh Parsley

REMAINING LAYERS

1 (24 oz) jar Pasta Sauce (about 3 cups) (I prefer marinara, use your favorite)

1/2 cup Chopped Spinach Leaves, *optional* (fresh, or frozen, thawed)

5-6 No Boil Lasagna Noodles (or regular uncooked lasagna noodles)

1/2 cup Mozzarella Cheese, shredded

1/2 cup Parmesan Cheese, grated

Instructions

Brown the Meat

1. Set pot to Sauté and add the beef, sausage, salt, pepper, onion powder, garlic powder, and Italian seasoning. Cook, stirring, until the meat is cooked.

2. Remove meat, drain, and set aside. Clean out pot and add 1 1/2 cups water to it.

Mix the Cheese Mixture

3. In a mixing bowl combine the ricotta, egg, mozzarella, parmesan, garlic powder, onion powder, Italian seasoning, oregano, salt, pepper, and parsley. Use a fork to mix thoroughly. Set aside.

Make the Lasagna

4. In a 7" x 3" or 6"x3" springform or push pan, make a layer of the noodles by breaking them and fitting them like a mosaic to cover the bottom of the pan.

5. Spread 1/3 of the pasta sauce over the noodles, covering them all. Spread 1/2 of the meat mixture over the sauce evenly. Then spread 1/2 of the cheese mixture evenly over the meat.

6. Sprinkle spinach (if using) over cheese mixture evenly, add another layer of noodles, press down on them a little.

7. Repeat step 5.

8. Add another layer of noodles, the last 1/3 of sauce, 1/2 cup mozzarella, and 1/2 cup parmesan.

9. Spray a piece of foil with nonstick spray and cover the pan with the foil so water can't get in.

10. Set the pan on a trivet with handles and lift them into the inner pot that has 1 1/2 cups of water in it. You can also use a sling to set the pan on the trivet in the pot.

11. Close the lid and lock in place. Turn the steam release knob to the Sealing position.

12. Press the Pressure Cook /Manual button and choose 24 minutes. High Pressure.

13. When the cook cycle has ended, let the pot sit undisturbed for 15 minute Natural Release. Then, turn the knob to the Venting position to release any remaining steam.

14. When the pin in the lid drops down, open the lid. Use silicone mitts, sling, or good pot holders that can get wet to lift the rack with the hot pan out of the pot to a cooling rack. Be VERY careful as it could slip off the rack.

15. Carefully remove the foil. Turn on broiler to 450° with oven rack in the middle of the oven.

16. Broil the cheese on top to your desired amount. Watch it closely as it doesn't take long.

17. Let the lasagna rest for a few minutes before releasing from the pan. This will help it maintain its shape and cool down just a bit.

18. Carefully (pan and lasagna very hot) release lasagna from springform pan while on a plate.

19. If you used a push pan, set a large can on a plate, then set the push pan on top of the can. Gently, and carefully push the sides of the pan straight down. Wear oven mitts or other hand protection. The pan and the lasagna will be very hot.

20. Slide another plate under the lasagna. You might need to use a spatula to help slide it over. Serve immediately.

Macaroni and Cheese

6 Servings | Prep Time: 10 mins. | Cook Time: 4 mins. | Total Time: 30 mins.

Ingredients

4 cups Water or Low Sodium Chicken Broth

4 Tbsp Butter, unsalted

1 tsp Ground Mustard

1/4 tsp Kosher Salt

1/2 tsp Seasoned Salt (optional, but it adds a nice flavor)

A Few Dashes of Hot Sauce (optional)

16 oz Pasta (1 lb macaroni, etc.)

2 cups Cheddar Cheese, shredded (freshly shredded for creamiest result)

1 cup Monterey Jack Cheese, shredded fresh

1/4 cup Parmesan Cheese

1/2 - 1 cup Heavy Cream (or half and half, evaporated milk, or whole milk) Add enough to get desired creaminess.

Instructions

1. Turn on the pot's Sauté setting.

2. Add the water, butter, ground mustard, salt, and seasoned salt to the pot and bring to a simmer.

3. Cancel the Sauté mode.

4. Stir in the pasta and close the lid. Set the steam release knob to the Sealing position.

5. Press the Manual (or Pressure Cook) button and use the +/- button to choose 4 minutes (or half of the time the pasta package directions indicate).

6. When the cook cycle ends, do a Quick Release of the pressure. Start slowly, using several small bursts of steam release, to make sure none of the sauce spews out with the steam (the butter helps keep the foam down). Then fully release the pressure.

7. When the pin in the lid drops, open the pot and give the contents a stir. You want some liquid in there, but if it looks too watery, take some out.

8. Add the cheeses, half at a time, and stir. Wait for it to melt before next step.

9. Add the cream and stir until blended with the cheese.

10. Adjust salt to taste.

11. Cover and let sit for a few minutes to soak everything up.

12. Serve hot.

Recipe Note
The mac and cheese thickens up as it cools. If you need to loosen it up, add more milk as needed.

Spaghetti with Meat Sauce

Ingredients

1 lb Lean Ground Beef or Turkey

1 sm Onion, chopped (or 1/2 tsp onion   powder)

3/4 tsp Salt

1/4 tsp Pepper

2 tsp Italian Seasoning

1/2 tsp Basil, dried

2 tsp garlic powder

16 oz Spaghetti Noodles (broken in thirds)

4 1/3 cups Low Sodium Broth or Water

1 (14 oz) can Diced Tomatoes, with juice

1 (24 oz) jar Spaghetti Sauce (or marinara)

Parmesan Cheese (for garnish)

Instructions

1. Turn your pot on to the Sauté setting. When it is hot, add the ground beef (If using ground turkey, add 1 Tbsp olive oil and add the onions, then add the ground turkey). Stir to break apart the meat.

2. Add the onion, salt, pepper, Italian seasoning, basil, and garlic powder. Cook for a few minutes, stirring occasionally, until the meat is mostly done, and the onions are turning translucent.

3. Scatter in the spaghetti noodles (broken in thirds) in a random fashion, so they are not al laying side-by-side. This keeps them from sticking together.

4. Pour in the broth/water and then the diced tomatoes evenly over the noodles (do not stir!).

5. Pour on the spaghetti sauce, evenly, completely covering all of the noodles (exposed noodles may not cook completely).

6. Close the lid. Set the steam release knob to the Sealing position. Cancel the Sauté setting.

7. Press the Pressure Cook/Manual button, then the +/- button to select 8 minutes (for softer noodles) or 6 minutes (for more al dente).

8. When the cooking cycle is finished, turn off the pot and do a controlled Quick Release of the pressure/steam. When the pin in the lid drops down, open the lid.

9. Stir the spaghetti well, and the sauce and noodles will blend nicely. If the noodles are not cooked enough for you, just put the lid back on and let it sit a few minutes while you get everything else for your meal ready. If a few noodles stick together, just use a fork to separate them (this rarely happens to me)

10. Garnish with parmesan cheese and serve with some French bread.

Spaghetti and Meatballs

5-6 Servings | Prep Time: 5 mins. | Cook Time: 9 mins. | Total Time: 29 mins.

Ingredients

2 lbs Meatballs, frozen - cooked

16 oz Spaghetti Noodles

1 (14 oz) can Diced Tomatoes w/juice

1 (24 oz) jar Spaghetti Sauce (or marinara sauce + Italian seasoning)

3 cups Water (fill the 24 oz jar once)

or use broth

Garnishes

Grated Parmesan Cheese

Shredded Mozzarella Cheese

Fresh Parsley or Basil

Instructions

1. Put meatballs in the bottom of the inner liner pot.

2. Break the spaghetti in half and sprinkle over meatballs in a random pattern, so not too many are side by side. This helps prevent them sticking together.

3. Pour the water/broth over the noodles.

4. Pour the diced tomatoes, if using over the noodles, and then the spaghetti sauce over the noodles, and cover as much of them as you can with the sauce. This helps them all get cooked.

5. Put on the lid and set the steam release knob to the Sealing position.

6. Press the Pressure Cook (Manual) button and then the +/- button or dial to select 9 minutes (7-8 minutes for more al dente).

7. After cook time has finished, turn off the pot and turn the steam release knob to the Venting position, and do a Quick Release of the steam so the pasta doesn't overcook.

8. Watch it closely, and if sauce starts to spew out with the steam, close the vent and release the steam in bursts until it looks like no more sauce will be spewing out.

9. After the pin in the lid drops down, open the lid and give the spaghetti a stir. If any noodles stuck together, just use a fork to separate them.

10. Serve with some bread, and garnish with parmesan cheese, mozzarella, or whatever you like!

Hamburger Stroganoff

Ingredients

1 Tbsp Olive Oil

2 Tbsp Butter

1 Yellow Onion, diced

1 lb Lean Ground Beef (or turkey)

1/2 tsp Thyme, dried

1 tsp Salt

1/2 tsp Pepper

3 cloves Garlic, pressed or minced

1 1/2 Tbsp Worcestershire Sauce

10 oz Mushrooms, sliced

4 cups Beef Broth

8 oz Wide Egg Noodles

To Finish

3 Tbsp Flour

3 Tbsp Cold Water

1 cup Sour Cream (plus extra for garnish)

1/4 cup Fresh Parsley, chopped

Instructions

1. Turn on Sauté setting. When pot is hot, add the oil, butter, and onion. Cook, stirring occasionally, until just starting to turn translucent.

2. Add the ground beef and stir, breaking up the meat, but leaving a few larger chunks. Cook, stirring occasionally, until just a little pink remains.

3. Add the thyme, salt, pepper, garlic, and Worcestershire sauce. Stir and cook for 1 minute.

4. Add the mushrooms and mix well. Cook for another minute.

5. Pour the broth in while stirring, and scraping the bottom of the pot to get up any brown bits.

6. Add the noodles. Press them gently into the mixture to submerge them as much as possible.

7. Cancel Sauté function. Press the Pressure Cook/Manual button, then press the +/- button to select 4 minutes.

8. After the cook cycle is finished, let the pot sit undisturbed for 2 minute natural release. Then do a Quick Release of the remaining pressure.

9. When the pin in the lid drops down, open the lid. Then turn on the sauté setting.

10. Mix together the flour and water. Add to the pot and stir well to combine. Turn off the pot.

11. In a small bowl, mix the sour cream with a little of the hot sauce from the pot. Then add a little more to temper the sour cream so it doesn't curdle when added to the hot stroganoff.

12. Add the sour cream and parsley to the pot. Stir gently to incorporate the ingredients. Taste and adjust salt, if needed.

13. Serve immediately, garnishing as desired.

Creamy Beef and Shells

6-7 Servings | Prep Time: 10 mins. | Cook Time: 20 mins. | Total Time: 30 mins.

Ingredients

1 1/2 lbs Ground Beef

1 sm Onion, diced

1/4 - 1/2 tsp Red Pepper Flakes (optional)

3 tsp Italian Seasoning

1 tsp Garlic Powder

1 tsp Salt

1/2 tsp Pepper

3 cups Beef Broth, low sodium (or 3 tsp beef bouillon and 3 cups water)

1 (12 oz) box Medium Shell Pasta*

1 (24 oz) jar Marinara Sauce

TO FINISH

1 cup Heavy Cream

1 cup Grated Parmesan Cheese

Instructions

1. Turn on the Sauté setting. Then add the ground beef. Cook, breaking up the meat, until about halfway done. Then add the onion and cook, stirring occasionally, until onion turns translucent..

2. Add the red pepper flakes (if using), Italian seasoning, garlic powder, salt, and pepper. Stir well.

3. Pour in the broth and stir.

4. Add the pasta in an even layer. Don't stir it. Gently press the pasta into the liquid.

5. Pour the marinara sauce over the pasta, covering it all. Don't stir it.

6. Turn off the Sauté setting. Close the lid and set the steam release knob to the Sealing position.

7. Press the Pressure Cook/Manual button or dial, then the +/- button or dial to select 5 minutes. High Pressure. The pot will take several minutes to come to pressure.

8. When the cook cycle has finished, turn the steam release knob to the Venting position to Quick Release the pressure.

9. When the pin in the lid drops back down, open the lid.

10. Stir in the heavy cream and parmesan cheese. Let the pasta sit for a few minutes to cool a little and thicken.

11. Serve hot!

Recipe Note

*If you want to use a full pound (16 oz) of pasta, increase the broth by 1 cup, add 1/2 tsp more of the Italian seasoning, and add more heavy cream to taste. The cook time stays the same.

Pizza Pasta Casserole

Ingredients

1 lb Italian Sausage

1/2 Onion, diced

1 1/2 tsp Italian Seasoning

1/2 tsp Oregano

2 tsp Garlic Powder

1/4 - 1/2 tsp Red Pepper Flakes

1/2 tsp Kosher Salt (or 1/4 tsp table salt)

1/4 tsp Pepper

1 Red Bell Pepper (optional) or green pepper, chopped

6 oz Mushrooms (optional) sliced

4 cups Low Sodium Chicken Broth

16 oz Rotini (or penne, ziti, etc)

24 oz jar Marinara Sauce

8 oz Mozzarella Cheese, shredded (plus more for garnish, if desired)

5 oz Pepperoni Slices (about 20-30 slices)

OPTIONAL ADD-INS

1/2 cup Sliced Black Olives

1/2 cup Cooked Bacon Pieces

1/2 cup Pineapple Chunks

Canadian Bacon (instead of pepperoni)

Instructions

1. Turn on the Sauté setting. Add sausage and onion. Cook until the meat is cooked through.

2. Add Italian seasoning, oregano, garlic powder (or garlic), red pepper flakes, salt, pepper, and bell pepper, and mushrooms, if using. Stir.

3. Add the broth or water and stir, scraping the bottom of the pot to deglaze (get up any browned bits).

4. Add the pasta evenly over the mixture. Do not stir.

5. Pour the marinara sauce over the pasta and cover it completely. Do not stir.

6. Cancel the Sauté function. Put the lid on the pot and turn the steam release knob to the Sealing position. Press the Pressure Cook (Manual) button, then the +/- button to select 4 minutes (for rotini). Or set cook time to half the time the package directions say to cook for.

7. When the cook cycle is finished, do a Quick Release of the pressure by turning the steam release knob to the Venting position.

8. When the pin in the lid drops down, open the lid and stir the pasta. Stir in half of the cheese and 3/4 of the pepperoni.

9. Stir in olives, if using, or any other add-ins you'd like.

10. Sprinkle the remaining cheese on top and arrange the remaining pepperoni on top of the cheese. Close the lid and let the cheese melt.

11. Serve from the pot or transfer to a casserole serving dish.

Cheeseburger Macaroni

Ingredients

1 lb lean Ground Beef or Turkey

1 Onion, chopped (or 1 tsp Onion Powder)

2 cloves Garlic, minced (or 1 tsp Garlic Powder)

3/4 tsp Seasoned Salt

1/2 tsp Kosher Salt (or 1/4 tsp table salt)

1/2 tsp Pepper

1 tsp Hot Sauce (optional)

1 tsp Dijon Mustard (or 2 tsp dry mustard)

3 cups Low Sodium Chicken Broth (or Water)

12 oz Small Macaroni (3 cups) uncooked

TO FINISH

2 cups Sharp Cheddar Cheese (shredded)

1 cup Monterey Jack Cheese (shredded)

1/4 - 2/3 cup Milk

GARNISH

Fresh Chopped Parsley, Sour Cream

Instructions

1. Turn on the pot's Sauté setting. When hot, add the ground beef and onion. Cook, stirring occasionally, until onions are tender, translucent, and the meat is browned.

2. Add the garlic. Stir.

3. Add all of the spices after browning the meat.

4. Add the hot sauce, if using, Dijon, and broth. Stir.

5. Put a glass lid, or other lid on to let the broth heat up to almost a simmer. If you have to use the IP's lid, make sure it is on Venting.

6. Next, remove glass lid and add the macaroni and make sure it is submerged.

7. Close the lid and set the steam release knob to Sealing. Then cancel the Sauté setting.

8. Press the Pressure Cook/Manual button, then the +/- button to select 4 minutes (or 1/2 the cook time the pasta's package directions indicate).

9. When the cook cycle is finished, turn the pot off and do a Controlled Quick Release* (explained below) of the pressure.

10. *A controlled quick release means you release the steam in short bursts, then longer bursts, until you can be sure none of the sauce spews out of the vent with the steam from the intense pressure. Then fully open the vent and let it go.

11. When the pin in the lid drops down, open the lid and stir the pasta.

12. Stir in the cheeses and then add as much milk as you want to make it as saucy as you like.

13. Add optional garnish and serve hot.

American Goulash

7-10 Servings | Prep Time: 15 mins. | Cook Time: 4 mins. | Total Time: 35 mins.

Ingredients

2 tsp Olive Oil (only if using gr. turkey)

1 lb Ground Beef or Turkey (lean)

1 Onion, diced

1/2 cup Diced Celery

2 Bay Leaves

1/4 tsp Red Pepper Flakes

2 tsp Italian Seasoning

1/2 tsp Pepper

1 tsp Salt (or more to taste)

5 cloves Garlic, pressed or minced

1 1/2 Tbsp Worcestershire Sauce (or Soy Sauce)

1 Green Bell Pepper, chopped

4 cups Chicken Broth, low sodium

2 cups (9 oz) Small Elbow Macaroni (If you use penne, you will need 3 cups. Weigh your pasta if you can)

1 Tbsp Paprika

1 (14 oz) can Diced Tomatoes (with juice)

1 (14 oz) can Tomato Sauce (or Marinara Sauce, 2 cups)

TO FINISH

1 1/2 cups Corn, frozen or canned

1/4 cup Fresh Parsley, chopped

Optional

1-2 cups Cheese, shredded

Instructions

1. Turn on the pressure cooker's Sauté setting. When the pot is hot add oil (if using ground turkey) or add the ground beef. Also add onion, celery, bay leaves. Cook until onion starts to turn translucent.

2. Add the red pepper flakes, Italian seasoning, pepper, salt, garlic, Worcestershire (or soy sauce), and green bell pepper. Stir, and sauté for a couple of minutes.

3. Pour in the broth and stir. Put a glass lid on the pot and let the broth heat up to barely a simmer. Then add the macaroni and paprika. Stir.

4. Add the diced tomatoes and the tomato sauce, but do not stir.

5. Put the lid on the pot and lock in place. Set the steam release knob to the Sealing position.

6. Cancel Sauté setting and press the Pressure Cook/Manual button, then the +/- button to choose 4 minutes (3 minutes for al dente pasta).

7. When the cook cycle is finished, do a Controlled Quick Release of the pressure by turning the knob towards the Venting position in bursts, until you feel confident that no sauce will come out of the vent with the steam. Then turn the knob all the way to the Venting position.

8. When the pin in the lid drops down, open the lid. Give the goulash a stir. Taste & adjust salt.

9. Add the corn and the parsley. Stir in the cheese, if you are using it and serve immediately.

Cheesy Taco Pasta

Ingredients

1 lb Lean Ground Beef or Turkey

2 1/2 Tbsp Taco Seasoning (see my recipe for homemade, or use 1 packet of store bought)

1 (16 oz) Container of Salsa

16 oz Pasta Shells, medium

4 cups Broth, low sodium (I prefer chicken broth)

2 cups Shredded Cheese (1 cup Monterey Jack + 1 cup sharp Cheddar)

Instructions

Brown the Meat

1. Turn pot on to Sauté mode. When hot, add the meat (use a little olive oil if using ground turkey). Cook until mostly done.

2. Add the taco seasoning, stir and finish cooking meat.

3. Add the salsa and broth. Stir. Put on a glass lid (or any lid that fits. If using the pressure cooker lid, make sure it is Venting). Let the broth start to simmer.

4. Add the pasta and stir. Cancel the sauté mode.

5. Put the pressure cooker lid on and set the steam release knob to Sealing.

Pressure Cook

6. Press the Manual (or Pressure Cook) button and use the +/- button to select 5 minutes for softer pasta, 4 minutes for more al dente (or half the time on the pasta package directions).

7. When cooking cycle ends, turn off the pressure cooker.

8. Do a controlled Quick Release of the pressure/steam. Start it in shorter bursts until you are sure no sauce will be spewing from the steam release knob. Then turn the knob all the way to Venting, and let it release the remaining pressure.

9. When the pin in the lid drops, open it and give the pasta a good stir.

10. Add the cheese, stir again, and serve.

11. Garnish with any of these: Avocado, Jalapeño, Sour Cream, Tortilla Chips, or Cilantro

Beef and Noodles

Ingredients

2 tsp Cooking Oil

1 (3 lb) Chuck Roast (or your favorite roast), cut into slightly larger than bite-sized cubes

2 cups Water

1 cup Beef Broth, low sodium

2 pkgs Beefy Onion Soup Mix (or regular onion soup mix)

2 (10.5 oz) cans Cream of Mushroom Soup

12 oz Wide Egg Noodles

1 cup Sour Cream (optional)

Instructions

1. Turn the pot on to Sauté setting. When the pot is hot, add the oil.

2. Add the Beef cubes in one layer (you will probably need to cook in 2 batches). Brown both sides lightly so they get some color. Don't cook them all the way through.

3. With all of the browned beef in the pot (still on sauté), add the water/broth, and stir, scraping up any brown bits from the bottom of the pot (deglaze).

4. Add the soup mix and stir well.

5. Add the Cream of mushroom soup on top of the meat, and do not stir it. Just leave it on top (this is so the mixture isn't too thick to come to pressure, avoiding a BURN message).

6. Place the lid on and set the steam release knob to the Sealing position.

7. Cancel the sauté and press the Pressure Cook/Manual button, and the +/- button to select 25 minutes.

8. When the cook cycle is finished, let the pot sit undisturbed for 10 minute natural release. Then turn the steam release knob to Venting to manually release the remaining pressure.

9. When the pin in the lid drops down, open the lid and give the beef mixture a stir.

10. Turn off the pot, then turn on the Sauté function to the Low setting, and add the noodles. Stir them in and submerge them.

11. Cover the pot with a glass lid, or the IP lid vented. Let the noodles cook until they are tender, about 5-8 minutes, stirring occasionally to make sure they don't stick.

12. When the noodles are done to your liking, turn off the pot and serve. If you are adding the sour cream, you can stir it in before serving, or top each serving with a dollop.

Loaded Taco Pasta

Ingredients

1 lb Lean Ground Beef (or ground turkey)

1 -1 oz Packet Taco Seasoning

1/2 tsp Onion Powder

1 tsp Garlic Powder

16 oz Salsa

1 (4 oz) can Mild Diced Green Chiles (optional)

3 cups Water (or low sodium broth)

1 (15 oz) can Black Beans, drained and rinsed

12 oz Medium Shells (or 12 oz other shape pasta)

1 (15 oz) can Corn Kernels (or 2 cups frozen kernels)

2 cups Cheddar Cheese, shredded

Instructions

Brown the Meat

1. Turn the pot on to the Sauté setting. When display reads Hot, add meat (use a little olive oil if using ground turkey). Cook, breaking up the meat, until mostly done.
2. Add the taco seasoning, onion powder, garlic powder. Stir and finish cooking the meat.
3. Add the salsa, green chiles if using, and broth. Stir. Put on a glass lid (or any lid that fits. If you use the pressure cooker lid, make sure it is on Venting). Let the broth heat up and start to simmer.
4. Add the black beans and the pasta. Stir and gently press the pasta down into the liquid.
5. Cancel the sauté setting.

Pressure Cook

6. Put the pressure cooker lid on and set the steam release knob to the Sealing position.
7. Press the Pressure Cook /Manual button or dial and then the + or - button to select 4 minutes (for medium shells), or half the time on the pasta package directions.
8. When cooking cycle ends, turn off the Instant Pot. Let it sit undisturbed for 1 minute to settle a bit.
9. Do a controlled Quick Release of the pressure/steam. Start it in smaller bursts until you are sure no sauce will be spewing from the steam release knob. Then I turn the knob all the way to Venting, and let it release the remaining steam/pressure.
10. When the pin in the lid drops down, open it and gently stir the pasta.
11. Add the corn, and then add the cheese. Stir again. If using frozen corn, let it sit a couple of minutes to heat it through.
12. Serve with any of the garnishes listed, or just as it is!

Garnish with any of these, if desired

13. Avocado, Jalapeño, Sour Cream, Tortilla Chips, Cilantro

Meatball Pasta Dinner

6-8 Servings | Prep Time: 10 mins. | Cook Time: 5 mins. | Total Time: 45 mins.

Ingredients

1 1/2-2 lbs Frozen Cooked Meatballs

3 3/4 cups Broth or Water

1 lb Pasta (I like penne or rotini best)

1 (24 oz) Jar of Pasta Sauce (I use Marinara)

1 (14.5 oz) can Diced Tomatoes, undrained

If using Marinara, Season with These Spices:

2 tsp Italian Seasoning

2 tsp Garlic Powder

3 tsp Dehydrated Onion

1/2 tsp Salt

1/2 tsp Pepper

Optional Toppings

1 cup Grated Parmesan

1 1/2 cups Shredded Mozzarella

Instructions

Layer the Ingredients in the Pot - Do Not Stir!

1. Put the meatballs in the pot.
2. Pour the broth/water over the meatballs.
3. Pour pasta on meatballs and spread out in an even layer.
4. Pour the can of tomatoes over the pasta, evenly.
5. Pour the jar of pasta sauce over, evenly, covering the pasta entirely.
6. Sprinkle the spices over the sauce.

Cook It

7. Put the lid on the Pot and set the knob to Sealing.
8. Press the Pressure Cook (or Manual) button, then the +/- button to choose 5 minutes (or half of the cooking time on the pasta package directions).

The pot may take up to 20 minutes to get to pressure, due to the frozen meatballs!

9. When the cooking cycle is done, do a Controlled Quick Release of the pressure until the pin drops. (A controlled quick release means you release the steam in short bursts, then longer bursts, until you are sure that no sauce will spew out of the vent with the steam from the intense pressure).
10. Open the lid, and stir contents, then mix in the parmesan cheese.
11. Taste and add more salt & pepper if needed.
12. Top with the Mozzarella cheese, if using, and cover the pot with a lid (or just use a plate) to help the cheese melt.
13. Serve hot!

Chicken Bacon Ranch Pasta

Ingredients

6 slices Thick Cut Bacon, cooked or uncooked, cut in bite-sized pieces

3 Tbsp Butter, unsalted

4 cups Chicken Broth, low sodium

1/2 cup Heavy Cream or Half and Half, (more if you like it saucier)

1 packet Ranch Dressing Powder

1/2 tsp Garlic Powder

16 oz Penne Pasta (or rotini, ziti, etc.)

2 (8 oz) Boneless Skinless Chicken Breast (cubed slightly larger than bite sized)

8 oz Cream Cheese, cubed

1 cup Sharp Cheddar Cheese, shredded (optional)

Instructions

1. Prepare all of the ingredients before you start. Cut the bacon and chicken, have the butter measured. Shred the cheese, and measure out the ranch & garlic powders, broth, and pasta. It will make the cooking process much easier and faster. Less stress!

2. **If you have uncooked bacon:** Turn on Sauté function. Add chopped bacon. Cook, stirring occasionally, until done. Remove to a paper towel. Drain the fat from the pot. Set aside.

3. Add the butter and a splash or two of the broth to the pot and stir, scraping the bottom of the pot so you can to get up all of the brown bits (fond).

4. Add the broth, heavy cream, ranch powder, and garlic powder, and stir well.

5. Add the pasta and stir.

6. Add the chicken and the cubes of cream cheese. Don't stir, but gently push down, using a spoon, to submerge the chicken and pasta. Cancel the Sauté function.

7. Place the lid on the pot and turn the steam release knob to the Sealing position.

8. Press Pressure Cook or Manual button, then the + or - button to choose 5 minutes. Your pasta may need a different time, usually half the time on the package directions.

9. When the cooking cycle ends, do a controlled Quick Release of the pressure, just until you are sure no sauce will spew out with the steam, then turn the knob all the way.

10. When the pin in the lid drops down, open it and give the contents a stir. It will be fairly soupy at this point.

11. Stir in the cheese and bacon. Let the cheese melt before serving. It will thicken as it cools.

Tuscan Chicken Pasta

Prep Time: 10 mins. | Cook Time: 3 mins. | Total Time: 23 mins.

Ingredients

3 Tbsp Butter

1 1/2 lbs Chicken Breast (boneless/skinless) cut a little larger than bite sized

4 cups Chicken Broth, low sodium

2 tsp Soy Sauce

1 (7 oz) jar Sun Dried Tomatoes, drained

5 cloves Garlic, pressed or finely minced (or 3 tsp garlic powder)

1/2 tsp Onion Powder

1 Tbsp Italian Seasoning

1 tsp Kosher Salt (or 1/2 tsp table salt)

1/2 tsp Pepper

8 oz Cream Cheese, cubed

16 oz Pasta (cavatappi, macaroni)

1 1/2 cups Heavy Cream, divided

TO FINISH

1 cup Grated Parmesan

3-4 cups Fresh Baby Spinach

4 Tbsp Fresh Basil, chopped

Instructions

1. Add the butter, chicken, broth, soy sauce, sun dried tomatoes, garlic powder, onion powder, Italian seasoning, salt, and pepper to the pot. Stir.

2. Add the cubes of cream cheese in a layer.

3. Pour in the pasta in an even layer and gently push it down into the liquid. Pour the heavy cream over the top.

4. Close the lid and set the steam release knob to the Sealing position.

5. Press the Pressure Cook/Manual button or dial, then the +/- button or dial to select 3 minutes (this time may vary for the type of pasta you use. I used cavatappi/corkscrew). High Pressure.

6. When the cook cycle is finished, Let the pot sit undisturbed for 3 minute natural release. Then turn the steam release knob to the Venting position to Quick Release the pressure. If the sauce starts to come out of the vent, close the vent and release the pressure in shorter bursts until you are able to open it fully with no sauce coming out.

7. When the pin in the lid drops down, open the lid. Stir the pasta well to incorporate the cream cheese as it may be lumpy at first.

8. Add the parmesan and the spinach. Stir well.

9. Add the remaining 1/2 cup of heavy cream and the basil and stir in.

10. Serve immediately.

Buffalo Chicken Pasta

Ingredients

3 1/2 cups Chicken Broth, low sodium

1 (12 oz) box Farfalle Pasta (Bow Tie)

8 oz Cream Cheese, cubed

1/2 cup Celery, diced (optional)

2 Chicken Breasts, boneless/ skinless cut in half cross-ways (or 3 cups cooked shredded)

1/3-1/2 cup Buffalo Hot Wing Sauce (such as Frank's Red Hot) plus extra for garnish

TO FINISH

1/2 cup Prepared Blue Cheese or Ranch Dressing

1 cup Cheddar Cheese, shredded

Green Onion or celery, for garnish

Instructions

1. Pour the chicken broth into the pot.

2. Pour in the pasta and even out the layer.

3. Dot the cubes of cream cheese and celery evenly over the pasta, do not stir.

4. Place the chicken breast pieces on top of the cream cheese/pasta (If using cooked chicken, add it after pressure cooking).

5. Pour the buffalo hot wing sauce over the chicken & pasta/cream cheese. Do not stir.

6. Place the lid on the pot and lock into place, setting the steam release knob to the Sealing position.

7. Press the Pressure Cook/Manual button, then the +/- button to select 6 minutes.

8. When the cook time has ended, do a Quick Release of the pressure. When the pin in the lid drops down, open the lid and remove the chicken to a plate. Stir the pasta mixture well until the cream cheese lumps have mixed in.

9. Shred the chicken with two forks and add back into the pot.

10. Add the cheese and stir.

11. Add the blue cheese or ranch dressing and stir (or just use it as a garnish at the end).

12. Garnish with green onion/celery and extra hot wing sauce or dressing, if desired.

Chicken and Noodles

6-8 Servings | Prep Time: 5 mins. | Cook Time: 18 mins. | Total Time: 58 mins.

Ingredients

2 large Chicken Breasts (skinless/boneless, fresh or frozen)

2 (10.75 oz) cans Cream of Chicken Soup

2 (14.5 oz) cans Chicken Broth (or 3 1/2 cups)

1 Stick of Butter, unsalted

1 Garlic Clove, pressed (or 1/2 tsp Garlic Powder)

1/4 tsp Poultry Seasoning

3/4 tsp Kosher Salt, divided (or 1/2 tsp table salt)

1/2 tsp Black Pepper

1 (24 oz) Bag Frozen Egg Noodles* or 12 oz dried

1-2 cups Frozen Mixed Vegetables (optional)

Instructions

1. Set your Instant Pot to Sauté mode (to get things warming up and start melting the butter).
2. Add the butter, broth, cream soup, 1/2 tsp of salt, pepper, garlic, and poultry seasoning. Stir.
3. Add the chicken breasts. Cancel sauté mode.
4. Put the lid on your pot, set the steam release knob to the Sealing position.
5. Press the Manual / Pressure Cook button, then +/- button to select 12 mins (If your chicken is frozen, do 18 minutes). High Pressure. Larger pieces of chicken need more cook time.
6. After cooking cycle ends, let the pot sit undisturbed for a 10 minute Natural Release, then manually release the remaining pressure, and when the pin drops, open the lid.
7. Remove the chicken and set on a plate. Turn off the pot.
8. Add the frozen egg noodles to the pot. Make sure they are submerged in the broth.
9. Put the lid on the pot and set the steam release knob to the Sealing position.
10. Then press the Manual / Pressure Cook button and set time for 6 minutes.
11. While noodles are cooking, shred the chicken using 2 forks. It should shred very easily. Sprinkle with the remaining 1/4 tsp salt.
12. When cooking cycle ends, let it do a 5 minute Natural Release, then do a Controlled Quick Release of the remaining pressure, and when the pin drops, open the lid.
13. Add the frozen mixed vegetables, if using, and stir.
14. Add the shredded chicken back into the pot. Stir. Let sit covered for a few minutes.

If You Don't Have the Frozen Noodles, use a 12 oz bag of dried wide egg noodles.

After removing the cooked chicken, turn on the Sauté function and add the noodles. Cook as you would on a stove top until they are done, then add the shredded chicken back in.

Cajun Pasta

6-8 Servings | Prep Time: 15 mins. | Cook Time: 5 mins. | Total Time: 35 mins.

Ingredients

1 Sweet Onion, diced

12 oz Farfalle or Penne Pasta, uncooked

1 tsp Garlic Powder

1 Tbsp Cajun or Creole Seasoning

1 Tbsp Smoked Paprika

3 cups Chicken Broth, low sodium*

1 cup Heavy Cream

1 lb Andouille or Kielbasa Sausage, sliced

To Finish

1 cup Grated Parmesan

1/2 cup Roasted Red Peppers, sliced

2-3 Tbsp Fresh Basil, chopped

Instructions

1. Layer the onion, then the pasta, garlic powder, Cajun seasoning, smoked paprika, broth, and heavy cream in the pot. Gently press down on the pasta to submerge it. Do not stir.

2. Add the sausage on top.

3. Place the lid on the pot and set the steam release knob to the Sealing position.

4. Press the Pressure Cook/Manual button and then the +/- button to select 5 minutes. The pot will take a few minutes to heat up and come to pressure.

5. When the cook cycle has ended, Do a *Controlled Quick Release of the pressure.

6. *A controlled quick release means you release the steam in short bursts, then longer bursts, until you can be sure none of the sauce spews out of the vent with the steam from the intense pressure. Then fully open the vent and let it go.

7. When the pin in the lid drops down, stir the pasta. Then add the parmesan and the roasted red peppers. Gently stir.

8. Place a lid on the pot and let it sit for 5 minutes before serving as it will thicken up.

9. Stir in the fresh basil just before serving. Serve hot.

Recipe Note
*Be sure to use low sodium broth or use water as this recipe has enough salt from the Cajun seasoning and sausage.

Tuna Noodle Casserole

6 Servings | Prep Time: 15 mins. | Cook Time: 13 mins. | Total Time: 38 mins.

Ingredients

1 Tbsp Olive Oil

3 Tbsp Unsalted Butter

1 sm Sweet Onion, diced

3 cups Chicken Broth, low sodium

1/2 tsp Kosher Salt

1/2 tsp Pepper

1 tsp Garlic Powder

1/2 tsp Onion Powder

1/2 tsp Dill Weed, dried

2 (6 oz) cans Chunk Light Tuna, in water, partially drained

12 oz Wide Egg Noodles, uncooked

2 (10.5 oz) cans Condensed Cream of Mushroom Soup (or 1 mushroom and 1 celery)

1 cup Half and Half

TO FINISH

2 cups Frozen Peas

2 cups Sharp Cheddar Cheese, shredded

2 Tbsp Fresh Parsley, chopped

Instructions

1. Turn on the Sauté setting. When hot, add the oil, butter and onion. Cook, stirring occasionally, until onion starts to turn translucent.
2. Add the broth, salt, pepper, garlic powder, onion powder, and dill. Stir.
3. Add the half and half. Turn off the Sauté setting.
4. Add the egg noodles. Do not stir.
5. Add the tuna, spreading evenly over the noodles. Do not stir.
6. Add the mushroom soup and spread to cover the noodles.
7. Close the lid and set the steam release knob to the Sealing position.
8. Press the Pressure Cook/Manual button, then the +/- button to select 3 minutes for soft noodles (2 minutes for firmer noodles). High Pressure.
9. When the cook cycle has finished, turn the steam release knob to the Venting position to Quick Release the steam/pressure. If any sauce comes out of the steam vent, close it and release the pressure in bursts until the pressure has gone down enough to open it fully.
10. When the pin in the lid drops back down, open the lid.
11. Carefully take the pot out of the pressure cooker housing and set on a heat safe surface.
12. Add the peas and give a gentle stir.
13. Add the cheese and stir. The casserole will thicken as it cools.
14. When the cheese has melted, serve with a sprinkle of parsley as a garnish.

Fettuccine Alfredo

Ingredients

3 Tbsp Butter, cut in a few pieces

4 cloves Garlic, pressed/minced (or 1 1/2 tsp Garlic Powder)

2 cups Chicken Broth

1 1/2 cups Heavy Cream

1 tsp Salt (or more to taste)

1/2 tsp Pepper

10 oz Fettuccine Noodles, broken in half

1 lb Chicken Breasts, uncooked cut in bite sized pieces (chicken is optional)

1 cup Parmesan Cheese, grated

Instructions

1. Place the butter and garlic in the pot.

2. Pour in the chicken broth and heavy cream.

3. Sprinkle in the fettuccine noodles, in a random pattern, and gently press them down.

4. **If Adding Chicken:** Add the chicken. Space evenly over the noodles. Sprinkle with salt & pepper.

5. Press down on the mixture to submerge as many of the noodle as possible. Then close the lid and set the steam release knob to the Sealing position.

6. Press the Pressure Cook/Manual button, then the +/- button to select 6 minutes (7 minutes for a softer noodle). After the cook cycle has finished, let the pot sit undisturbed for 5 minute natural release.

7. Manually release the remaining pressure in short bursts at first, until you are sure no sauce will spew out with the steam.

8. Carefully open the lid and give the mixture a good stir. It may be a little soupy, but it will thicken up.

9. Add the grated parmesan and stir it in. If it's still a little too thin, just add a more parmesan cheese to thicken. It will thicken as it cools, also.

10. Serve with some nice bread and a salad.

Cheesy Garlic Orzo

4-6 Servings | Prep Time: 10 mins. | Cook Time: 4 mins. | Total Time: 14 mins.

Ingredients

2 tsp Olive Oil

2 tsp Butter

1/2 sm Onion, diced

3 cloves Garlic

1/2 tsp Salt (or to taste)

2 cups Chicken Broth (or vegetable broth)

8 oz Orzo Pasta (1 1/2 cups dry)

1 1/2 cups Grated Parmesan Cheese

1 cup Mozzarella Cheese, shredded

1 cup Half and Half

1 tsp Fresh Thyme Leaves, optional garnish

Instructions

1. Turn on the pressure cooker's Sauté function. When hot, add the oil and butter.

2. Add the onions and cook until translucent, stirring occasionally.

3. Add the garlic and cook for about 30 seconds, stirring constantly.

4. Add the salt and broth. Stir, and let come to a simmer.

5. Stir in the Orzo. Then place the lid on, locking in place. Set the Steam Release Knob to Sealing.

6. Cancel the sauté function.

7. Press the Pressure Cook/Manual button, then the +/- button to select 4 minutes.

8. When the cooking cycle has finished, immediately turn the Steam Release Knob to the Venting position (Quick Release). When all of the steam has vented, and the pin in the lid drops down, open the lid.

9. Stir in the parmesan cheese, then stir in the mozzarella.

10. Stir in the half and half.

11. Serve immediately, garnish with fresh thyme if desired.

> **This recipe makes a great side dish to go with chicken, ham, or pork tenderloin.**

Entrées

beef, pork, chicken, fish, veg.

Mississippi Pot Roast

6-10 Servings | Prep Time: 10 mins. | Cook Time: 1 hr. | Total Time: 1 hr. 35 mins.

Ingredients

3-6 lbs Chuck Roast, cut into 1 pound chunks of even thickness

3 Tbsp Vegetable Oil

1 sm Onion, chopped

9 Pepperoncinis, whole or chopped

1/2 cup Pepperoncini Juice from the jar

3/4 cup Low Sodium Beef Broth (or water)

1 (1 oz) packet Dry Ranch Dressing Mix

1 (1 oz) packet Au Jus (or brown gravy mix)

1/2 - 1 Stick of Butter, unsalted

FOR GRAVY

3 Tbsp Flour

3 Tbsp Softened Butter, unsalted

Instructions

1. Turn pot on Sauté mode (normal). When hot, add the oil.
2. Place meat in one layer into the pot and don't move for 5 minutes (Don't brown for less than that).
3. Turn meat over and cook for another 5 full minutes.
4. Remove the meat to foil or a dish you can cover. Wrap it to keep it warm.
5. **Deglaze the pot**: Add onion to pot and stir, add a bit of the beef broth or a small amount of water if there is not enough moisture to loosen the brown bits from the bottom of the pot. Stir, scraping the bottom of the pot until the bottom is free of the stuck on brown bits.
6. Add the pepperoncinis and their juice, beef broth, au jus and ranch packets, and butter.
7. Turn off the sauté mode. Add the meat back into the pot.

The above step is optional. You can just add everything to the pot (except oil), and start pressure cooking it. Browning the meat first gives an added depth of flavor.

8. Close lid and set the steam release knob to the Sealing position.
9. Press the Pressure Cook/Manual button then the +/- button to select 60 minutes. High Pressure. It will take several minutes to build pressure.
10. When the cooking cycle ends, let the pot sit undisturbed for 15 minute natural release.
11. Turn off the pot and manually release the remaining pressure by turning the steam release knob to the Venting position.
12. When the pin in the lid drops back down, open the lid.

Make the Gravy

13. Remove the pot roast to a plate and cover.
14. Turn the Sauté function back on.
15. Mix the flour and butter together until well combined.
16. When the liquid is starting to simmer, add the mixture to the pot, stirring well until thickened. Then turn off the pot and add the roast back in.
17. Enjoy with mashed or baked potatoes, or over rice.

Beef and Broccoli

Ingredients

SAUCE

1/2 cup Soy Sauce, low sodium

1 cup Beef Broth, low sodium

1 1/2 Tbsp Sesame Oil

1/3 cup Brown Sugar

1 tsp Ginger Powder (or 1 Tbsp fresh grated)

1/4 tsp Red Pepper Flakes

TO SAUTÉ

2 Tbsp Peanut or Canola Oil

2 lbs Chuck Roast or Flank Steak, sliced thinly against the grain

1 medium Onion, sliced into half moons

5 cloves Garlic, finely minced (2 Tbsp)

1 1/2 lbs Broccoli Florets, fresh or frozen

TO THICKEN

3 Tbsp Corn Starch

1/4 cup Cold Water

Optional - If you want to cook rice with the beef (you'll need a tall trivet and 7" pan)

2 cups Long Grain White Rice, well rinsed

2 cups Water

GARNISHES

1 Tbsp Sesame Seeds

2 Green Onions, sliced

Instructions

1. Gather all of your ingredients together and have everything chopped and ready to go, and the sauce made before you start.

2. Combine all of the sauce ingredients in a large measuring cup or a medium size bowl. Whisk it well. Set aside.

3. Turn on the Sauté setting, and when hot, add the oil. Add half of the beef strips and brown them a couple minutes on both sides (don't cook fully). Remove them to a plate and repeat with the second half.

4. After the second batch has browned, add the first batch back into the pot and add the onion and garlic. Cook for a couple of minutes, stirring frequently.

5. Pour in the sauce and stir.

6. Turn off the Sauté setting. If you are making rice, set the tall trivet into the pot and set the pan of rice/water on the trivet. Then close the lid and set the steam release knob to Sealing.

7. Press the Pressure Cook/Manual button or dial, then the +/- button or dial to select 10 minutes. High Pressure.

8. After cooking cycle has ended, let the pot sit undisturbed for 5 minutes. Then do a Quick Release of the remaining pressure/steam. When the pin in the lid drops down, you can open the lid.

9. Then carefully remove the pan of rice and the trivet and set aside. Add the broccoli to the pot, pour in the cornstarch slurry, and pressure cook again, for 0 (zero) minutes. Then Quick Release as soon as the cooking cycle has finished.

10. Meanwhile, fluff the rice with a fork and transfer to a serving bowl.

11. After you open the pot again, stir well. Serve over hot rice and garnish as desired.

Saucy Beef Brisket

5-7 Servings | **Prep Time: 10 mins.** | **Cook Time: 1 hr. 30 mins.** | **Total Time: 1 hr. 55 mins.**

Ingredients

3 lb Beef Brisket, (flat) cut in 3 equal pieces, against the grain

2 tsp Kosher Salt, divided

1 tsp Pepper

2 tsp Olive Oil

1 1/2 cups Apple Cider (2 cups for 8 qt pot)

1 small Onion, sliced

1 tsp Garlic Powder

1/2 tsp Liquid Smoke (optional)

1 (12 oz) bottle Chili Sauce (such as Heinz)

3 Tbsp Brown Sugar

3-4 Tbsp Cornstarch + 3-4 Tbsp cold water

Instructions

1. Trim excess fat from the brisket and cut in half, across the grain. Salt and pepper both sides.

2. Turn on the pressure cooker's sauté setting. When hot, add the oil, then the brisket halves. Brown a few minutes on each side to get a bit of a crust. Remove to a plate.

3. Pour the apple cider/juice into the pot and scrape the brown bits from the bottom of the pot (deglaze). Turn off the sauté function.

4. Add the onion, garlic powder, and liquid smoke, and stir.

5. Place the brisket halves in the liquid and pour the chili sauce over the meat. Do not stir.

6. Place the lid on the pot and lock in place. Set the steam release knob to Sealing.

7. Press the Pressure Cook/Manual button, then the +/- button to select 90 minutes. High Pressure.

8. When the cooking cycle ends, let the pot sit undisturbed for 15 minute Natural Release. Then turn the steam release knob to Venting to release remaining pressure.

9. When the pin in the lid drops down, open the lid.

10. Test the tenderness of the brisket using a fork. If the meat isn't tender enough, immediately put the lid back on and cook for another 10 minutes with a 10 minute natural release.

11. Use tongs to remove the brisket to a plate and cover with foil.

12. Turn the sauté function back on.

13. Stir in the brown sugar. Taste and add as much of the reserved tsp of salt as desired.

14. Mix the cornstarch with the cold water and stir to make a slurry. Whisk into the simmering sauce. If it doesn't get thick enough after a couple of minutes, make some more slurry and add a little at a time until sauce has desired thickness.

15. Slice the brisket across the grain and add the slices into the sauce. Let them stay in the sauce. Serve with mashed potatoes or rice, or on buns.

Corned Beef and Cabbage

Ingredients

6 cloves Garlic, roughly chopped

1 Yellow Onion, quartered

2-4 lb Corned Beef Brisket, rinsed (with the spice packet). If larger than 3lbs, cut in half

1 (12 oz) bottle Guinness Beer, or other Stout beer

2-3 cups Water (2 for a small brisket, and 3 for a larger one)

3 med Carrots, cut in 3" pieces

2 med Potatoes, cut into fourths or sixths

1 small head Cabbage, cut in fourths or sixths

Recipe Note

If you don't want to use beer, you can substitute 2 cups of low sodium Beef Broth or Water

Instructions

1. Add the garlic and onion to the pot.

2. Place the brisket in the pot with the fat side down.

3. Sprinkle spice packet over and around the brisket.

4. Pour the beer (or other liquid), and water in the pot, trying not to wash off all of the spices from the meat.

5. Place the lid on the pot and lock in place. Set the steam release knob to sealing.

6. Press the Pressure Cook/Manual button, then the +/- button to select 90 minutes. High pressure.

7. When cooking cycle is finished, turn off the pot and let it sit undisturbed for 15 minute natural release. Then manually release the remaining pressure (slowly at first, in short bursts so you know only steam will spew from the knob) until the pin in the lid drops down. Then open the lid and use tongs to carefully remove the meat to a dish, spoon some of the hot cooking liquid over it and cover to let it rest.

8. Add the carrots, potatoes, and cabbage to the pot and close the lid, set it to sealing, and set the cook time for 3 minutes. Do a controlled (slowly at first, in short bursts so you know only steam will spew from the knob) Quick Release when the cook cycle is finished.

9. Slice the brisket against the grain for the most tender and easy to eat meat. Then place the meat and vegetables in a dish with enough cooking liquid poured over to make it nice and juicy.

10. Serve with some crusty bread to sop up that wonderful broth!

Beef Short Ribs

4-5 Servings | Prep Time: 20 mins. | Cook Time: 1 hr. 10 mins. | Total Time: 1 hr. 35 mins.

Ingredients

3/4 cup Flour

1 tsp Salt

3/4 tsp Pepper

3-4 lbs Beef Short Ribs (6-8 pieces)

6 slices Bacon, chopped

1 lg Onion, chopped

2 lg Carrots, diced lg

1 rib Celery, diced

5 cloves Garlic, minced

1/2 cup Red Wine

1/2 cup Beef Broth, low sodium

2 sprigs Fresh Rosemary

3-4 sprigs Fresh Thyme

1 Bay Leaf

1 Tbsp Tomato Paste

2 tsp Balsamic Vinegar

Instructions

1. Mix together the flour, salt, and pepper. Dredge the short ribs in the flour mixture, lightly coating all sides, and set aside. Discard the flour mixture.
2. Turn on the Sauté setting and add the chopped bacon. Cook until fat is rendered out and the bacon is just crisp. Remove bacon to a plate and set aside. Remove the bacon fat (don't throw it out), keeping 2 Tbsp in the pot.
3. Turn the Sauté temperature to the high setting. Brown the short ribs in the pot on all sides. Add more of the bacon fat if needed. Then remove them to a plate and set aside.
4. Add the onions, carrots, and garlic to the pot. Cook, stirring frequently for 1 minute.
5. Add the wine and beef broth and stir, scraping up the browned bits from the bottom of the pot. I like to use a wooden spoon for this.
6. Add the rosemary, thyme, bay leaf, and reserved bacon to the pot and stir.
7. Add the tomato paste but don't stir. This keeps the liquid from getting too thick.
8. Place the short ribs in the pot, nestling them down into the veggies and broth. They don't need to be covered, just sitting in there.
9. Cancel the Sauté setting and close the lid, setting the steam release knob to Sealing.
10. Press the Pressure Cook/Manual button. Then press the +/- button to select 40 minutes. High Pressure. It will take a few minutes to come to pressure.
11. When the cook time is finished, let the pot sit undisturbed for 10 minute natural release. Then turn the steam release knob to Venting to release the remaining pressure.
12. When the pin in the lid drops down, open the lid and carefully remove the short ribs using tongs. Set them on a plate.
13. Carefully skim off the fat from the top of the cooking liquid and remove the bay leaf and rosemary & thyme stems. Discard.
14. Stir the balsamic vinegar into the cooking sauce.
15. Serve the short ribs on a bed of mashed potatoes, mashed cauliflower, or alone, with some of the sauce poured over them.

Pot Roast

Ingredients

1 1/2 tsp Kosher Salt (more to taste)

1 tsp Pepper

2 Tbsp Olive Oil

3 lbs Chuck Roast, well marbled

2 large Yellow Onions, cut in quarters

1/2 cup Red Wine, (or beef broth)

3 cloves Garlic, smashed

2 sprigs Rosemary

3 sprigs Thyme

1 can Beef Consommé, (or 2 cups of rich beef broth)

1 Tbsp Soy Sauce, low sodium

4 large Carrots**, cut in large 3" pieces

8 oz Sliced Mushrooms (optional)

TO THICKEN THE GRAVY

1/3 cup Flour

4 Tbsp Butter, softened

Instructions

1. Sprinkle salt and pepper over all sides of the roast. Set aside.

2. Turn on the Sauté setting of the pressure cooker and when it is hot add the olive oil. Then add the roast and brown it for 5 minutes on each side. Remove to a plate.

3. Add the onion quarters and brown them on each side

4. Pour in the red wine and deglaze the pot by stirring, scraping up all of the browned bits from the bottom of the pot. Feel free to replace the wine with more beef broth.

5. Add the garlic, rosemary, thyme, beef broth, soy sauce, carrots, and mushrooms. Give the contents of the pot a good stir. Make sure the herbs and garlic are submerged in the broth.

6. Add roast back into the pot, then place the lid on and set the steam release knob to Sealing.

7. Cancel the Sauté function, then press the Pressure Cook/Manual button, then the +/- button to select 60 minutes. High Pressure.

8. Meanwhile, mix the flour and butter together very well. If you have to, microwave for 5-10 seconds to soften butter further. Set aside.

9. When the cooking cycle has finished, let the pot sit undisturbed for 15 minute natural release. Then turn the steam release knob to Venting to manually release any remaining pressure.

10. When the pin in the lid drops down you can open the lid. Skim off the fat with a spoon, then take out the roast and set it on a plate. Remove the rosemary and thyme stems and discard.

11. ** To cook carrots and/or potatoes separately from the roast, add them to the pot after the roast cooks and place the lid back on, seal it, and set the cook time for 3 to 5 minutes (this will depend on how large the veggie pieces are. Baby carrots will only take 3 minutes). Then Quick Release.

12. Turn the Sauté setting on and when it starts to simmer, stir in the flour/butter mixture. Let that simmer, stirring occasionally, for just enough time as it takes for the gravy to thicken. Then turn off the pot.

13. Serve the roast with a big spoonful of the veggies and gravy. This goes well with mashed potatoes.

French Dip Sandwiches

Ingredients

- 1 Tbsp Cooking Oil
- 1-2 tsp Salt
- 1 tsp Pepper
- 3-4 lb Beef Bottom Round Roast (or Chuck roast) cut in half
- 1 Onion, sliced
- 1 Bay Leaf
- 2 cloves Garlic, minced
- 3 sprigs Fresh Thyme (or 1/4 tsp dried)
- 2 cups Beef Broth
- 2 Tbsp Soy Sauce
- 1 (10.75 oz) can French Onion Soup, condensed
- French or Hoagie Rolls
- Butter, for rolls
- 3 slices per sandwich Provolone Cheese (or Swiss, etc.)

Instructions

1. Lightly salt and pepper the two halves of the roast. Set aside.
2. Turn on the pot's Sauté function. When hot, add the oil. Then add the roast and brown it a few minutes on each side. Remove to a plate and set aside.
3. Add the onion slices and stir (add a splash of the beef broth if too dry). Cook, stirring occasionally, and scraping the bottom of the pot to get the browned bits off (deglaze), until onion turns translucent.
4. Add the bay leaf, garlic, thyme. Stir for a minute (add another splash of the broth if it gets dry).
5. Stir in the beef broth, soy sauce, and French onion soup.
6. Add the roast back in and close the lid. Set the steam release knob to the Sealing position.
7. Cancel the Sauté function and press the Pressure Cook/Manual button. Then use the +/- button to select 70 minutes. When cook cycle is done, let the pot sit undisturbed for 15 minute Natural Release.
8. Turn the steam release knob to the Venting position and release the remaining steam/pressure.
9. After opening the lid, check to make sure the roast is tender. If not as tender as you'd like, put the lid back on and set for another 10 minutes.
10. Remove the meat to a cutting board and slice or shred.
11. Strain the au jus into a fat separator. Save the onions and pour the defatted au jus into ramekins or small dishes.
12. Spread the butter on the rolls and toast them in a frying pan, toaster oven, or in the oven. Pile some roast onto a roll, add some of the onion, and then layer 3 on slices of the cheese. Broil to melt, if desired.
13. Serve sandwich with a ramekin of au jus for dipping.

Italian Beef

6-8 Servings | Prep Time: 10 mins. | Cook Time: 1 hr. | Total Time: 1 hr. 10 mins.

Ingredients

3-4 lb Chuck Roast, cut into large chunks

1 (1 oz) packet Zesty Italian Dressing Mix

1 tsp Dried Oregano

1 tsp Dried Basil

4 cloves Garlic, minced

1/2 (16 oz) jar Mild Pepperoncinis

1/3 cup Pepperoncini Juice from the Jar

1/4 cup Red Wine (optional)

1 (10.5 oz) can Beef Broth or Consommé

1 (16 oz) jar Giardiniera (Italian pickled vegetables)

6 Hoagie Rolls

6-12 slices Provolone or Swiss Cheese

Instructions

1. Add the meat to the pot. Sprinkle with the Italian dressing mix, oregano, basil, and the minced garlic.

2. Add the pepperoncinis, just use half of the 16 oz jar, and save the rest for garnish.

3. Add about 1/3 cup (or more to taste) of the juice from the pepperoncini jar to the pot.

4. Add the red wine, if using. Then pour the beef broth over everything and give it a stir.

5. Close the lid and set the steam release knob to the Sealing position.

6. Press the Pressure Cook/Manual button or dial, then the +/- button or dial to select 60 minutes. High Pressure. The pot will take several minutes to come to pressure.

7. When the cook cycle has finished, turn off the pot and let it sit undisturbed for 15 minute natural release. Then turn the steam release knob to the Venting position to release the remaining pressure.

8. When the pin in the lid drops down, open the lid and skim off the fat that is on top.

9. Shred the beef. You may need to remove it to a plate to do this. Then just add it right back into the pot.

To Make a Sandwich

10. Use a slotted spoon to put some of the shredded beef onto a hoagie roll, top with provolone cheese, then add some of the giardiniera and pepperoncinis on top.

11. You can use the au jus from the pot to dip the sandwiches in, if you like!

Recipe Note
You can also serve this flavorful shredded beef over mashed potatoes or rice.

Honey Garlic Pork Tenderloin

Ingredients

1 lb Pork Tenderloin (not pork loin roast)

Dry Rub

1/2 tsp Salt

1/2 tsp Onion Powder

1/2 tsp Chili Powder

1/2 tsp Thyme

1 tsp Rosemary

Sauce

1/2 cup Orange Juice

1 1/2 Tbsp Garlic, (7 to 9 cloves) pressed or finely minced

1/2 cup Soy Sauce, low sodium

3 Tbsp Brown Sugar

1 tsp Grated Ginger

1/2 cup Honey

For Browning the Pork

1 tsp Olive Oil

3 Tbsp Butter

To Thicken (whisk together)

3 Tbsp Corn Starch

4 Tbsp Cold Water

For Serving

2-3 cups Hot Cooked Rice

Instructions

1. First, note how much your pork tenderloin weighs (they are typically 1 to 1 1/2 lbs) and measure across to find out how thick it is. This recipe is for a 1 lb tenderloin at 1.5" thick. If yours is larger, it will need to rest longer after pressure cooking.

Prepare the Pork

2. Mix the dry rub ingredients together and coat the pork tenderloin on all sides. Set aside.

Make the Sauce and Slurry

3. In a bowl, whisk together the sauce ingredients until the honey is fully dissolved. Set aside.

4. Mix together the corn starch and water. Set aside.

Brown the Pork

5. Turn on the Sauté setting. When it is hot, add the olive oil and the butter. Then place the pork in the pot and brown in on all sides about 2-3 minutes each side. Then remove it to a plate.

6. Add the sauce to the pot and stir, scraping the bottom of the pot to get up any of the fond (browned bits). This is also called deglazing. Turn off the pot.

7. Place the pork back in the pot and coat with the sauce.

Pressure Cook the Pork

8. Close the lid and set the steam release knob to the Sealing position.

9. Press the Pressure Cook/Manual button, then the +/- button to select 1 minute (for a 1 lb tenderloin, 1.5" thick). LOW Pressure. If your pot doesn't have Low pressure, cook a 1 lb tenderloin (1.5" thick) for 0 (zero) minutes at High pressure.

10. When the cook cycle has finished, turn off the pot and let it sit undisturbed for 15 minute natural release. Use a timer. Turn the steam release knob to Venting to release remaining steam/pressure. There may not be any. When the pin in the lid drops down, open the lid.

11. Check the temperature of the pork. It should be 145°. If it's a little higher than that, it's okay. If it's a little lower, put the lid on and let it rest a few more minutes.

12. Remove the tenderloin to a baking pan and cover loosely with foil. Turn on your Broiler to start heating it up.

Thicken the Sauce

13. Turn on the Sauté setting. When it starts to simmer, add the corn starch slurry. Stirring until thickened.

Broil to Caramelize

14. Remove the foil from the tenderloin and spoon some of the sauce over it. Place under the broiler and caramelize the coating. Watch it so it doesn't burn!

Serve

15. Serve the tenderloin sliced into medallions, on top of some rice with more sauce over it.

> **Recipe Note**
> You can cook more than one pork tenderloin at the same time. Make sure they are the same size. Keep the cook time the same.

Meatloaf and Mashed Potatoes

Ingredients

To Cook Potatoes

2 1/2 lbs Potatoes, peeled and quartered

1 1/2 cups Chicken Broth (or water, veggie broth, beef broth, etc.) If using 8 qt pot increase to 2 cups

2-3 cloves Garlic (optional, to make garlic mashed potatoes)

Meatloaf Mixture

2 lbs Ground Beef (I use 85%-90% lean)

1/2 cup Bread Crumbs (panko or crushed crackers)

1/3 cup Milk

2 Eggs

1/3 cup Ketchup (or bbq sauce)

1/2 cup Onion (finely minced or grated on a cheese grater)

1 1/2 tsp Garlic Powder

1 1/2 tsp Smoked Paprika (optional)

1/2 tsp Oregano

1/4 tsp Thyme

2 Tbsp Chives, chopped (or parsley, dried or fresh)

1 tsp Salt

1/2 tsp Pepper

Meatloaf Topping

1/3 cup Ketchup

1/3 cup BBQ Sauce

1 Tbsp Yellow Mustard

1 Tbsp Brown Sugar (optional)

To Make the Mashed Potatoes

4 Tbsp Butter

1 tsp Salt

1/2 cup Heavy Cream (or half and half) As needed to get desired creaminess.

1/2 cup Sour Cream (optional)

Instructions

Set up the Pot and Potatoes

1. Put the quartered potatoes in the bottom of the pot. Add the broth and garlic, if using. Set the trivet right on top of the potatoes.

Make the Meatloaf

2. Add the meatloaf ingredients to a large bowl and use your fingertips lightly to combine.

3. Place mixture onto a piece of heavy duty foil and shape the meat into a loaf of even thickness. Try not to make it too a thick. If it's too thick you will need to cook it longer.

4. Fold the sides of the foil up to make a bowl shape (this will collect the drippings).

5. Lift the meatloaf in the foil bowl into the pot and set on the trivet. Make sure there is a little room around it for the steam to circulate.

Cook the Meatloaf

6. Place the lid on the pot and set the steam release knob to the Sealing position. Then press the Pressure Cook/Manual button, then the +/- button to select 30 minutes.

7. While the meatloaf and potatoes are cooking, mix up the topping by adding the ketchup, BBQ sauce, mustard, and brown sugar, if using, in a bowl. Set aside.

8. When the cook cycle ends, turn off the pot and let it sit for 10 minute natural release. Then turn the steam release knob to Venting to do a Quick Release of the remaining pressure.

9. When the pin in the lid drops down, open it and get a meat thermometer and take the temperature of the meatloaf. Beef should be 160°, turkey should be 165°.

10. If it isn't done, put the lid back on and set time for another 10 minutes.

11. Get a turkey baster and a baking sheet pan.

12. Use the turkey baster to suction out most of the drippings so that when you lift the meatloaf out of the pot, hot drippings won't spill on you. Just put them in a coffee cup.

13. Lift the foil with the meatloaf on it out of the pot and onto the baking sheet. Spread the topping on the meatloaf and put under the broiler at 425° until it's caramelized to your liking.

Make the Mashed Potatoes

14. While the meatloaf is broiling, add butter and salt to potatoes, still in the pot, and stir/mash.

15. Don't forget about your meatloaf under the broiler! Check on it so it doesn't burn.

16. Add as much heavy cream as you like, and sour cream, if using. Taste, adjust salt, if needed.

17. After you remove the meatloaf from the oven, let it rest 5 minutes before serving.

Stuffed Peppers

3-5 Servings | Prep Time: 15 mins. | Cook Time: 9 mins. | Total Time: 34 mins.

Ingredients

1 cup Water, for the Pressure Cooker

For the Peppers

4 med-large Bell Peppers (any color)

1 cup Cooked Rice (or parboiled rice)

1/2 lb Lean Ground Turkey or Beef (85% to 93% lean)

1 Egg, beaten

1 tsp Garlic Powder

1/2 small Onion, diced (or 1/2 tsp Onion Powder)

1 tsp Salt

1/2 tsp Pepper

3 Tbsp Bread Crumbs

2 tsp Italian Seasoning

2 tsp Paprika

2 tsp Worcestershire Sauce

1 cup Shredded Cheese, divided

1 (14 oz) can Tomato Sauce, divided

Instructions

1. Add the cup of water to the inner liner of the pressure cooker. Also place the trivet in the pot for the peppers to sit on.

2. Rinse the peppers and cut the tops off. Deseed and remove the membrane.

3. To a mixing bowl, add the rice, ground turkey or beef (raw) and all other ingredients (except for half of the tomato sauce and half the cheese). Mix to combine thoroughly with the rice.

4. Fill each pepper with enough of the meat mixture to come a little bit above the top of the pepper. Don't pack them too tightly or they won't cook evenly.

5. Place stuffed peppers on the trivet in the pot. They will be sitting above the water.

6. Pour remaining tomato sauce on top of the peppers.

7. Put the lid on and close it, turning the steam release knob to the Sealing position.

8. Press the Pressure Cook/Manual button, then the +/- button to select 9 minutes. High Pressure.

9. After the cooking cycle ends, turn the steam release knob to the Venting position to do a Quick Release of the pressure.

10. When the pin in the lid drops and all of the remaining pressure is released open the lid.

11. Check the internal temperature using an instant read thermometer. The temp should be at least 165° for ground turkey, and 160° for ground beef.

12. If they aren't fully cooked, put the lid back on and wait for 2 to 5 minutes, then check again.

13. Sprinkle reserved cheese on top of each pepper and put the lid on to melt it.

14. Remove peppers with tongs to serve.

Porcupine Meatballs

Ingredients

Meatballs

1 lb Ground Beef (80% to 90% Lean)

1 Tbsp Onion, grated or finely diced

1 Egg

1/4 cup Long Grain White Rice (uncooked)

2 tsp Worcestershire Sauce

1 tsp Kosher Salt (or 3/4 tsp table salt)

1/2 tsp Pepper

1 tsp Garlic Powder

Optional (if you have leaner meat)

3 Tbsp Heavy Cream (or half and half)

2 Tbsp Bread Crumbs

Sauce

1 (10.75 oz) Can Condensed Tomato Soup

1 can Water or Broth (use the soup can)

2 tsp Worcestershire Sauce

1 tsp Brown Sugar

1 tsp Red Wine Vinegar

Instructions

Meatballs

1. Mix all the ingredients for the meatballs together and form 12 to 14 small meatballs. Set aside.

Sauce

2. Mix the sauce ingredients together and stir well to combine. Pour into the pot and turn on the Sauté mode to start the sauce warming up.

Pressure Cook the Meatballs

3. When the sauce is just starting to simmer, stir it and carefully add the meatballs to the pot.

4. Close the lid of the pressure cooker and set the steam release knob to the Sealing position

5. Cancel the Sauté mode.

6. Press the Manual/Pressure Cook button, then the +/- button to choose 25 minutes.

7. When the cooking cycle ends, let the pot sit and naturally release for 15 minutes. Then manually release the remaining pressure until the pin in the lid drops.

8. Open the lid and serve the meatballs with some sauce over them.

9. These Porcupine Meatballs go well with mashed potatoes or crusty bread.

Recipe Note
While cooking Porcupine Meatballs, try cooking some halved russet potatoes at the same time in the sauce.

Swedish Meatballs

Ingredients

MEATBALL MIXTURE
1 lb Ground Beef (90% lean)
1/2 lb Ground Pork
1/2 cup Panko Bread Crumbs
1/2 cup Milk
1 small Sweet Onion, grated on a cheese grater
1 tsp Salt
1/2 tsp Pepper
1/4 tsp Allspice
1/4 tsp Nutmeg
1 tsp Garlic Powder
1 Egg, beaten

1/4 cup Fresh Parsley, finely chopped, divided

SAUCE
2 Tbsp Olive Oil
6 Tbsp Butter, divided
2 (10 oz) cans Beef Consommé (or good beef broth, 2 1/2 cups)
1 tsp Dijon Mustard
1 tsp Worcestershire Sauce
2 cups Heavy Cream, divided
1/4 cup Flour
Salt & Pepper to taste

Instructions

1. In a mixing bowl add ground beef, ground pork, panko, milk (pour over the crumbs), onion, salt, pepper, allspice, nutmeg, garlic powder, beaten egg, and 2 Tbsp of the parsley. Mix together well to combine the ingredients.

2. Form 30 meatballs and set them on parchment paper.

3. Turn on the pot's Sauté setting, and when it is hot, add the olive oil and 2 Tbsp of the butter.

4. Add 15 of the meatballs and brown lightly on outside. Do not cook completely. Remove to a plate and repeat with the second batch.

5. Add the beef consommé and stir, scraping the bottom of the pot to get up any of the browned bits (deglaze).

6. Add the remaining 4 Tbsp of butter, Dijon, Worcestershire, and 1 cup of the heavy cream (reserve the remaining 1 cup). Stir well.

7. Cancel the Sauté setting.

8. Add the meatballs back into the pot. Close the lid and set the steam release knob to the Sealing position.

9. Press the Pressure Cook/Manual button (High pressure), and then the +/- button to select 4 minutes. When the cook time is finished, let pot sit undisturbed for 6 minutes.

10. While the meatballs are cooking, mix the flour with the remaining 1 cup of heavy cream. Whisk it well so there are no lumps. Set aside.

11. Do a Controlled Quick Release, (see page 2).

12. When the pin in the lid drops down, you can open it.

13. Remove the meatballs to a plate and cover. Turn on the Sauté setting and bring to a simmer. Whisk in the flour/cream mixture, stirring frequently, until thickened. Cancel the Sauté setting.

14. Taste the sauce and adjust salt & pepper, if needed. You can either add the meatballs back in, or serve and pour the sauce over them. Garnish with remaining parsley.

15. Instant Pot Swedish Meatballs go great over noodles, rice, or mashed potatoes.

Salisbury Steaks

5-8 Servings | Prep Time: 30 mins. | Cook Time: 19 mins. | Total Time: 49 mins.

Ingredients

Meat Mixture
1 Egg
1/4 cup Grated Onion
2 tsp Garlic Powder
1/2 tsp Onion Powder
3 tsp Dried Parsley
3 tsp Worcestershire Sauce
1/4 cup Bread Crumbs
1 lb Ground Beef (85%-90% lean)
1/2 lb Ground Sausage
For Browning the Patties
2 Tbsp Olive Oil

Gravy Mixture
1 lg Onion, sliced thin or diced
1/3 cup Red Wine*
2 Tbsp Butter
8 oz Crimini Mushrooms, sliced
2 lg cloves Garlic, finely minced
1 tsp Salt
1/2 tsp Pepper
2 cups Beef Broth
3 Tbsp Ketchup
Slurry To Thicken
3 Tbsp Corn Starch + 3 Tbsp Cold Water

Instructions

1. In a mixing bowl, add the egg and beat it. Then add the grated onion, garlic powder, onion powder, parsley, Worcestershire, and bread crumbs. Mix well to combine.

2. Add the ground beef and the ground sausage. Mix together to combine.

3. Form 8 small, thin patties (about 3 oz ea.) and place them on a plate and cover with plastic wrap. Try to let sit for at least 1 hour to give the flavors time to develop.

4. Turn on the Sauté setting. When hot, add the oil.

5. Brown the patties in two batches, moving to a plate when done. Don't cook all the way through, just do a quick sear on each side. Set aside.

6. Add the onion and stir, scraping up the browned bits from the bottom of the pan. Add the red wine and stir some more.

7. Add the butter and the mushrooms. Cook for 2-3 minutes, stirring occasionally and scraping the bottom of the pot.

8. Add garlic, salt, and pepper. Cook, stirring constantly, for 30 seconds.

9. Mix the beef broth and the ketchup together and pour into the pot.

10. Add the patties back into the pot. Be sure to cover with the sauce as much as possible.

11. Turn off sauté setting. Close the lid and set the steam release knob to the Sealing position.

12. Press the Pressure Cook/Manual button, then the +/- button to select 7 minutes. High Pressure.

13. When the cook cycle is finished, turn off the pot and let it sit undisturbed for 10 minute natural release. Then turn the steam release knob to Venting to release the remaining pressure.

14. When the pin in the lid drops back down, open the lid.

15. Remove the patties to a plate and turn the sauté setting back on.

16. Mix corn starch & water together. Stir into simmering sauce. Stir constantly until it thickens. If you like your gravy thicker, use another Tbsp of corn starch mixed with 1 Tbsp of cold water.

17. Turn off the sauté setting and add the patties back into the pot and cover with the gravy.

18. Serve over mashed potatoes, rice, mashed cauliflower, bread, or whatever you like!

Recipe Notes
*If you don't want to use wine, try unsweetened grape juice, or more beef broth.
A Tablespoon of balsamic vinegar is also good in addition.

Korean Ground Beef

5-7 Servings | Prep Time: 20 mins. | Cook Time: 11 mins. | Total Time: 31 mins.

Ingredients

2 tsp Vegetable Oil

1 1/2 lbs Lean Ground Beef or Ground Turkey

7 cloves Garlic (or 1 Tbsp pressed garlic)

1/3 cup Soy Sauce, low sodium

1/2 cup Water

3 Tbsp Brown Sugar

1 Tbsp Sesame Oil

1 Tbsp Ginger Root, grated (or 1 1/2 tsp powdered ginger)

1/2 Asian Pear, grated (optional)

3/4 tsp Red Pepper Flakes (or more to taste)

1/2 tsp White Pepper (or black)

1 1/2 cups Jasmine Rice, rinsed

1 1/2 cups Water

2 Tbsp Butter

TO SERVE

Tortillas (for tacos)

Lettuce Leaves (for lettuce wraps)

GARNISH

2 Green Onions, sliced

Sesame Seeds

Instructions

1. Get all of your ingredients together and measured out. This will make the process go smoother. Also have the rice in the pan and ready to go.

2. Turn on the pot's Sauté setting. When it is hot, add the oil, and then the ground beef. Cook beef until it loses the pink color. I use 90% lean beef, so I don't drain, but drain the excess fat if there is more than a few teaspoons.

3. Add garlic, soy sauce, water, brown sugar, sesame oil, ginger, Asian pear (if using), red pepper flakes, and white pepper. Mix well, scraping the bottom of the pot to get up any browned bits so you don't get the Burn error.

4. Cancel the Sauté setting. Set the trivet in the pot right over the beef.

5. Put the rice, water, and butter in the pan and set on top of the trivet.

6. Close the lid and set the steam release knob to the Sealing position.

7. Press the Pressure Cook/Manual button and the +/- button to select 3 minutes.

8. When the cook cycle is finished, let the pot sit undisturbed for 9 minute Natural Release. Turn the steam release knob to Venting to release the remaining pressure.

9. When the pin in the lid drops down, open the lid and carefully remove the pan of rice. Then fluff the rice with a fork.

10. Remove the trivet and stir the beef.

11. Serve the beef over rice, on lettuce leaves, in taco shells/tortillas, garnish, and enjoy!

Beef Taco Bowls

5-7 Servings | Prep Time: 15 mins. | Cook Time: 23 mins. | Total Time: 46 mins.

Ingredients

1 - 1 1/2 lbs Lean Ground Beef or Ground Turkey (I use 93%)

1/2 tsp Onion Powder

1 tsp Garlic Powder

1 (1 1/4 oz) pkg Taco Seasoning (or 2 1/2 Tbsp homemade)

1 (15 oz) can Black Beans, drained & rinsed

1 1/2 cups Frozen Corn Kernels

2 cups Salsa (not too thick)

1 (4 oz) can Diced Green Chiles

1 1/2 cups Long Grain White Rice, well rinsed

1 3/4 cups Beef or Chicken Broth, low sodium

GARNISHES

1 cup Shredded Cheddar Cheese

1/4 cup Cilantro, chopped

Sour Cream, Salsa, Avocado

Tortilla Chips, Hot Sauce

Lime Wedges

Instructions

1. Turn on the pot's Sauté setting and add the ground beef. Cook, stirring occasionally, until mostly done. Cancel the Sauté setting and drain excess fat.

2. Add the onion powder, garlic powder, and taco seasoning and stir well.

3. Layer on the black beans, corn, salsa, green chiles, and rice. Do not stir.

4. Pour the broth over the layers, but do not stir. Use a fork or back of a spoon to gently press the rice down into the broth. It's okay if it is not completely submerged.

5. Place the lid on the pot and set the steam release knob to the Sealing position.

6. Press the Pressure Cook/Manual button or dial, and then the +/- button to select 8 minutes. The pot will take several minutes to come to pressure.

7. After the cook time has ended, do a Quick Release of the pressure by turning the steam release knob to the Venting position.

8. When the pin in the lid drops down you can open the lid.

9. Fluff the rice with a fork and then stir the taco bowl mixture.

10. Serve with any of your favorite garnishes/toppings.

11. If you are meal prepping, dish up into your containers and let cool before you put the lids on and put in the refrigerator.

Hamburgers

4 Servings | Prep Time: 10 mins. | Cook Time: 15 mins. | Total Time: 32 mins.

Ingredients

Hamburger Meat Mixture #1

1 lb Ground Beef (80% - 85% lean)

1 tsp Salt

1/2 tsp Pepper

1 tsp Garlic Powder

1/4 cup Onion, finely chopped or grated (or 1 Tbsp dried onion or 1/2 tsp onion Powder)

1 tsp Smoked Paprika (optional)

2 tsp Worcestershire Sauce

Hamburger Meat Mixture #2

1 lb Ground Beef (80% - 85% lean)

1 (1 oz) Packet of Onion Soup Mix (mix with the meat)

Fixings

4 Hamburger Buns

Cheese Slices, Tomato Slices, Lettuce, Mayo, Ketchup, Mustard

Instructions

1. Add 1 1/2 cups of water and trivet to the inner stainless liner of the 6 qt pressure cooker (2 1/2 cups for 8 qt).

2. Mix all of the hamburger meat mixture ingredients together in a bowl with the meat.

3. If making Version #2, mix the soup packet with the ground meat.

4. Divide the meat mixture into 4 equal (4 oz) patties, 3 (5 oz) patties, or 2 (8 oz patties). press your thumb into the center of each patty to make an indentation.

5. Wrap patties in foil or parchment. The wrapping and cooking under pressure is what steams them.

6. Stack the wrapped patties on the trivet in a staggered pattern. Then place the lid on the pot and set the steam release knob to the Sealing position.

7. Press the Pressure Cook/Manual button, then the + /- button to select:

    11 minutes for 4 oz patties (7 minutes for a touch rare)

    13 minutes for 5 oz patties (9 minutes for a touch rare)

    15 minutes for 8 oz patties (11 minutes for a touch rare)

8. High pressure.

9. When the cook cycle is finished, do a Quick Release of the pressure.

10. Carefully remove the patties from the pot using tongs. Let them rest for 5 minutes. Then unwrap them on a plate to catch the drippings, and make up your hamburger with all of your favorite fixin's!

Sloppy Joes

5 Servings | Prep Time: 15 mins. | Cook Time: 14 mins. | Total Time: 32 mins.

Ingredients

1 1/2 lbs Ground Beef or Ground Turkey (lean)

1 sm Onion, diced

1/4 tsp Red Pepper Flakes

1/4 tsp Salt

1/2 tsp Pepper

2 cloves Garlic, pressed or minced

1 Green Bell Pepper, diced

1 Tbsp Worcestershire Sauce

1 Tbsp Soy Sauce

2 tsp Dijon Mustard

1 1/2 Tbsp Brown Sugar

1/2 cup Beef Broth* (or water)

1/2 cup Ketchup

1 (6 oz can) Tomato Paste**

5 Hamburger Buns

Instructions

1. Turn on the pot's Sauté setting. Add the ground beef (if using ground turkey, add some oil to the pot first). Cook, stirring occasionally, until the meat is mostly done. Use a spoon or turkey baster to remove the extra fat.

2. Add the onion, salt, and pepper, and cook for a couple of minutes to soften. Scrape the bottom of the pot as you stir.

3. Add the garlic, bell pepper, red pepper flakes, Worcestershire, soy sauce, Dijon, brown sugar, and beef broth, Stir well, scraping the bottom of the pot to get up any brown bits.

4. Add the tomato paste and ketchup. Do not stir. Just leave it sitting on top of the meat mixture.

5. Put the lid on and lock into place. Set the steam release knob to the Sealing position.

6. Cancel the Sauté setting and press the Pressure Cook/Manual button. Then press the +/- button to select 4 minutes. The pot will take a few minutes to come to pressure.

7. After the cooking cycle is finished, let the pot sit undisturbed for 5 minute Natural Release. Then turn the steam release knob to Venting and manually release the remaining pressure.

8. When the pin in the lid drops down, open it and stir the Sloppy Joe mixture to incorporate the tomato paste and ketchup. Taste and adjust salt.

9. Serve on soft hamburger buns.

Recipe Notes
*If using the 8 qt size pot, increase broth/water to 3/4 cup.
**Don't stir the tomato paste. It will thicken the sauce and possibly cause a BURN error.

Unstuffed Cabbage Rolls

6-8 Servings | Prep Time: 15 mins. | Cook Time: 18 mins. | Total Time: 33 mins.

Ingredients

1 lb Ground Beef or Ground Turkey, or use sausage or half sausage for added flavor

1 large Yellow Onion, chopped

2 Bay Leaves

4 large cloves Garlic, pressed or minced

2 tsp Paprika

1 1/2 tsp Kosher Salt (or 1 tsp table salt)

1 tsp Pepper

1/4 tsp Oregano

1 med Head of Green Cabbage, chopped

3 1/2 cups Beef Broth,* low sodium (or chicken, if using gr. turkey)

1 Tbsp Balsamic Vinegar

1 Tbsp Worcestershire Sauce

1 cup Long Grain White Rice, rinsed, uncooked

1 (14 oz) can Diced Tomatoes, with juice

1 Tbsp Tomato Paste

2 tsp Sugar

Instructions

1. Get all of your veggies chopped, and all other ingredients ready to go. Then turn on the pressure cooker's Sauté setting.

2. If using ground beef, add it to the pot and start browning it. Then add the onions, If using ground turkey, add some olive oil to the pot and add the onions first. Then add the ground turkey when the onions just start to turn translucent.

3. Add the bay leaves and garlic. Sauté, stirring frequently, for a minute.

4. Add the paprika, salt, pepper, oregano, cabbage, broth*, balsamic vinegar, and Worcestershire. Stir well and let heat up for a few minutes.

5. Add the rice and stir well.

6. Pour the can of diced tomatoes, tomato paste, and sugar over the cabbage mixture. Don't stir.

7. Put the lid on the pot and lock in place.

8. Set the steam release knob to the Sealing position.

9. Cancel the Sauté function and then press the Pressure Cook/Manual button. Use the +/- button to choose 5 minutes.

10. When the cook cycle is finished, let the pot sit undisturbed for 8 minutes. Then do a *Controlled Quick Release* (page 2)to manually release the remaining pressure. This will take a few minutes as the pot is full.

11. When the pin in the lid drops down, open the lid carefully and give the contents a stir.

12. Taste and adjust salt, if desired and serve hot.

Picadillo

6-7 Servings | Prep Time: 12 mins. | Cook Time: 7 mins. | Total Time: 19 mins.

Ingredients

1 1/2 lbs Lean Ground Beef or Turkey

1 med Sweet Onion (or yellow)

2 Bay Leaves

1/4 tsp Cinnamon

1 Tbsp Cumin

2 tsp Oregano (Mexican is best)

1 tsp Salt

4 cloves Garlic, pressed or minced

1 Jalapeño, seeded and diced

1 Red Bell Pepper, Chopped

1/2 cup Green Olives, sliced (or half capers and half olives)

1 Tbsp Green Olive Juice (from jar)

2 tsp Worcestershire Sauce

1 Tbsp Red Wine Vinegar

1/8-1/4 cup Raisins (golden or black)

1 (14 oz) can Diced Tomatoes (w/juice)

Instructions

1. Turn on your pot's sauté setting. Add the ground beef and cook, stirring to break up the meat, until almost done (if using ground turkey, add 2 tsp olive oil to pot before adding turkey).

2. Add the onion, bay leaves, cinnamon, cumin, oregano, and salt. Cook, stirring occasionally, until onion starts to soften.

3. Add garlic, jalapeño, and red bell pepper. Cook, stirring frequently, for a minute.

4. Add green olives, olive juice, Worcestershire, and red wine vinegar. Stir together.

5. Sprinkle raisins over the top, then pour the diced tomatoes evenly over the meat mixture. Do not stir.

6. Cancel the Sauté function. Place the lid on the pot and lock it into position. Set the steam release knob to Sealing.

7. Press the Pressure Cook/Manual button, then the +/- to choose 7 minutes. High pressure.

8. When the cook cycle ends, let the pot sit undisturbed for 5 minute Natural Release. Then Manually release the remaining steam/pressure until the pin in the lid drops down. Open the lid and stir. Taste and adjust salt, if desired.

9. Serve over hot rice, or in tacos, burritos, etc.

Taco Pie

4-6 Servings | Prep Time: 15 mins. | Cook Time: 25 mins. | Total Time: 40 mins.

Ingredients

1 lb Lean Ground Beef or Turkey

1 (1 oz) Taco Seasoning Packet (or 2-3 Tbsp *Easy Taco Seasoning* pg. 360)

1 1/2 cups Refried Beans

1/3 cup Salsa

4 (8 inch) Flour Tortillas

2 Tbsp Enchilada Sauce (optional)

2 1/2 cups Shredded Cheese or to taste. (I use sharp cheddar + Monterey Jack)

Garnish

Sour Cream, Cilantro, Extra Salsa, Hot Sauce

Instructions

1. Use the Sauté setting on your pressure cooker (or use a frying pan) to brown the meat, stirring in the taco seasoning about halfway through. Cook until done. Set aside. Cancel sauté setting.

2. Wash/Rinse out the pot and put 1 1/2 cups of water in it.

3. Mix the refried beans with the salsa.

4. Spray a 7"x3" springform or push pan with cooking spray. Place 1 of the tortillas in the bottom of the pan and spread 1/2 cup of the refried bean mixture over it.

5. Sprinkle on 1 cup of the meat evenly, then the enchilada sauce, and 1 cup of the cheese.

6. Place a second tortilla in the pan, then 1/2 cup of the refried bean mixture, 1 cup of the meat, and then 1/2 cup of the cheese (the first layer has 1 cup of cheese, that is correct).

7. Add a third tortilla, then 1/2 cup refried bean mixture, 1 cup of the meat, and 1/2 cup of cheese.

8. Place the final tortilla on and gently press in place.

9. Cover the pan with foil and place on the trivet/rack, and use the handles to place them in the pot. You can also use a sling, and set the pan on the trivet that you will put in the pot first.

10. Place the lid on the pot and lock in place. Turn the steam release knob to the Sealing position.

11. Press the Pressure Cook/Manual button. Use the +/- button to choose 17 minutes. High pressure.

12. When the cooking cycle has ended, let the pot sit undisturbed for 10 minute Natural Release. Then turn the steam release knob to Venting to release the remaining pressure.

13. After the pin in the lid drops, open the lid. Use silicone mitts, or oven mitts to carefully remove the pan and trivet. If you used a sling, gather up the two ends of the sling and carefully lift out the pan to a cooling rack. Be very careful as the pan and the water is hot.

14. Turn on your broiler to 450° (F). Remove the foil from the pan and sprinkle on the remaining 1/2 cup of cheese (or more, up to 1 cup).

15. Place the pan on the middle oven rack and let the cheese brown to your desired amount. Don't leave it unattended as it could get too brown if you don't watch it!

16. Remove from oven to a plate and let it sit for a few minutes to set up and cool a bit.

17. Run a butter knife around the edge to loosen it. Carefully unlock the springform pan and lift the ring off. Use a spatula to slide pie off of the pan bottom, or just leave it and serve from it.

18. If you used a push pan, loosen the edge with a knife, and set a large can on a plate and set the pan on top of the can and gently push downward. The pie will be sitting on the pan bottom. Carefully slide the pie onto another plate and serve. Use caution as it's hot.

19. Cut taco pie into desired serving sizes and garnish as desired.

Balsamic Pork Loin Roast

Ingredients

2 lb Pork Loin Roast (not tenderloin) boneless

2 tsp Kosher Salt, divided

1 tsp Pepper, divided

1 Tbsp Olive Oil

1 Onion, sliced into thick rounds

1 tsp Garlic Powder

1/3 cup Apple Cider

1/3 cup Balsamic Vinegar

1 Apple, sliced thick (core it, don't peel)

To Finish

3 Tbsp Corn Starch + 3 Tbsp Cold Water

2 Tbsp Honey

Instructions

1. Salt & pepper all sides of the roast, using 1 tsp of the salt and 1/2 tsp of the pepper. Set aside.
2. Turn on the Sauté setting. When hot, add the oil.
3. Add the pork roast and onion. Brown the roast for 2-3 minutes per side. Remove to a plate.
4. Sprinkle the garlic powder, and remaining salt and pepper over the onions.
5. Add the apple cider, and when it starts to simmer, stir, scraping the bottom of the pot to get up all of the browned bits (deglaze).
6. Pour in the balsamic vinegar.
7. Add the apple slices to the pot and then set the roast on top. Cancel the sauté setting.
8. Close the lid and set the steam release knob to the Sealing position.
9. Press the Pressure Cook/Manual button, then the +/- button to select 30 minutes. High Pressure. (if roast is larger than 2.5 pounds, or bone-in, add 10 min cook time per pound).
10. When the cook cycle is finished, let the pot sit undisturbed for 10 minute natural release. Then turn the steam release knob to Venting to release remaining pressure.
11. When the pin in the lid drops back down, open the lid.
12. Take the temperature of the roast. It should be close to 140° F. If it is much below that (by 5 degrees or more), place the lid back on the pot and seal it. Then set time for "0" minutes and after it is done, let it sit 5 minutes before releasing pressure and opening it.
13. Remove the roast to a plate and loosely cover with foil.
14. Whisk together the corn starch and the cold water. Set aside.
15. Turn the sauté setting on and when it starts to simmer, stir in the corn starch slurry. Keep stirring until the sauce thickens.
16. Turn off the pot and stir in the honey. Taste the sauce and adjust seasonings if desired
17. Transfer roast to a serving dish, slice it, and pour some of the sauce over it.
18. Serve each portion with some of the extra sauce.

Baby Back Ribs

4-5 Servings | Prep Time: 15 mins. | Cook Time: 25 mins. | Total Time: 50 mins.

Ingredients

FOR THE POT

1 1/2 cups Water (or Apple Cider)

2-3 Tbsp. Liquid Smoke (put in the water)

1/3 cup Apple Cider Vinegar (ACV)

FOR THE RIBS

1-2 racks Baby Back Ribs (or other pork ribs)

1/2 - 1 cup Dry Spice Rub Use your favorite, or make a batch of Ribs Spice Rub, pg. 362

1 cup BBQ Sauce

Instructions

1. Put a trivet in the inner liner of the pot. Add the water or juice, liquid smoke, and ACV.
PREPARE THE RIBS

2. Lay out the rack of ribs, meaty side down, on a baking sheet. Remove the thin membrane (also called silver skin, if it's still on there) by grasping it with your bare hands, or a paper towel, and pulling down the length of the rack. It should come off pretty easily.

3. Sprinkle dry spice rub liberally over both sides of the ribs and gently rub it in.

4. Carefully roll the rack into a "C" shape and put it in the pot sideways (the meaty side will face the outside of the pot. You can also cut the rack into a few pieces and stack it in the pot.

5. Put the lid on the pot and close it, turning the venting knob to the Sealing position.

6. Press the Pressure Cook/Manual button, then the +/- button to choose 25 minutes.

7. After cook time ends, let the pot sit undisturbed for 10 minutes.

8. Then turn the steam release knob to venting and release the rest of the pressure until the pin in the lid drops, and open the lid.

9. Remove the rack of ribs using tongs, and place on a baking sheet.

10. Pour the BBQ sauce on the hot ribs and use a brush or a spatula to cover them generously.

OPTIONAL: Turn your oven to BROIL at 425° and set the oven rack about 8-10 inches from element.

Put the pan under the broiler for a few minutes, until the sauce gets bubbly. Be careful not to leave them in there too long as they might dry out. No one wants dry ribs! Enjoy!

Balsamic Apple Pork Tenderloin

4 Servings | Prep Time: 10 mins. | Cook Time: 7 mins. | Total Time: 27 mins.

Ingredients

1 Tbsp Cooking Oil, neutral (canola or sunflower)

1 1/2 lbs Pork Tenderloin* (not loin roast)

1 sm Onion, cut in half and thinly sliced

2 cloves Garlic, pressed or finely minced

2 1/2 Tbsps Balsamic Vinegar

1/2 cup Apple Juice or Chicken Broth, low sodium

2 Apples, chopped (any variety)

1/2 tsp Kosher Salt (or 1/4 tsp table salt)

1 (3") sprig Fresh Rosemary

3 sprigs Fresh Thyme

TO FINISH

2 Tbsps Honey

1 Tbsp Butter

2 1/2 tsps Corn Starch

Instructions

1. Turn on Sauté setting. When hot, add the oil.

2. Place the tenderloin in the pot and let it cook for 2-4 minutes (depending on thickness), undisturbed, Then flip it over and do the same on that side. Brown all sides.

3. Remove the tenderloin to a plate. Set aside.

4. Add the onion and cook until tender, stirring frequently, scraping up all of the brown bits from the bottom of the pot. You might need to add a small splash of the broth to help loosen it.

5. Add the garlic. Stir.

6. Add the balsamic vinegar. Stir.

7. Add the juice/broth, apple, salt, rosemary, and thyme. Stir well.

8. Add the tenderloin back in and nestle it down into the broth mixture.

9. Put the lid on the pot and lock it in place. Set the steam release knob to the Sealing position. Cancel the Sauté function.

10. Press Pressure Cook (Manual) and adjust the pressure to Low Pressure, then the +/- to choose 2 minutes (smaller tenderloins use 0-1 minute, depending on thickness).

11. When the cook cycle ends, Turn the pot off or unplug it (so the warming doesn't get activated) and let the pot sit for 15 minutes (natural release). Then turn the steam release knob to Venting to release the remaining pressure (there may not be any, and that's okay).

12. When the pin in the lid drops, open the lid and use a meat thermometer to take the internal

temperature of the tenderloin. If it reads 140° (F) or more, you are good to remove the tenderloin to a plate and cover with foil to rest (it will continue to cook and heat to the safe 145° (F) temp).

13. If the tenderloin isn't up to temp, Remove the tenderloin and complete the next 3 steps. Then add tenderloin to mixture and let it cook for a few minutes, turning once. Check temperature again before removing and covering with foil. Then proceed to adding the corn starch, etc.

14. Turn the Sauté function back on. Add the honey and stir well to incorporate.

15. Add the butter and stir.

16. Cook for about 5 minutes to let the mixture reduce a little and the flavors concentrate.

17. Scoop out about 1/3 cup of the liquid into a cup and whisk in the corn starch. Pour mixture into the simmering sauce and stir well to thicken. Turn off the pot.

18. Slice the tenderloin into medallions and serve with a generous portion of the balsamic-apple sauce.

19. Garnish if desired (photo shows thyme and pomegranate arils).

Recipe Notes: *If you have a smaller tenderloin, say 1 pound, you will only cook for 0 (zero) minutes instead of 2. Same natural release time. Please use a meat thermometer.

Teriyaki Pork Tenderloin

Ingredients

SAUCE (mix together)

1/2 cup Teriyaki Sauce

1/2 cup Low Sodium Chicken Broth (or water)

4 cloves Garlic, pressed or finely minced

4 Tbsp Brown Sugar

1 tsp Ginger, fresh or ground Pork

2 Tbsp Olive Oil

1 1/2 lbs Pork Tenderloin (not pork loin roast)

1/2 sm Sweet Onion, finely minced

TO THICKEN SAUCE (whisk together)

3 Tbsp Corn Starch

3 Tbsp Cold Water

TO SERVE

3-4 cups Cooked Hot Rice

Sliced Green Onions, garnish

Instructions

1. Before cooking, mix together your sauce and set aside.

2. Turn on the Sauté setting. When hot add olive oil. Add the pork tenderloin and brown 2-3 minutes on each side. Then remove to a plate.

3. Meanwhile, mix together the corn starch and water. Set aside.

4. Add the onion and cook until tender, stirring and scraping the bottom of the pot with a wood spoon, until you get up all of the browned bits from the bottom (deglaze). You may need a little splash of water to help get up the browned bits.

5. Turn off the pot. Add the pork tenderloin on top of the onions.

6. Pour the sauce over the pork.

7. Close the lid and set the steam release knob to the Sealing position.

8. Press the Pressure Cook/Manual button, then the +/- button to select 0 (zero) minutes. High Pressure. The pot will take several minutes to come to pressure.

9. When the cook cycle has finished, turn off the pot and let it sit undisturbed for 15 minute natural release. Then turn the steam release knob to Venting to release remaining pressure.

10. When the pin in the lid drops back down, open the lid and check the temperature of the meat with an instant read thermometer. You want 143° to 145° at the thickest part. If it is under 140°, close the lid and let it rest a few minutes longer. Then check again.

11. Remove the pork to a plate and loosely cover with foil.

12. Turn on the Sauté setting. When the sauce starts to simmer, stir in the corn starch slurry. Stir until thickened, then turn off the pot.

13. Serve the tenderloin sliced into medallions, with some of the sauce over it. Garnish with green onion slices. Delicious over hot rice.

Peach Glazed Ham

Ingredients

5-9 lb Ham* (spiral cut, cooked) soaked and rinsed well

2 (14 oz) cans Sliced Peaches, in juice (divided)

TO FINISH

1 cup Peach Preserves

2 tsp Ginger, fresh or grated

1 tsp Cinnamon

1/4 tsp Ground Cloves (optional)

1/4 to 1/2 tsp Red Pepper Flakes

1/2 to 1 cup Brown Sugar

TO THICKEN (mix these together while ham is cooking and set aside)

2 to 3 Tbsp Corn Starch

2 to 3 Tbsp Cold Water

Instructions

1. Soak your ham in cold water for an hour if you can, then drain and rinse it well. If you can't soak it, just rinse it very well. This reduces the saltiness of the ham.

2. Add ham to the pot, cut side down, if possible. I can fit a 9 lb spiral ham in an 8 qt pot, depending on the shape. I can fit up to a 7 lb ham in my 6 qt, depending on the shape.

3. Add one can of the peaches to the pot, and add the juice of the second can to the pot, reserving the peaches from that can (If using an 8 qt pot, add 1/4 cup of water just to be sure there is enough, but not too much, liquid to get the pot to pressure).

4. Put the lid on the pot and set the steam release knob to the Sealing position. Then press the Pressure Cook/Manual button, then the +/- button to select 3 minutes (If your ham is 8 to 9 lbs. If cooking a 4 to 7 lb ham, do 2 minutes). High pressure.

5. When the cook time is finished let the pot sit for 5 minute natural release, then turn the steam release knob to Venting to release the remaining pressure.

6. Turn off the pot. Remove ham to a platter or pan and wrap in foil to keep it moist.

7. Turn on the Sauté setting.

8. Add the peach preserves, ginger, cinnamon, cloves, red pepper flakes, and brown sugar. Stir well.

9. When it starts to simmer, add the corn starch slurry. Stir until thickened. Turn off the pot.

10. Slather the glaze all over the ham, reserving some for serving at the table.

11. At this point you can broil in the oven to caramelize the outside, or serve as is.

12. Garnish with the reserved peaches.

Recipe Note: *If your ham is uncut, increase the cook time to about 20 minutes.*

Bone-In Ham

3-8 lb Ham | Prep Time: 15 mins. | Cook Time: 37-50 mins. | Total Time: 1 hr. 15 mins.

Ingredients

1 (3-3 lb) Bone-in Ham* (Uncut, Fully Cooked shank or butt "portion")

2 (20 oz) cans Pineapple Chunks (with juice) Reserve 1/4 cup juice

1/2 tsp Ground Cloves, or 1 tsp whole (optional)

2 Tbsp Ground Dry Mustard (or 1

Tbsp prepared Dijon)

1/2 cup Honey

To Finish

1/4-1/3 cup Brown Sugar, divided

3 Tbsp Corn Starch

1/4 cup Cold Water

Instructions

1. Pour the cans of pineapple and their juice into the pot, reserving 1/4 cup of the juice.

2. Add the cloves and mustard. Stir well.

3. Place the ham on a trivet (I like to use a silicone steamer with handles) in the pot with the fat side up. If it doesn't fit well, cut off a piece and fit it into the pot along side the larger piece.

4. Make sure the ham is below the level of the pot so the lid goes on without obstruction. I can fit an 8-9 lb ham in my 8 quart pot, and a 6 to 7 lb ham in my 6 qt.

5. Pour the honey over the ham.

6. Place the lid on the Instant Pot and set the steam release knob to Sealing.

7. Press the Pressure Cook/Manual button, then the +/- button to select the cook time minutes.

8. Your ham's cook time will depend on the weight/thickness. Use High pressure.

> 4-5 pounds - 12 minutes plus 25 minutes Natural Release
> 6-7 pounds - 17 minutes plus 25 minutes Natural Release
> 8-9 pounds - 22 minutes plus 25 minutes Natural Release
> (For a spiral cut ham, only cook 3 minutes with a 15 minute NPR).

9. When cook cycle finishes, let the pot naturally release pressure for 25 minutes. Then quick release any remaining pressure by turning the steam release knob to Venting.

10. When the pin in the lid drops, open the lid and take the temperature of the ham. It should read 110° to 115° (F) or just under (If it reads just under, you don't have to cook it longer, just let it rest a few more minutes. Then take the temperature again). If the temp is less than 85°, put the lid on and set it for 3 minutes more cook time and a 10 minute NPR.

11. Carefully remove the ham to a baking sheet.

12. Ladle the liquid from the pot to a fat separator (straining out the pineapple chunks) and discard the extra fat. Then add the defatted liquid and pineapple chunks back into the pot.

13. Turn on the Sauté setting (Low or Less temperature).

14. Mix in a half of the brown sugar. Taste and adjust sugar, mustard, or cloves, if desired.

15. Add the corn starch slurry to the simmering liquid and stir until glaze is thickened. Then turn off the Sauté setting.

If You Want To Glaze/Caramelize the Outside of the Ham

16. Turn on the broiler to 425°.

17. Mix the corn starch and reserved pineapple juice together to make a slurry. Add the slurry to the simmering liquid and stir until it is thickened. Then turn off the pot.

18. Pour some of the glaze over the ham and place the ham under the broiler to caramelize for a few minutes. Check it often to make sure it doesn't burn!

19. Remove ham from oven to a serving platter and serve. Serve the extra glaze as a gravy.

Country Style Ribs

4-5 Servings | Prep Time: 10 mins. | Cook Time: 25 mins. | Total Time: 50 mins.

Ingredients

3-4 lbs Country Style Pork Ribs (boneless or bone-in)

1/3 cup Spice Rub* (something smoky)

2 cups Apple Juice

1 Tbsp Liquid Smoke

1/4 cup Apple Cider Vinegar

1-2 cups Barbecue Sauce (your favorite brand or homemade)

Instructions

1. Rub the ribs with the spice rub on all sides. Let the ribs sit while you prepare the pressure cooker.

2. Add the apple juice, liquid smoke, and apple cider vinegar to the inner liner pot of the pressure cooker. Place the metal trivet/rack in the pot.

3. Place the ribs on the trivet, trying not to overlap by much.

4. Place the lid on the pot and set the steam release knob to the Sealing position.

5. Press the Pressure Cook/Manual button, then the +/- button to select 25 minutes.

6. When the cook time is finished, let the pot sit undisturbed for 10 minute Natural Release. Then turn the steam release knob to Venting to Quick Release the remaining pressure.

7. When the pin in the lid drops down, open the lid.

8. Set the oven broiler to 350° to start heating up.

9. Use tongs to remove the ribs to a foil lined baking pan. Slather barbecue sauce all over them.

10. Place under a 350° broiler for a few minutes to caramelize the sauce (this step is optional. Sometimes I just sauce them up and eat them). Watch them to make sure they don't burn or get dried out.

11. Serve with a little extra bbq sauce for dipping.

Beef Tips

Ingredients

SEASONING RUB

3 Tbsp Flour

2 tsp Steak Seasoning

2 tsp Garlic Powder

1 tsp Onion Powder

1 1/4 tsp Kosher Salt

1/2 tsp Pepper

TO BROWN THE BEEF

2 lbs Beef Sirloin Roast, cut in 2" cubes

2 Tbsp Olive Oil

GRAVY

2 Tbsp Butter

1 Onion, chopped

2 lg cloves Garlic, minced

1/3 cup Red Wine (or beef broth)

1 tsp Beef Bouillon

1 (10.5) oz can Beef Consommé

1 Tbsp Worcestershire Sauce

1 tsp Thyme Leaves (not ground)

Instructions

MAKE THE SEASONING RUB

1. In a gallon sized baggie, mix together the seasoning ingredients. Set aside.

BROWN THE MEAT

2. Turn on the pot's Sauté setting (high temperature).

3. Cut the roast into 2 inch cubes and put them into the baggie with the seasoning mixture. Shake the baggie to coat all of the meat with the seasoning.

4. When the pot is hot, add the oil. Then add half of the steak cubes in one layer. Brown both sides, but don't cook through, and remove to a plate. Repeat with the second half of the meat.

MAKE THE GRAVY

5. Add the butter and onion to the pot. Stir and scrape the bottom of the pot, getting up all of the browned bits.

6. Add the garlic, stir. Cook about 20 seconds, then add the red wine.

7. Add the bouillon, consommé, Worcestershire sauce, and thyme leaves. Mix well to dissolve the bouillon.

8. Cancel the Sauté setting.

COOK THE BEEF TIPS

9. Add the beef tips back into the pot. Close the lid and seal it.

10. Set the cook time for 25 minutes. High pressure.

11. When the cook time finishes, let the pot sit undisturbed for a 10 minute natural release.

12. Turn the steam release knob to Venting and release the remaining pressure.

13. Stir, taste the gravy and adjust salt, if necessary.

14. Serve over mashed potatoes, rice, or cauliflower rice.

Autumn Apple Pork Chops

2-4 Servings | Prep Time: 10 mins. | Cook Time: 25 mins. | Total Time: 45 mins.

Ingredients

3 Apples, sliced about 1/4" thick

1 sm Sweet Onion (Walla Walla, Vidalia, etc) Cut in half and thinly sliced.

2-4 Pork Chops (I prefer bone-in 3/4")

3/4 tsp Salt

1/8 tsp Pepper

1 Tbsp Vegetable Oil

1/4 cup plus 1 Tbsp Water (divided)

4 Tbsp Butter (unsalted)

4 Tbsp Brown Sugar

1/4 tsp Cinnamon

1/4 tsp Nutmeg

Pinch of Salt

2 Tbsp Corn Starch

3 Tbsp Cold Water

Optional

2-4 sm Potatoes (cook with pork chops as a side dish)

Garnish

Chopped Pecans (optional)

Instructions

1. Season the pork chops with salt & pepper on each side. Set aside while the pot warms up.
2. Turn the IP to Sauté mode. When the pot is hot, add the oil to the pot.
3. Add the pork chops, two at a time, and brown on each side for about 4 minutes per side. Remove to a plate and set aside.
4. Add the onion and 1 Tbsp water. Cook the onion, stirring frequently and scraping to deglaze the pot (get all of the brown bits off the bottom). I like to use a wooden spoon.
5. When the onions are translucent and tender, add the butter and stir until melted.
6. Add the apples and 1/4 cup water. Stir well.
7. Add the pork chops (and any juices on the plate) back in and set them on top of the apples. Don't stir.
8. If you are cooking potatoes with this dish, set them on top of the pork chops. Leave them (whole small or quartered potatoes).
9. Put the lid on the pot and set the steam release knob to Sealing. Cancel the Sauté mode.
10. Press the Manual/Pressure Cook button, then the +/- button to select 10 minutes (8 minutes for thinner chops).

**The pot will come to pressure with only 1/4 cup of water in it. This is because the apples will release water as the pot is heating up and building pressure.

11. While the pork chops are cooking, mix together the brown sugar, cinnamon, nutmeg, and

a pinch of salt. Set aside.

12. When the cook cycle ends and the pot beeps, don't do anything to it, just let it naturally release pressure for 10 minutes (the counter will begin counting up). After the 10 minutes is up, turn the steam release knob to manually release the remaining pressure.

13. When the pin in the lid drops, open the lid. Remove the pork chops (and potatoes) to a plate and cover with foil or a lid to keep warm.

14. Turn the Sauté back on.

15. Add the brown sugar mixture to the apple mixture and stir.

16. Mix the corn starch and cold water. Stir the corn starch slurry into the apple gravy, stirring constantly.

17. When the mixture thickens, turn off the pot. Remove apple gravy to a serving bowl.

18. Serve the pork chops smothered in the warm apple gravy. Yum! Garnish with chopped pecans, if desired.

Pork Chops with Mushroom Gravy

4-6 Servings | Prep Time: 10 mins. | Cook Time: 18 mins. | Total Time: 45 mins.

Ingredients

4-6 Pork Chops

3 Tbsp Oil

8 oz Mushrooms, sliced

1 cup Low Sodium Chicken Broth (divided)
or replace 1/4 cup of the broth with sherry

1 sm Onion, diced

3 cloves Garlic minced or pressed

2 tsp Worcestershire Sauce

1 tsp Soy Sauce, low sodium

1/2 tsp Salt

1/2 tsp Pepper

1 can Cream of Mushroom Soup

1/4 cup Flour

1/2 cup Sour Cream (or Greek yogurt)

Instructions

1. Turn on the pot's sauté setting to the highest heat level. When the pot is hot, add the oil.

2. Brown the pork chops on both sides, in two batches. Then set browned chops on a plate.

3. Add the mushrooms to the pot and cook a couple of minutes. Then add 1/4 cup of the chicken broth (or sherry, if using) and deglaze the pot, using a wooden spoon to scrape up the browned bits from the bottom of the pot.

4. Add the onion and cook for 5 minutes, until it starts to turn translucent.

5. Add in the garlic and cook for 1 minute.

6. Add soy sauce, salt, pepper, Worcestershire, and remaining 3/4 cup chicken broth. Stir well.

7. Place the pork chops back in the pot and turn off the Sauté setting.

8. Pour the cream of mushroom soup on top but do not stir. Place the lid on the pot and set the steam release knob to the Sealing position.

9. Press the Pressure Cook/Manual button, then the +/- button to select 10 minutes (for 1 1/2" thick) or (7 or 8 minutes for smaller, thinner chops, 12 minutes for thicker chops)

10. When the cooking cycle has finished, let the pot sit undisturbed for 8 minute natural release.

11. Remove the chops to a dish and spoon some of the gravy over them to keep them moist.

12. Turn the Sauté setting on and mix the flour with some of the hot liquid in a mug. Then pour the mixture into the pot and stir to thicken. Stir a little water into the gravy if it is too thick.

13. Turn off the Sauté setting.

14. Stir in the sour cream.

15. Serve pork chops with some of the mushroom gravy. Yummy with mashed potatoes or rice.

Pork Carnitas

Ingredients

2 Tbsp Olive Oil

1 tsp Kosher Salt

1/2 tsp Black Pepper

1 tsp Oregano

1 Tbsp Cumin

2 tsp Chili Powder

2 tsp Paprika

2 tsp Garlic Powder

1 tsp Adobo Powder

1 tsp Ground Coriander

3 lbs Pork Shoulder, cut into large chunks

1 Onion, diced

1 cup Orange Juice

1 Cinnamon Stick

OPTIONAL

1/4 tsp Cayenne Powder

1 Jalapeño Pepper, chopped

Instructions

1. In a mixing bowl add the olive oil and spices. Mix well.

2. Add the pork chunks and stir them to make sure they are completely coated with the oil/spice mixture. Set aside.

3. Pour the orange juice into the pressure cooker's inner liner.

4. Add the cinnamon stick, pork chunks and the chopped onion to the pot and stir.

5. Place the lid on the pot and set steam release knob to the Sealing position.

6. Press the Pressure Cook (or Manual button), and then the +/- buttons to set time to 35 minutes. High Pressure.

7. After cook cycle ends, let it naturally release pressure for 15 minutes.

8. Turn steam release knob to Venting to release the remaining pressure.

9. When the pin on the lid drops, open it and remove meat to a plate or bowl and shred, using two forks. Don't shred too much as you want to have some slightly bigger pieces.

10. Very carefully strain the liquid in the pot, (saving the onions, and discarding the cinnamon stick) into a fat separator.

11. Pour as much of the degreased liquid as you want into a large serving bowl with the pork and the onions, and mix well.

> **Recipe Note**
>
> Serve on warm tortillas, on a bun, in a salad, over corn bread.
> Garnish with cilantro, avocado, tomatoes, green onion, salsa, Cotija cheese, sour cream, lime juice.

Pulled Pork

Ingredients

SPICE RUB

3 Tbsp Brown Sugar

1 1/2 Tbsp Smoked Paprika

2 tsp Salt

1 tsp Pepper

1 tsp Garlic Powder

1/2 tsp Onion Powder

3 tsp Chili Powder

2 tsp Cumin

1/4 tsp Cayenne Powder (optional)

PORK

3-4 lbs Pork Shoulder Roast (Pork Butt) Fat trimmed off, and cut in 1 lb chunks

1 Onion, cut in eighths

1 (12 oz) can Dr. Pepper or Cola (or 1 1/2 cups chicken stock)

2 Tbsp Brown Sugar (or more to taste)

1/2 tsp Salt (or more to taste)

Instructions

1. Mix the spices together for the rub. Remove 2 Tbsps and set aside for later.

2. Rub all sides of the pork roast chunks generously with the spice rub. Set meat aside.

3. Cut the onion into 8 pieces (cut in half, then cut each half into 4 pieces). Put the onion into the inner cooking pot of the pressure cooker.

4. Pour the can of pop into the pot over the onion.

5. Set the pork chunks on top of the onions. Sprinkle the brown sugar over the pork.

6. Place the lid on and lock in place. Set the steam release knob to the sealing position.

7. Press the Pressure Cook/Manual Button, then the +/- button to choose 65 minutes.

8. After the cook time is finished, let the pot sit undisturbed for 15 minute natural release. Then turn the steam release knob to Venting to Release the remaining pressure.

9. When the pin in the lid drops down, open it and remove the meat to a large bowl. Use a slotted spoon to get the onions out and add to the meat. Use two forks to shred the meat.

10. Sprinkle the reserved spice rub and 1/2 tsp salt onto the meat. Mix well. Taste and add more salt and/or brown sugar, if desired.

11. Use a large spoon (or a fat separator) to skim off the fat from the cooking liquid. Then add 1/2 cup of the liquid to the meat and mix in. You can add more of the liquid to the meat if you like it more moist.

12. Serve on buns, or over rice or potatoes, or in tortillas.

Kalua Pork

Ingredients

5-7 lbs Pork Shoulder (Pork Butt)

7 Garlic Cloves, peeled and cut in thick slivers

1-2 Tbsp Hawaiian Red Alaea Sea Salt (or pink Himalayan sea salt) As much as needed to coat the meat

2-3 slices Smoky Bacon, thick cut (or 2 tsp liquid smoke)

3/4 cup Water

1 med Head Green Cabbage, cut in 4-6 wedges

1 lb Baby Carrots, (optional) cut in half

Instructions

1. Cut the pork shoulder into 3 equal pieces.

2. Cut slits in the pork meat and stuff with the garlic slivers.

3. Sprinkle the red sea salt all over each piece of the pork.

4. Wrap bacon around each piece of pork (if using liquid smoke instead, add it with the water).

5. Add the water to the inner liner of the pressure cooker (and liquid smoke, if using).

6. Place the pork pieces in the pot.

7. Place the lid on the pot and set the steam release knob to the Sealing position.

8. Press the Pressure Cook/Manual button and then the + or - button to select 90 minutes.

9. When the cook cycle is finished, leave the pot undisturbed for a 20 minute natural release. Then turn steam release knob to Venting to manually release the remaining pressure.

10. After the pin in the lid drops down, open it and remove the pork with tongs to a large bowl.

11. Defat the liquid/drippings (if desired) and add the cabbage wedges (and carrots, if using) to the liquid in the pot. Close the lid and set to Sealing. Use the +/- button to choose 3 minutes.

12. Meanwhile, use two forks to shred the pork. Then cover and wait for the cabbage to finish.

13. When the veggies are done cooking, do a Quick Release of the pressure. Then open the lid once the pin has dropped down.

14. Remove the veggies to a serving bowl, and place the shredded pork on top of it. Taste the liquid in the pot and adjust salt if needed. Then ladle some over the meat and cabbage to flavor it and keep it moist.

Alaea Hawaiian Red Sea Salt is a traditional, native salt blend of the Hawaiian Islands. Sometimes referred to as Hawaiian red salt, it is an unrefined sea salt that has been mixed with an iron oxide rich volcanic clay called 'alaea', that gives the salt its brick red color.

Sausage and White Beans

6-8 Servings | Prep Time: 10 mins. | Cook Time: 45 mins. | Total Time: 1 hr. 10 mins.

Ingredients

2 tsp Olive Oil

1 1/2 lbs Smoked Kielbasa Sausage (or Smoked Turkey Sausage), cut in 3/4" rounds

1 lg Yellow Onion, chopped

1 lg Bay Leaf

4 Carrots, chopped (~ 1 1/2 cups)

3 Celery Ribs, chopped (~ 1 cup)

4 sprigs Fresh Thyme (or 1/2 tsp dried)

1 - 4" Sprig of Fresh Rosemary

1/2 tsp Oregano, dried

4 cloves Garlic, pressed or minced

1/2 tsp Pepper

6 cups Chicken Broth, low sodium (use 7 cups if you like it a little soupier)

1 lb Navy Beans,*** dry (rinsed & sorted) or 2 cans of white beans*

OPTIONAL

3 cups Fresh Baby Spinach or Kale

Salt to taste (Add after cooking)

Instructions

1. Turn the pot to the Sauté setting. When hot add the oil and sausage. Lightly brown all sides.

2. Add the onion, bay leaf, carrots and celery. Stir and cook until the onion starts to turn translucent. Make sure to scrape any brown bits from the bottom of the pot (deglaze).

3. Add the thyme, rosemary, oregano, and garlic. Cook, stirring for 30 seconds.

4. Add pepper, and broth. Stir, and put a glass lid on the pot. Let contents come to a simmer.

5. Once the broth is simmering, add the beans and stir. Put the lid on, and set the steam release knob to the Sealing position.

6. Cancel the sauté function and press Pressure Cook/Manual button, then the +/- button to choose 40 minutes.** High pressure.

7. The pot may take 10 minutes to come to pressure, but since the contents are already hot, it will pressurize quicker. Once the cooking cycle has finished, let the pot sit undisturbed for 15 minute Natural Release.

8. Turn the steam release knob to Venting to release remaining pressure. Use caution.

9. When the pin in the lid drops down, open the lid. Gently stir the beans. Taste a few to test for tenderness and for salt, and add salt if needed.

10. If beans aren't tender enough (sometimes old beans take longer), just put the lid back on and cook them for 5 more minutes under pressure, and a 15 minute natural release.

11. If adding spinach or kale, stir it into the beans after pressure cooking. Let the pot sit for a few minutes until the greens are wilted and soft.

12. Serve with some crusty bread.

Recipe Notes
*If using canned white beans, rinse & drain them, add at the same time you would add the dry beans, and adjust broth to 4 cups, and cook time to 5 minutes, with a 10 minute natural release. Canned white beans are soft, so they may break apart easily.

**If you soaked your beans for at least 8 hours, adjust cook time to 25 minutes and reduce broth to 4 cups.

***Old beans can take longer to cook. If you think yours are old, soak them or prepare for longer cook time.

Drunken Beans

6-8 Serving | Prep Time: 15 mins. | Cook Time: 40 mins. | Total Time: 1 hr. 15 mins.

Ingredients

3/4 lb Bacon (chopped)

1 lg Yellow Onion (diced)

1/2 Green Bell Pepper (diced)

1 Red Bell Pepper (diced)

1 Pasilla or Hatch Chile (chopped)

1 Jalapeño Pepper (seeded & diced)

5 Garlic Cloves (minced)

(14 oz) can Diced Tomatoes (w/juices)

1 Tbsp Chili Powder

1 Tbsp Cumin

2 tsp Mexican Oregano (or 1 tsp regular)

2 tsp Kosher Salt (or 1 tsp table salt)

1 (12 oz) Beer (Mexican dark or a Lager) or 1 1/4 cup more broth

3 1/2 cups Chicken Broth* (low sodium)

2 Bay Leaves

Bundle of Cilantro Stems (tied with butcher's string for easy removal)

1 lb Dry Pinto Beans** (rinsed & sorted) or 2 cans of prepared pinto beans

TO FINISH

1/2 cup Cilantro Leaves (chopped)

GARNISHES

Reserved Cooked Bacon, Avocado

Sour Cream, Cilantro Cotija Cheese

Instructions

1. Turn on the Sauté mode. When hot, add the bacon. Cook, stirring occasionally, until just turning crisp. Remove from pot and set aside. Discard all but 2 Tbsp of the bacon fat.

2. Add onion and stir. Cook until it starts turning translucent, scraping the bottom of the pot.

3. Add the green pepper, red pepper, pasilla, and jalapeño. Stir well.

4. Add the garlic and cook, stirring frequently, for 1 minute.

5. Add the tomatoes, chili powder, cumin, oregano, and salt. Stir well.

6. Add the beer, broth, bay leaves, cilantro stems bundle, and the beans. Stir well.

7. Add 3/4 of the cooked bacon back in, reserving 1/4 of it for garnishing. Stir.

8. Place the lid on the pot and lock in place. Set the steam release knob to Sealing.

9. Turn off Sauté. Press the Manual / Pressure Cook button, then the +/- to choose 45 minutes.

10. When the cook cycle ends, let the pot naturally release pressure for 20 minutes. Then manually release the remaining pressure by turning the steam release knob to Venting.

11. When the pin in the lid drops, open the pot and stir the beans. Discard bay leaves and cilantro stems bundle.

12. Stir in the 1/2 cup chopped cilantro leaves. Taste and adjust salt, if needed.

13. Garnish as desired and serve. These are great over rice or corn bread!

Cowboy Beans

Ingredients

1 1/2 lbs Ground Beef (90% lean)

1/2 lb Thick Cut Bacon, chopped (about 6-8 slices)

1 lg Onion, diced

6 cloves Garlic, minced

3/4 cup Water*

1 lb Kielbasa Sausage, smoked (cut into 1 1/2" pieces)

2 (28 oz) cans Pork & Beans (or baked beans)

1/2 cup Ketchup

1 (14 oz) can Red Kidney Beans*, drained & rinsed

1/2 cup Barbecue Sauce

1 1/2 Tbsp Dijon Mustard

1/3 cup Molasses

1/2 tsp Pepper

1 Tbsp Chili Powder

1 Tbsp Smoked Paprika

1 tsp Liquid Smoke (optional for smoky flavor)

To Finish

1/4 cup Brown Sugar

Instructions

1. Have everything ready before you start cooking. This helps the process go smoothly.
2. Turn on the Sauté setting and add the ground beef, bacon, and onion. Cook until meat is no longer pink (you shouldn't have to drain it. Leave some fat in there).
3. Add the garlic and stir. Let cook for a minute.
4. Add the water and kielbasa. Stir and scrape the bottom of the pot with a wood spoon.
5. Add the remaining ingredients in order (except brown sugar), and *do not stir*, just push them down into the mixture to cover them.
6. Close the lid and set the steam release knob to the Sealing position. Cancel the Sauté setting.
7. Press the Pressure Cook/Manual button, then the +/- button to select 8 minutes.
8. Watch the pot until it comes to pressure. This is a thick mixture, and you don't want the burn message. If you get one, remove the lid if the pin is still down (otherwise release pressure first) and get a wood spoon in there and scrape the bottom. Add 1/4 cup of water if it is too thick, close the lid, reset time.
9. When the cook time is done, turn the pot off and let it sit undisturbed for 15 minutes. Then release remaining pressure in bursts, until you are sure no sauce will spew out with the steam.
10. When the pin in the lid drops down, open and carefully stir the beans. Stir in the brown sugar.
11. Serve with corn bread.

Red Beans and Rice with Sausage

6-8 Servings | Prep Time: 15 mins. | Cook Time: 55 mins. | Total Time: 1 hr. 10 mins.

Ingredients

- 1/4 lb Bacon (or 2 Tbsp bacon fat)
- 1 Large Yellow Onion (2 cups diced)
- 3-4 stalks Celery, (2 cups diced)
- 7 cloves Garlic, pressed or minced
- 3 Bay Leaves
- 1 Green Bell Pepper, chopped
- 1 Red Bell Pepper, chopped
- 1/2 tsp Sage, dried
- 1/2 tsp Basil, dried
- 1 Tbsp Cajun / Creole Seasoning (Cajun Spice Blend, pg. 360)
- 5 cups Chicken Broth, low sodium
- 1 lb Small Red Beans (such as Camellia)
- 1 1/2 lbs Andouille Sausage (or a smoky Kielbasa) sliced in 3/4" rounds
- 1/4 cup Parsley, chopped
- 2 cups Cooked White Rice
- Garnish: Green Onions, Hot Sauce

Instructions

1. Turn on the Sauté setting. Add the bacon and cook, stirring occasionally, until it renders the fat. Remove the bacon and set aside (You won't be adding it in, you just want the fat). If using bacon fat, let it heat up and proceed.

2. If you are using Andouille sausage, add it and brown on both sides. Then remove. If using kielbasa, don't brown it, add it with the beans.

3. Add the onions and celery. Cook for a couple of minutes, scraping the bottom of the pot to get the brown bits up (deglaze). You may need to add just a splash of the broth to help loosen it.

4. Add the garlic, bay leaves, green and red bell peppers, sage, and basil. Cook, stirring frequently, until onion is translucent.

5. Add the Cajun/Creole seasoning, broth, beans, and sausage. Stir and put the lid on the pot and lock it in place. Set the steam release knob to the Sealing position.

6. Cancel the Sauté function and press the Pressure Cook/Manual button, then the +/- button to choose 40 minutes (High Pressure).

7. When the cook cycle has finished, let the pot sit undisturbed for 20 minute natural release. Turn the steam release knob to Venting to manually release the remaining pressure.

8. When the pin in the lid drops down, open the lid. Carefully stir the beans.

9. Taste a few of the beans to make sure they are tender. If not, cook for 5 more minutes.

10. Mash some of the beans to make a creamy consistency. Taste and add more seasoning if desired. Stir in the chopped parsley.

11. Serve over cooked white rice and garnish with green onions and hot sauce.

Hawaiian Pineapple Pork

5-7 Servings | Prep Time: 30 mins. | Cook Time: 25 mins. | Total Time: 1 hr. 15 mins.

Ingredients

1 (20 oz) can Pineapple Chunks, drained (reserve the juice, divided)

2 Tbsp Cooking Oil (or coconut oil), divided

1 Onion, chopped

1 Bay Leaf

2 Red Bell Peppers, chopped in 1" pieces

2 Jalapeños, seeded & diced

5 cloves Garlic, minced

1 Tbsp Ginger, grated

2-3 lbs Pork Shoulder, cut in slightly larger than bite-sized pieces

1/4 tsp Red Pepper Flakes (or to taste)

1/2 tsp Salt

1/3 cup Brown Sugar

Sauce (mix together and set aside)

3/4 cup Reserved Pineapple Juice

1/3 cup Soy Sauce

1 Tbsp Rice Wine Vinegar

1 tsp Fish Sauce

1/2 cup Chicken Broth

To Finish Sauce

1/4 cup Reserved Pineapple Juice (if there's enough. or use water or broth)

2 Tbsp Corn Starch

Instructions

1. Before you start cooking, gather everything together and get it all chopped and measured. This makes it so much easier!

2. Drain the pineapple chunks, and reserve the juice from the can.

3. Mix together the sauce: 3/4 cup pineapple juice, soy sauce, rice wine vinegar, fish sauce, and chicken broth. Set aside.

Sauté the Veggies

4. Turn on the Sauté setting and when it is hot, add the oil. Then add the onion and bay leaf and sauté until soft.

5. Add the red bell pepper and jalapeño, and sauté until the red bell pepper is softened, but still a little firm. Then remove the mixture from the pot into a bowl and set aside.

Sauté the Pork and Pineapple

6. Add another Tbsp of oil to the pot and add the garlic and ginger. Stir and cook a few seconds, then add the pork chunks, pineapple chunks, and red pepper flakes. Cook, stirring occasionally, until the pork is slightly cooked on all sides. Scrape the bottom of the pot to loosen up any browned bits.

7. Pour the sauce over the pork, sprinkle salt and the brown sugar over (don't stir) and close the lid. Turn the steam release knob to the Sealing position.

Pressure Cook the Pork

8. Turn off Sauté. Press Pressure Cook/Manual button, then the +/- button to select 10 minutes.

9. While the pork is cooking, mix 2 Tbsp cornstarch with 1/4 cup of reserved pineapple juice to make a slurry. Set aside.

10. When the cooking cycle is finished, let the pot sit undisturbed for 10 minute natural release. Then turn the steam release knob to Venting and manually release remaining pressure.

11. When the pin in the lid drops down, open, use a slotted spoon to remove the pork to a bowl.

Thicken the Sauce

12. Turn the sauté setting on. When sauce starts to simmer, stir in cornstarch slurry. Cook until sauce thickens. Turn off pot, add pork, and red bell pepper/onion mixture in. Stir to combine.

13. Serve over hot cooked rice.

Kielbasa and Sauerkraut

Ingredients

2 Tbsp Vegetable Oil

1 1/2 lbs Kielbasa, cut in 1 ½" rounds

1 med Onion, diced

3 med Carrots cut in 1 ½ inch pieces

2 cloves Garlic, pressed or minced

1/2 tsp Kosher Salt

1/2 tsp Black Pepper

1 Tbsp Caraway Seeds

1/3 cup Dry White Wine (or apple juice)

2 cups Chicken Broth

3 sm Gold Potatoes, cubed

1 Apple (cored, peeled and large diced)

1 (32 oz) Jar Sauerkraut (drain 1/2 of the liquid)

Parsley Garnish (optional)

Instructions

1. Turn on the Sauté setting, and when it is hot, add the vegetable oil. Wait a few seconds, then add the kielbasa. Brown it and remove to a bowl.

2. Add the onion and carrots to the pot and stir. Let it cook for a minute or two.

3. Add the garlic, salt, pepper, and caraway seeds, stir.

4. Add the wine and broth. Stir, scraping the bottom of the pot to get the brown bits up.

5. Add the potatoes and apple, stir.

6. Add the kielbasa back in, juices and all.

7. Add sauerkraut. Stir well to combine.

8. Put the lid on the pot, and set the knob to Sealing. Cancel the sauté mode.

9. Press the Pressure Cook (or Manual) button, then use the +/- button to select 8 minutes. High Pressure.

10. After the cook cycle ends, leave pot undisturbed for 10 minute Natural Release.

11. Turn the steam release knob to Venting to release the remaining pressure and when the pin drops, open the lid and give the food a good stir.

12. The contents will be very hot, so when you dish it up you may want to wait a few minutes before eating it. Garnish with a little fresh parsley, and ENJOY!

Recipe Notes
Serve with a slice of buttered crusty bread, or a biscuit. This is one of those meals that is better the next day! It reheats very well.

Leg of Lamb

Ingredients

5 cloves Garlic, divided

4 lbs Boneless Leg of Lamb

3 tsp Kosher Salt, divided

1 tsp Pepper

1 Tbsp Olive Oil

1 Onion, chopped

1/2 cup Red Wine

3 sprigs Fresh Thyme

2 sprigs Fresh Rosemary

1 cup Chicken Broth, low sodium

2 tsp Red Wine Vinegar

Optional - To Thicken

2 Tbsp Corn Starch + 2 Tbsp Cold Water

Instructions

1. Slice 4 of the garlic cloves lengthwise. Pierce the lamb in several places and push the garlic slivers into the cuts. Then sprinkle 2 tsp of the salt and the pepper over the entire roast.

2. If the roast is coming apart from the bone being removed, tie it together with butcher's string.

3. Turn on the pot's sauté setting. Wait for it to get hot, then add the oil. Brown the lamb roast for several minutes. Then turn it over and brown the other side. Remove it to a plate.

4. Add onion and cook a few minutes, scraping the bottom of the pot, using a wooden spoon.

5. Add the wine and cook, scraping up the browned bits from the bottom of the pot.

6. Add the rosemary, thyme, remaining tsp of salt, remaining clove of garlic (minced), chicken broth, and the red wine vinegar. Stir well. Then turn off the sauté setting.

7. Add the lamb roast back into the pot.

8. Press the Pressure Cook/Manual button. Press the +/- button to select 70 minutes (20-30 minutes for a rare roast). For a bone-in roast, select 85 minutes. This will yield a fork tender leg of lamb. If your roast is larger than 4 lbs, increase the time by 5 minutes.

9. When cook time ends, let the pot sit undisturbed for 20 minutes (10 minutes for a rare roast). Turn the steam release knob to Venting to release remaining pressure. Turn off the pot.

10. When the pin in the lid drops down, open the lid. Remove roast to a platter and cover. Remove the herb stems from the pot and discard.

11. Skim the fat off the top of the liquid in the pot, or use a fat separator to defat the liquid.

12. OPTIONAL: Return the liquid to the pot and turn on the sauté setting. Mix up a slurry of 2 Tbsp corn Starch to 2 Tbsp cold water. When the liquid is simmering, whisk in the slurry and stir until it thickens.

13. Serve the roast sliced, with some of the defatted sauce over it.

Whole Chicken

Prep Time: 10 mins. | **Cook Time:** 20 mins. | **Total Time:** 45 mins.

Ingredients

1 cup Water (for the pressure cooker. 8 qt pot use 2 cups)

1 Whole Chicken (any size that will fit in your pot)

Spice Rub or Salt & Pepper

1/2 med Onion, cut in wedges

1/2 Lemon, cut in wedges

OPTIONAL

1 sm Apple, cut in wedges

Fresh Herbs

Instructions

1. Pour the cup of water into the inner cooking liner of the pressure cooker.

2. Rub the chicken with a spice rub, such as my **Rotisserie Chicken Spice Rub**, pg 363, or salt & pepper.

3. Stuff the cavity of the chicken loosely with the onion, lemon, and apple wedges (herbs too, if using).

4. Set the chicken on the trivet/rack and lower into the pot (you don't have to use the trivet, but it does make it easier to get the cooked chicken out of the pot).

5. Close the lid and set the vent to the Sealing position. Press the Pressure Cook/Manual button or dial, and then the +/- button to select the cook time in minutes (High pressure): 6 minutes per pound, and a 15 minute Natural Release (So a 4 lb chicken will cook for 24 minutes, rest for 15 min.).

6. After the cooking cycle has finished, let the pot sit undisturbed for 15 minutes (15 minute natural release). Turn the steam release knob to Venting position to release remaining steam/pressure.

7. Carefully open the lid once the pin has dropped down. Remove the chicken to a platter, or to a baking sheet if you are going to broil it to crisp up the skin.

8. If you are broiling it, set the broiler to 450° and set the chicken under it until the desired crispness is achieved.

9. Serve immediately, or let cool and store for use in recipes that call for cooked chicken meat.

Recipe Note
Make your chicken look special by placing it on a bed of greens with herbs and fruit.

Chicken Breast

1-8 Servings | **Prep Time: 10 mins.** | **Cook Time: 7 mins.** | **Total Time: 27 mins.**

Ingredients

1 cup Water (2 cups for 8 qt pot)

2 (8 oz) Chicken Breasts
(skinless/boneless)

2 tsp Olive Oil

1 Tbsp Spice Rub (optional)

Instructions

1. Pour the water into the inner liner of the pressure cooker. Set the trivet/metal rack in the pot also.

2. Rub the chicken breasts with the olive oil.

3. Rub the spice rub on all sides of the chicken breasts. Set them on the trivet/rack in the pot.

4. Place the lid on the pot and set the steam release knob to the Sealing position.

5. Press the Pressure Cook (Manual) button, and then the +/- button to select 7 minutes for an 8 oz breast, (a little less than 1 minute per ounce). If cooking multiple breasts, set time for the average size (High Pressure).

6. When the cook time is finished, let the pot sit undisturbed for 10 minute natural release. Then manually release any remaining pressure/steam.

7. Open the lid and take the temperature with a meat thermometer. It should read at least 160° and will cook a little more as it rests.

8. Remove the chicken to a plate and let rest 5-10 minutes, tented with foil, before cutting it as this will help it retain its juices.

Recipe Notes

1. For best results, weigh the chicken breasts.
2. You can add up the weight and cook for an averaged amount of time (a little less than 1 minute per ounce).
3. Rub the chicken breast with a little olive oil to help it stay moist and tender.
4. Use the trivet/rack to keep the chicken above the water so it doesn't boil.
5. Use an instant-read meat thermometer to check for doneness.
6. The best results with this method is for chicken breasts from about 5 to 10 ounces, and about 1 1/2 inches thick. If one end is a lot thicker, just pound it with a meat mallet, heavy wood spoon, or rolling pin, to thin it out a bit.

Try my Baked Chicken Spice Rub

Chicken Wings 3 Ways

4-6 Servings | Prep Time: 10 mins. | Cook Time: 20 mins. | Total Time: 30 mins.

Ingredients

Chicken Wings (Use 2 1/2 - 3 lbs *per recipe*)

1 cup Water

2 1/2 lbs Chicken Wings, cut into flat and drumette pieces

BUFFALO WINGS

1/2 cup Frank's Red Hot Sauce®, original version

1/2 cup Unsalted Butter, melted

1/2 tsp Worcestershire Sauce

1/4 tsp Garlic Powder

1/8 tsp Cayenne Pepper

BARBECUE WINGS

1 cup Barbecue Sauce

TERIYAKI WINGS (This sauce needs to be brought to a low boil on the stove in a small saucepan before coating the wings)

1/4 cup Soy Sauce, low sodium

1/8 cup Dry Sherry

1/8 cup Vegetable Oil

1 tsp Rice Vinegar

2 tsp Orange Juice

1 tsp Fish Sauce

1 tsp Hoisin Sauce

1 Clove Garlic, pressed

2 tsp Fresh Ginger, grated

1/3 cup Brown Sugar

3 tsp Corn Starch

Instructions

Cook the Wings

1. Add 1 cup of water to the inner liner of the pressure cooker.

2. Put the wing pieces in a steamer basket, vertically, and set on the trivet/rack in the Pot.

3. Close the lid and set the steam release knob to the Sealing position.

4. Press the Pressure Cook/Manual button, then the +/- button to select 5 minutes (if your wings are whole, do 8 minutes).

5. After cooking cycle ends, let Naturally Release the for 7 minutes. Then manually release the remaining pressure. Open the lid after the pin drops.

6. Spread the wings on a baking sheet and let air dry for a few minutes.

Flavor the Wings

7. Add the sauce ingredients for the flavor you are making into a bowl, and whisk well (if making barbecue wings, just put the barbecue sauce into the bowl).

8. Add the wings to the bowl and stir them around to coat with the sauce.

9. You can serve them at this point, but they are even better if you broil them in a 400° oven for 5 minutes per side.

Salsa Chicken

Ingredients

3 - 4 Chicken Breasts**, skinless/boneless (approx. 8 oz ea)

Salt, to season meat

Pepper, to season meat

2 tsp Garlic Powder, to season meat

1 Tbsp Taco Seasoning

1 tsp Oregano (If you can get Mexican Oregano, it's really good)

16 oz Salsa*

Instructions

1. Season chicken breasts on all sides with salt, pepper, and garlic powder.

2. Put 1/2 cup of salsa in the inner pot of the pressure cooker. Then add the chicken breasts to the pot, setting them on the salsa.

3. Sprinkle the oregano and taco seasoning over the chicken.

4. Pour the remaining salsa over the chicken, covering it. *If your salsa is really thick, you can add 1/4 cup of water to help the pressure build, but I have never needed to. I use a salsa that is from the refrigerated section of the store, and it works nicely, with good flavor.

5. Put the lid on the pot and set the steam release knob to the Sealing position.

6. Press the Pressure Cook/Manual button, then the +/- button to choose 10-12 minutes** depending on the weight/thickness of the breasts. You don't need to add any additional liquid to the pot, the salsa and chicken have enough to bring it to pressure.

7. When the cooking cycle has ended, let the pot sit undisturbed for 10 minutes natural release. Then, manually release any remaining pressure (there may not be any, and that's okay) by turning the steam release knob to Venting.

8. Remove the chicken to a large bowl and shred it, using two forks. Then add it back into the pot. If there is too much liquid for your taste, just scoop some out. Leave some, as it has a lot of flavor, and will also keep the meat moist (the liquid is also great over rice).

Recipe Notes
**If your chicken breasts are the really large (11 oz or more) sized, increase cook time by 3 minutes.

Crack Chicken

Ingredients

1/2 cup Water

2 lbs Boneless Skinless Chicken Breasts (about 4 8-oz breasts)

1 (1 oz) packet Ranch Dressing Mix

1 tsp Garlic Powder

1/2 tsp Onion Powder

1/2 tsp Dill Weed, dried

2 tsp Parsley, dried

1/4 tsp Pepper

1/4 tsp Smoked Paprika

1 (8 oz) block Cream Cheese (room temperature)

TO FINISH

1 cup Cheddar Cheese (shredded, not from a bag)

8 slices Cooked Thick Cut Bacon, chopped

3 Green Onions, chopped

Instructions

If you cook the bacon in the pot, set it aside to cool, and wipe out the pot. Continue with recipe.

1. Add the water to the inner liner pot of the pressure cooker.

2. Add the chicken breasts to the pot, overlapping as little as possible for even cooking.

3. Sprinkle the ranch dressing over the chicken.

4. Sprinkle the garlic powder, onion powder, dill weed, parsley, pepper, and smoked paprika over the chicken.

5. Break the block of cream cheese up into chunks and put them in the pot.

6. Close the lid and set the steam release knob to the Sealing position.

7. Press the Pressure Cook/Manual button, then the +/- button to select 12 minutes. High Pressure. Smaller, thinner chicken breasts need less cook time.

8. When the cook cycle has finished, turn off the pot and let it sit undisturbed for 10 minute natural release. Then turn the steam release knob to the Venting position to release any remaining pressure.

9. When the pin in the lid drops back down, open the lid and turn off the pot.

10. Remove the chicken breasts to a plate.

11. Whisk the cream cheese liquid left in the pot. Then gradually whisk in the cheddar cheese until it melts.

12. Using two forks, shred the chicken and add it back into the pot.

13. Add the bacon and green onion to the pot and stir well to combine.

14. The mixture may look just a little watery, but it will not stay that way. If it is too watery (this might be the case if you used frozen chicken) you can turn on the sauté setting for a short time and stir to cook off some of the water.

15. Serve on buns, or over rice, or with pasta.

Mississippi Chicken

Ingredients

2-3 lbs Chicken Thighs or Breasts (Boneless/skinless. Fresh or frozen)

1/2 cup Water

1/3 (16 oz) jar Pepperoncinis (with juice) Leave whole or slice as desired

1 (1 oz) packet Au Jus or Brown Gravy Mix*

1 (1 oz) packet Ranch Dressing Mix** (low sodium, if possible)

1/2 stick Unsalted Butter (4 Tbsp)

With Rice (you will need a tall trivet and a 6" or 7" pan)

1 1/2 cups White Long Grain Rice (rinsed)

1 1/2 cups Water

Instructions

1. Put chicken in the bottom of the inner pot of the pressure cooker. (If using chicken breasts, cut them in half, if possible).

2. Add all of the other ingredients and close the lid and lock it in place. Turn the steam release knob to the sealing position.

3. Press the Pressure Cook/Manual Button and the +/- button to select 8 minutes (if using frozen breasts that you can't cut in half, set time to 15 minutes).

4. When the cook time is finished, let the pot sit undisturbed for 5 minute Natural Release. Then turn the steam release knob to Venting to Quick Release the remaining pressure.

To Cook Rice with the Chicken

5. After adding all ingredients, set the trivet in the pot and make sure it touches the bottom of the pot.

6. Put the rinsed rice and water in the pan and set it on the trivet (A pan gripper helps with this). Close lid and proceed with cooking directions.

7. When the cooking cycle finishes, let the pot sit undisturbed for a 5 minute natural release. Then turn the steam release knob to the Venting position to Quick Release the remaining steam/pressure.

Finish it Up

8. When the pin in the lid drops down, open it and use a pan gripper or silicone mitts to remove the pan of rice (if making rice)

9. Use tongs to remove the chicken and shred it.

10. If you want to thicken the cooking liquid, turn on the Sauté function and stir in 2 Tbsp of cornstarch mixed with some of the hot liquid. Pour into the pot and stir until thickened.

11. Mix the chicken back into the cooking liquid.

12. Serve over rice, or potatoes, on tortillas, etc

Recipe Note
*This recipe can be a bit salty. Try finding low sodium au jus and/or ranch dressing mix.

Butter Chicken

5-7 Servings | Prep Time: 25 mins. | Cook Time: 20 mins. | Total Time: 53 mins.

Ingredients

SPICES

1 1/4 tsp Cumin

1 1/2 tsp Coriander Seed, ground

2 tsp Garam Masala, plus 1 tsp to finish

1 tsp Turmeric

1/2 tsp Cinnamon

1 1/2 tsp Sweet Paprika

3/4 tsp Coarse Salt

1/4 tsp Cayenne Pepper (more if you like it spicy)

1 tsp Fenugreek (optional)

FOR THE SAUCE

1 Tbsp Neutral Oil (Peanut, Sunflower, etc.)

6 Tbsp Butter, divided (4 Tbsp, 2 Tbsp to finish)

2 sm Bay Leaves

1/2 Cinnamon Stick

6 Garlic Cloves, pressed or finely minced

1 sm Onion, finely minced

1 Tbsp Fresh Ginger, grated (or 1 tsp powered)

1 Tbsp Lime Juice

1 (14.5 oz) Can Diced Tomatoes, undrained

1/2 cup Chicken Broth, low sodium

1 Tbsp Tomato Paste

2 lbs Chicken Thigh Meat, Cut in 2" cubes

TO FINISH

1 tsp Garam Masala

2 Tbsp Butter

1/2 cup Heavy Cream

1 (14 oz) can Coconut Milk Cream (just the thick, cream from the can. Save the watery part for another recipe)

GARNISH

Cilantro Leaves chopped

Instructions

1. Combine the dry spices in a bowl and set aside.

Make the Sauce

2. Turn on the Sauté setting of your pot. When Hot, add the oil and 4 Tbsp of the butter.

3. Add the bay leaf, cinnamon stick, garlic, and onion. Stir and let cook for a minute, stirring frequently. Don't let it burn.

4. Add the fresh ginger, if using. Stir and cook for a couple of minutes. Add the spices. Stir well.

5. Add the tomatoes, broth, and lime juice. Stir well. Add the tomato paste, but don't stir it. You want it in there, but you don't want to risk it burning.

6. Add the chicken and don't stir too much. Just spread it out.

7. Turn off the sauté setting.

If You Are Also Making Rice

8. Place a tall trivet over the chicken and set the pan of rice/water on it. I like to use Jasmine or Basmati rice, with a 1:1 rice/water ratio.

Pressure Cook It

9. Close the lid. Set the steam release knob to the Sealing position.

10. Press the Manual (or Pressure Cook) button, then the +/- button to select 8 minutes.

11. After cook cycle ends, let the pot naturally release the pressure for 8 minutes. Then manually release the remaining pressure and open the lid.

12. Use a slotted spoon to take out the chicken, and set it aside in a bowl covered with foil.

13. Use an immersion blender to make the sauce really smooth. You could use a blender if you want. Either way, be very careful since the contents are so hot!

14. Add remaining 1 teaspoon of Garam Masala and the remaining 2 Tbsp of butter. Stir until butter is melted.

15. Add the heavy cream & coconut milk cream if using, and the chicken, and stir until combined. Taste and adjust salt if necessary.

16. Serve over rice, or with naan, and garnish with cilantro leaves and toasted cashews (optional).

Chicken Taco Bowls

4-6 Servings | Prep Time: 15 mins. | Cook Time: 10 mins. | Total Time: 35 mins.

Ingredients

1 1/2 cup Low Sodium Chicken Broth, divided

2-3 Chicken Breasts (boneless/skinless)

1 (1 1/4 oz) packet Taco Seasoning (or 2 1/2 Tbsp homemade)

1 (15 oz can) Black Beans, drained & rinsed

1 1/2 cups Corn Kernels (frozen, fresh, or 1 can drained)

16 oz Salsa (not too thick)

1 (4 oz) can Diced Green Chiles (mild or hot)

1 1/2 cups Long Grain White Rice, rinsed well

1 cup Shredded Cheddar Cheese

GARNISHES

Lime wedges, Hot Sauce

Sour Cream (or Greek yogurt)

Cilantro, Red Onion

Diced Tomato, Avocado

Instructions

1. Pour 1/2 cup of the chicken broth into the inner pot. Then set the chicken breasts in the pot in a single layer.

2. Sprinkle the taco seasoning over the chicken, covering it.

3. Add the black beans in one layer.

4. Add the corn in a layer.

5. Add the salsa, spread evenly over in a layer.

6. Add the diced chiles.

7. Sprinkle on the rice in an even layer.

8. Pour the remaining 1 cup of broth over the rice.

9. Use a fork to gently press down on the rice to submerge it in the liquid. Do not stir.

10. Place the lid on the pot and set the steam release knob to the Sealing position. Then press the Pressure Cook/Manual button, then press the +/- button to select 10 minutes. High pressure.

11. When the cook time has ended, immediately turn the steam release knob to the Venting position to do a Quick Release of the steam/pressure.

12. When the pin in the lid drops down, open the pot and remove the chicken breasts to a plate.

13. Fluff the rice with a fork.

14. Use 2 forks to shred the chicken, then return it to the pot. Stir well.

15. Serve with some of the cheddar cheese sprinkled on top, and any of the garnishes you prefer. I love to load up on all of them!

16. If making this for meal prep, divide between the containers and let cool before refrigerating.

Chicken Taco Pie

4-6 Servings | Prep Time: 15 mins. | Cook Time: 20 mins. | Total Time: 45 mins.

Ingredients

1 1/2 cups Water (for pressure cooker)

1 small whole Rotisserie Chicken, (or other cooked chicken) deboned, skinless & shredded (about 3 cups of meat)

1 can Refried Beans

1/4 cup Salsa

2 Tbsp Diced Green Chiles

1 Tbsp Taco Seasoning

1-2 cups Pepper Jack Cheese, shredded (or Monterey Jack) plus extra for the top layer

1-2 cups Cheddar Cheese, shredded (plus extra for the top layer)

4 (8") Flour Tortillas (if using 7" pan)

Garnishes (choose your favorite)

Sour Cream, Salsa, Cilantro, Avocado

Hot Sauce

Instructions

1. Gather and prepare everything you will need. Prepare the rotisserie chicken, or other cooked chicken, shred the cheese, spray the pan with cooking spray, etc.

2. Add the water to the pressure cooker's removable inner pot/liner.

3. Set the pot to the Sauté setting. This will start the water heating up, which will bring the pot to pressure faster.

4. In a small bowl, mix the can of refried beans with the salsa and taco seasoning.

5. Place a tortilla in the pan and press it down (it will be slightly bigger than the pan, and that's okay).

6. Spread on 1/3 of the bean mixture, then 1/3 of the shredded chicken, and 1/3 of the cheese.

7. Place another tortilla in the pan and press it down. Spread on 1/3 of the bean mixture, then 1/3 of the shredded chicken, and 1/3 of the cheese.

8. Place a third tortilla in the pan and press it down. Spread on 1/3 of the bean mixture, then 1/3 of the shredded chicken, and 1/3 of the cheese.

9. Place a fourth tortilla in the pan and press it down. Nothing goes on top of this layer yet.

10. Wrap a piece of foil over the top and crimp it around the edges (so no water gets in).

11. Set the pan on the trivet and use the handles to carefully lower it into the pot.

12. Cancel the Sauté setting. Place the lid on the pot and set the knob to the sealing position.

13. Press the Pressure Cook/Manual button, then the +/- button to select 20 minutes.

14. When the cook cycle ends, do a Quick Release of the pressure and when the pin in the lid drops down, open the lid and very carefully remove the trivet/pan.

15. Carefully remove the foil and sprinkle on the remaining cheese.

16. Turn on the broiler to 425° and set the pan under it and broil until the cheese melts.

17. Let sit for just a few minutes to cool a bit and set up. Then remove from the pan.

18. Garnish with sour cream, avocado, salsa, cilantro, hot sauce, etc., and serve!

Hawaiian Chicken and Rice

5-7 Servings | Prep Time: 20 mins. | Cook Time: 13 mins. | Total Time: 48 mins.

Ingredients

2 lbs Skinless Boneless Chicken Breasts (3-4) cut larger than bite sized pieces

2 tsp Kosher Salt, divided

1/2 tsp Pepper

2 1/2 Tbsp Cooking Oil, divided

1 Red or Green Bell Pepper, large dice

1 sm Sweet Onion, chopped

2 tsp Ginger, grated (or 1 tsp powdered)

4 cloves Garlic, finely minced

1/4 tsp Red Pepper Flakes, or more to taste

1 (20 oz) can Pineapple Chunks in Juice

3/4 cup Barbecue Sauce, (something smoky and just a little sweet, not honey)

TO FINISH

1/3 cup Brown Sugar

3 tsp Apple Cider Vinegar

To Thicken
(Mix together while chicken cooks)

3 Tbsp Corn Starch

4 Tbsp Cold Water

GARNISH

2 Green Onions, sliced

FOR THE RICE

2 cups White Long Grain Rice, rinsed

2 cups Water

Instructions

1. Salt and pepper the chicken pieces, saving 1 tsp of the salt for later. Set aside.

2. Rinse the rice and add to a 7"x2.5" pan (stainless is best), and add the water to the pan. Set aside.

3. Turn on the Sauté setting. When it is hot, add half of the oil, then add the bell pepper. Cook just until softened, then remove to a plate and set aside.

4. Add the remaining oil, then add the chicken. Cook, turning every couple of minutes, just to get a little color on the outside.

5. Add the onion, stir and sauté for a couple of minutes.

6. Add the ginger, garlic, remaining 1 tsp salt, and red pepper flakes. Cook, stirring frequently, for a minute.

7. Add the can of pineapple chunks, along with the juice. Don't stir.

8. Pour on the BBQ sauce, but don't stir.

ADD RICE

9. Place a long legged trivet in the pan right on the chicken and pineapple. Make sure the legs of the trivet are about 3" tall.

10. Set the pan of rice on the trivet. Cancel the Sauté setting. Close the lid and set the steam release knob to the Sealing position.

PRESSURE COOK

11. Press the Pressure Cook/Manual button or dial, then the +/- button to select 3 minutes. High Pressure. The pot will take several minutes to come to pressure.

12. When the cook cycle has finished, turn off the pot and let it sit undisturbed for 10 minute natural release. Then turn the steam release knob to the Venting position to release the remaining steam/pressure.

13. When the pin in the lid drops back down, open the lid. Remove the pan of rice to a heat safe surface (be careful!). Take out the trivet.

FINISH

14. Add the brown sugar and the apple cider vinegar to the chicken in the pot. Stir. Taste and adjust salt, if needed.

THICKEN

15. Turn on the Sauté setting and add the corn starch slurry. Stir. When thickened, turn off the pot.

16. Add the bell peppers back in and stir.

SERVE

17. Fluff the rice with a fork and serve the Hawaiian chicken over the rice. Garnish with green onion.

Cashew Chicken

4-6 Servings | Prep Time: 20 mins. | Cook Time: 5 mins. | Total Time: 25 mins.

Ingredients

1 1/2 lbs Chicken Thighs or Breasts, skinless/boneless, cut in 2" pieces

1 med Carrot, cut into matchsticks (optional)

6 oz Mushrooms (optional)

1 bunch Green Onions, sliced & divided

1 can Water Chestnuts, drained & rough chopped

SAUCE

1/4 cup Low Sodium Soy Sauce

1 Tbsp Oyster Sauce (or Hoisin)

1 Tbsp Rice Wine Vinegar

1-2 Tbsp Brown Sugar (to taste) or use Honey

2 tsp Toasted Sesame Oil

1/3 cup Low Sodium Chicken Broth

3 tsp Grated Fresh Ginger

2 tsp Sriracha (or 1/2 tsp Red Pepper Flakes)

5 cloves Garlic, finely minced or pressed

ADD AFTER PRESSURE COOKING

1 sm Red Bell Pepper, thinly sliced

1 handful Snow Peas (optional)

TO THICKEN

1 1/2 Tbsp Corn Starch

2 Tbsp Cold Water

ADD AT THE END

1 cup Roasted Cashews (I buy raw and roast them)

Reserved Green Onions

To Make Rice At the Same Time

2 cups White Rice (or basmati, jasmine)

2 cups Water

1 Tbsp Butter, or 2 tsp Olive Oil

Instructions

1. Add the chicken pieces to the inner stainless liner of the pressure cooker.
2. Add the carrot, mushrooms, water chestnuts, and the white parts of the green onions (save the green parts).
3. Mix together the soy sauce, oyster sauce, vinegar, brown sugar, sesame oil, chicken broth, ginger, Sriracha, and garlic. Pour over the chicken and vegetables. Stir.
4. Mix together the corn starch and water and set aside.

If Making Rice With the Chicken

5. Place the tall legged trivet in the pot right down in the chicken/sauce. Then place the pan on the trivet. Add the rice, water, and butter. Stir. No need to cover it.
6. Close the lid and set the steam release knob to the Sealing position.
7. Press the Pressure Cook/Manual button, then the +/- button to select 3 minutes. High Pressure.
8. When cook cycle is finished, turn off the pot. Leave undisturbed for 9 minute natural release. Turn the steam release knob to Venting position to release remaining steam/pressure.
9. When the pin in the lid drops back down, open the lid.
10. Turn on the Sauté setting. When the sauce starts to simmer, stir in the red pepper, snow peas, if using, and the corn starch slurry. Stir until thickened.
11. Turn off the pot and stir in cashews and remaining green onion slices. Taste and adjust salt.
12. Serve hot.

Chicken Broccoli Rice Casserole

Ingredients

- 1 Tbsp Olive Oil
- 2 Tbsp Unsalted Butter
- 1 med Onion, chopped
- 1 1/2 lbs Chicken Breast, cubed
- 1 1/4 tsp Kosher Salt
- 1/2 tsp Pepper
- 1 1/2 tsp Garlic Powder
- 1/2 tsp Onion Powder

- 1/4 tsp Thyme Leaves (dried, not ground)
- 4 cloves Garlic, finely minced
- 1 1/2 cups Long Grain White Rice, rinsed
- 2 1/2 cups Chicken Broth, low sodium
- 2 1/2 cups Shredded Sharp Cheddar Cheese
- 2 lbs Frozen Broccoli Florets

Instructions

1. Turn on the Sauté setting. When it is hot, add the olive oil and butter.

2. Add the onion and cook for about 3 minutes, stirring occasionally, until turning translucent.

3. Add the chicken. Sprinkle the salt, pepper, garlic powder, onion powder, and thyme over it. Stir. Cook, stirring occasionally, until just the outside of the chicken turns white.

4. Add the garlic and stir.

5. Add the rice and the broth. Scrape up any browned bits from the bottom of the pot

6. Gently press the rice and chicken into the broth, then put the lid on the pressure cooker and set the steam release knob to the Sealing position. Turn off the Sauté setting.

7. Press the Pressure Cook/Manual button, then the +/- button to select 3 minutes. High Pressure.

8. While the chicken and rice is cooking, run the frozen broccoli florets under hot water and drain. Set aside. If using fresh broccoli, you may need to microwave it with a little water for a few minutes to soften it, as it won't cook in the pot with the residual heat. If the florets are large, cut them in half.

9. When the cook cycle is finished, turn off the pot and let it sit undisturbed for 10 minute natural release. Then turn the steam release knob to Venting to release the remaining pressure.

10. When the pin in the lid drops back down, open the lid and stir in the cheese.

11. Add the broccoli florets, stir. Close the lid so it cooks in the residual heat of the rice/chicken.

12. Take the lid off and stir. Serve immediately. Makes good leftovers.

Chicken Thighs and Potatoes

Ingredients

SPICE RUB MIXTURE

1/4 tsp Onion Powder

1/4 tsp Black Pepper

1/4 tsp Poultry Seasoning

1/2 tsp Garlic Powder

1/2 tsp Paprika

1/2 tsp Kosher Salt

FOR COOKING

2 Tbsp Olive Oil

6 Chicken Thighs (I use skin on, bone in)

1 1/2 cups Chicken Broth low sodium

3 Large Red Potatoes, cut in fourths

1 Tbsp Butter

1 Small Sprig Rosemary

1/2 Lemon

Instructions

1. Mix the spices together in a small dish. Sprinkle on both sides of the chicken thighs.
2. Turn on the Sauté setting. When hot, add the olive oil.
3. Add 3 or 4 chicken thighs, skin side down, and brown them on both sides, about 4 minutes per side. Repeat with the remaining thighs. Set aside on a plate.
4. When all of the thighs are browned, carefully remove any remaining oil from the pot. If the bits on the bottom of the pot are too blackened, add a little water and use a wooden spoon to scrape them off and discard. Otherwise, keep the browned bits in there for flavor.
5. Add the broth to the pot (still on Sauté mode). Stir and scrape any remaining brown bits on the bottom of the pot.
6. Add the potatoes, butter, and the rosemary.
7. Put a tall trivet over the potatoes.
8. Set a steamer basket on top of the trivet and add the chicken thighs to it (make sure they don't set up above the rim of the pot. You need to be able to comfortably get the lid on).
9. Squeeze the lemon juice over the chicken.
10. Close the lid and set the steam release knob to the Sealing position. Cancel the sauté mode.
11. Press the Pressure Cook/Manual button, then the +/- button to choose 13 minutes.
12. When cooking cycle ends, let it naturally release pressure for 5 minutes.
13. Turn off the pot. Then manually release the remaining pressure, and when the pin in the lid drops, carefully open the lid.
14. Carefully remove the steamer basket with the chicken to a plate, then remove the trivet.
15. At this point you can either use a potato masher to mash the potatoes right in the pot, or remove them with a slotted spoon and make gravy from the drippings. If you choose to remove them, set them aside and turn on the pot to the sauté mode to make gravy.
16. Add a cornstarch slurry to the liquid in the pot (mix 2 Tbsp cornstarch and 2 Tbsp cold water, and whisk it into the hot liquid in the pot). Keep stirring until it thickens.
17. Turn off the pot and serve the gravy over the potatoes, and the chicken thighs if you'd like.

Turkey Breast & Potatoes

Ingredients

1 cup Water for pressure cooker

FOR THE TURKEY

1 Tbsp Olive Oil

2 tsp Poultry Seasoning

3 tsp Rubbed Sage

1 tsp Kosher Salt

1/2 tsp Black Pepper

1 tsp Garlic Powder

2-6 lb Turkey Breast

3-4 lg Potatoes, halved

OPTIONAL ADD-INS

(cook with turkey breast)

1 sm Onion, chopped

2 Garlic Cloves, minced

FOR THE GRAVY

1/3 cup Butter + 1/3 cup Flour

Instructions

1. Put the water in the inner liner of the Instant Pot, and put the wire rack/trivet in also.
2. Rub the turkey breast with the olive oil and rub the spices all over it.
3. Place the turkey breast in the pressure cooker, however it fits best (I try to put mine meaty side down, but have cooked some on their sides). Also add in the onion and garlic, if using.
4. Put the lid on the pot and set the steam release knob to the Sealing position.
5. Press the Pressure Cook/Manual button, then the +/- button to choose the time in minutes (about 26 minutes for a small 3-4 pound breast, about 30 minutes for a 5-6 pound breast, about 40 minutes for a 7 lb breast).
6. When the cooking cycle has ended, let the pot sit and naturally release for 10 minutes. Then manually release the remaining pressure. When the pin in the lid drops, open the pot.
7. Take the temperature and f it is below 160° F, put the lid back on the pot and let it set for a few more minutes. 165° F is fully cooked.
8. Remove the turkey breast to a baking pan. Also remove the wire rack/trivet.

Cook the Potatoes

9. Put the potatoes in the pot, close the lid and set the steam release knob to Sealing.
10. Press the Manual/ Pressure Cook button, then the +/ - button to choose 10 minutes. When cook cycle is done, do a Quick Release of the pressure.
11. Remove potatoes and set aside while you make the gravy.
12. Set your oven rack to the lowest position. Turn broiler to 425° F to begin warming up.
13. Place the turkey breast, skin side up, under the broiler. Brown a few minutes on each side. If you don't want to brown it, just skip this step and let it rest, covered, while the potatoes cook.

Make the Gravy

14. Press the Sauté button on the pressure cooker.
15. In a microwave safe dish, mix the butter and flour and microwave for about 20 seconds.
16. When the drippings in the pot start to simmer, stir in the butter/flour mixture. Keep stirring until the gravy thickens.

Turkey Meatloaf

6-8 Servings | Prep Time: 10 mins. | Cook Time: 35 mins. | Total Time: 45 mins.

Ingredients

1 1/2 cups Water for Pressure Cooker

MEATLOAF

2 lbs 85% Lean Ground Turkey

1/2 cup Bread Crumbs (Panko)

2 Tbsp Dehydrated Onion (or 1/2 cup of fresh, finely diced)

1 1/2 tsp Coarse Salt

1 tsp Black Pepper

2 tsp Garlic Powder (or 3 cloves garlic)

1/2 tsp Poultry Seasoning

1/2 cup Whole Milk

2 Eggs

1/3 cup Ketchup

2 tsp Worcestershire Sauce

1 tsp Liquid Smoke

GLAZE TOPPING

1/2 cup Ketchup

1/4 cup Brown Sugar

1 tsp Mustard

Instructions

1. Mix all of the meatloaf ingredients together and combine thoroughly.
2. Put 1 1/2 cups of water in the pressure cooker, and the trivet/steamer rack.
3. Place the meat mixture on a piece of foil and form it into a rounded loaf shape (not a ball), making it an even thickness end to end (not too thick), for cooking consistency.
4. Grab the foil by the opposite corners, like a sling, and lift the meatloaf into the pot and set it on the rack. Close the lid and set the steam release knob to the Sealing position.
5. Press the Pressure Cook/Manual button, and use the +/- button to select 35 minutes.
6. When the cook cycle is ends, leave it to do a natural pressure release of 10 minutes. Quick release the remaining pressure.

Before you take the meatloaf out, do 2 things.

7. **First**, take the internal temperature of the meatloaf and make sure it is 160° F (it will come up to 165° by the time you finish broiling it).
8. **Second**, use a small knife to poke a few holes in the foil, and the drippings will drain to the water below.
9. Carefully lift the meatloaf out of the pot and onto a baking tray.
10. Turn on broiler to 450° F. Rack in the middle.
11. Spread the glaze topping all over the meatloaf and put it under the broiler for a few minutes to caramelize the topping. Just keep an eye on it so it doesn't burn.
12. Serve with a side of potatoes or rice, a veggie or salad, and you'll have a great meal!

Egg Roll in a Bowl

4-6 Servings | Prep Time: 10 mins. | Cook Time: 10 mins. | Total Time: 25 mins.

Ingredients

1 lb Ground Pork (or Turkey, Chicken, Beef)

1/2 small Sweet Onion, sliced

1 Tbsp Grated Fresh Ginger (or 1 Tbsp Ground Ginger)

4 cloves Garlic, Pressed (or 3 tsp Garlic Powder)

2 Tbsp Low Sodium Tamari (or Coconut Aminos, Low Sodium Soy Sauce)

1 tsp Rice Wine Vinegar

2 Tbsp Toasted Sesame Oil (more for taste)

1/2 cup Chicken Broth, low sodium

1 (14 oz) bag Coleslaw Mix (or Broccoli Slaw)

3 Green Onions, sliced

1-2 tsp Sriracha

Instructions

1. Turn on the pot's Sauté setting. When hot, add the pork and onion and cook, stirring occasionally, until almost fully cooked.

2. Add the ginger and garlic and cook, stirring constantly, for 30 seconds to 1 minute. Don't let it burn!

3. Add the tamari, vinegar, sesame oil, and chicken broth. Stir, scraping the bottom of the pot to get up all of the browned bits (deglaze).

4. Turn off the pot.

5. Pour the coleslaw mix into the pot, but do not stir.

6. Close the lid and set the steam release knob to the Sealing position.

7. Press the Pressure Cook/Manual button, then press the +/- button to select 0 (zero) minutes. High pressure. The pot will take a few minutes to come to pressure.

8. As soon as the cooking cycle has ended, turn the steam release knob to the Venting position to do a Quick Release of the pressure.

9. When the pin in the lid drops down, open the lid and give the mixture a good stir.

10. Garnish with green onions, Sriracha, and a little more sesame oil, if desired. Serve hot.

Recipe Note
Bulk it up with the addition of other veggies: broccoli, cauliflower, snap peas, bamboo shoots, corn, or even mushrooms.

Lemon Butter Salmon

Ingredients

1 cup Water (for pressure cooker)
2 cups for 8 qt
2 (5-6 oz) Salmon Fillets (w/skin)
1/4 tsp Salt
1 pinch Pepper
2 cloves Garlic (pressed)
1 Tbsp Fresh Chopped Dill (or 1 1/2 tsp dried)
4-6 Fresh Lemon Slices (thinly sliced)

2 Tbsp Butter (sliced into 4 pats)
2 Tbsp Water (or white wine)
2 Tbsp Fresh Lemon Juice

Tools

- Metal Trivet/Rack, for pan to sit on
- 7"x3" or 6"x3" metal cake pan
- Cooking Spray

Instructions

1. Pour 1 cup of water into the inner liner of the pressure cooker. Then set the trivet/rack inside.
2. Place the salmon fillets into the pan, skin side down.
3. Sprinkle the fillets with the salt, pepper, and the garlic.
4. Place the dill on the salmon, followed by the lemon slices, then the butter pats on top.
5. Add the water and lemon juice to the pan.
6. Place the pan into the pressure cooker, onto the trivet.
7. Close the lid and set the steam release knob to the Sealing position.
8. Press the Pressure Cook/Manual button, then the +/- button to select 5 minutes*. High Pressure (use Low pressure for thinner fillets, as well as shorter cook time).
9. When the cook cycle has finished, immediately turn the steam release knob to the Venting position to Quick Release the pressure.
10. When the pin in the lid drops back down, open the lid and carefully remove the pan.
11. Serve immediately with some of the lemon butter sauce over the fillets.

Recipe Notes
*Larger (thicker) fillets and frozen will need additional cook time.

Low Country Shrimp Boil

6-8 Servings | Prep Time: 20 mins. | Cook Time: 2 mins. | Total Time: 45 mins.

Ingredients

2 cups Water

1 1/2 Tbsp Old Bay Seasoning, divided (or Shrimp & Crab Boil liquid)

1 tsp Kosher Salt (or 1/2 tsp table salt)

1 lb New Potatoes, small, 4 oz size

1 Onion, cut in thick slices

6 cloves Garlic, roughly chopped

2 Bay Leaves

1 Lemon, quartered

2 tsp Cajun Seasoning, divided

2 ears Corn on the Cob, cut in thirds

1 lb Smoked Sausage, cut in 2" pieces

2 lbs Shrimp, raw, jumbo size (easy peel, or split & deveined) partially frozen is best

Serve With

Butter for dipping, Crusty Bread

Instructions

1. Have all of your veggies and sausage chopped or cut before you start cooking. Also have the spices there with you as it will help everything cook at the proper times.

2. Add 2 cups of water to the pressure cooker on Sauté setting to get the water warming up.

3. Add the Old Bay seasoning (or shrimp boil seasoning), and salt.

4. Add Potatoes, onion, garlic, bay leaves, and lemon. Sprinkle with some Cajun seasoning.

5. Add the corn and sprinkle it with a little more of the Cajun seasoning..

6. Add the sausage and the shrimp. Sprinkle with more Cajun Seasoning and Old Bay.

7. Close the lid and set the steam release knob to Sealing. Cancel the Sauté setting.

8. Press the Pressure Cook/Manual button, then the +/- button to select 2 minutes for frozen shrimp (1 minute for fresh shrimp) High Pressure. It will take a long time to come to pressure.

9. When the cook cycle is finished, turn the steam release knob to the Venting position and do a Quick Release of the steam/pressure. This will take a few minutes as the pot is full.

10. Open the lid once the pin has dropped down. Turn off the pot.

11. Use a large slotted spoon to scoop the shrimp boil contents to a large bowl.

12. At this point you can dump it onto a table lined with newspaper or butcher paper, or put it on a baking sheet pan and serve it from there.

13. Melt some butter for dipping, and serve with some crusty bread.

Recipe Note
If you keep the shells on the shrimp, and keep them partially frozen, they are less likely to be overcooked.

Jambalaya

6 Servings | Prep Time: 35 mins. | Cook Time: 25 mins. | Total Time: 1 hr. 10 mins.

Ingredients

1 lb Shrimp (41-50 count) peeled & deveined

1 1/2 Tbsp Cajun Seasoning, divided (or use Creole)

3 Tbsp Olive Oil, divided

1 lb Chicken Breast, cubed (or use thighs)

1 lb Andouille Sausage, cut in 1/2" rounds

1 lg Onion, chopped

2 ribs Celery, chopped

1 Bay Leaf

4 lg cloves Garlic, pressed or finely minced

1 lg Jalapeño, deseeded and diced

1 Green Bell Pepper, seeded and chopped

1/2 tsp Kosher Salt

1/2 tsp Marjoram, dried

1 tsp Thyme Leaves, dried (not ground)

2 cups Chicken Broth, low sodium

1 Tbsp Worcestershire Sauce

1 1/2 cup Long Grain White Rice, rinsed

1 (14.25 oz) can Diced Tomatoes, with juice

GARNISH

2 Tbsp Parsley, chopped

Instructions

1. Before you begin cooking, have all of your ingredients prepped. Veggies cut, meats cut, rice rinsed, spices measured, and have it all right there with your pot.

2. Sprinkle the shrimp with 2 tsp of the Cajun seasoning. Toss to coat and set aside.

3. Turn on the pot's Sauté setting. When it is hot, add 2 Tablespoons of the olive oil.

4. Add the Sausage pieces and let brown on one side. Then flip them over and brown on the other side. Remove them to a paper towel lined plate.

5. Add the shrimp to the pot and cook them, stirring frequently, until they are halfway cooked. Remove them to a paper towel lined plate.

6. Add the chicken and cook for a couple of minutes, just long enough to get a little color on all sides, but not fully cooked. Remove to a paper towel lined plate.

7. Add the remaining Tablespoon of olive oil and the onions, celery, and bay leaf. Cook, stirring occasionally, until the veggies soften a little. Add a little more olive oil if needed.

8. Add the garlic, jalapeño, and green pepper. Cook, stirring constantly for 30 seconds.

9. Add the salt, marjoram, thyme, and the remaining Cajun seasoning. Stir well.

10. Add the chicken broth and Worcestershire sauce. Stir.

11. Add the rice in an even layer on top, but don't stir it in.

12. Pour the diced tomatoes on top of the rice evenly. Don't stir.

13. Add the chicken back into the pot in an even layer. Just press it down it doesn't have to be completely submerged.

14. Turn off the Sauté setting.

15. Close the lid and set the steam release knob to the Sealing position.

16. Press the Pressure Cook/Manual button, then the +/- button to select 6 minutes. High Pressure. The pot will take several minutes to come to pressure.

17. When cook cycle is finished, turn off the pot and let it sit undisturbed for 4 minute natural release. Turn the steam release knob to Venting to release remaining pressure.

18. When the pin in the lid drops back down, open the lid.

19. Add the shrimp and the sausage. Gently stir in and put the lid back on, but don't close the steam valve, leave it on venting. Let it sit for 5 minutes to finish cooking the shrimp.

20. Open the lid and give it a stir. Taste the rice and adjust salt and/or seasoning as desired.

21. Serve with parsley on top, and some hot sauce, if desired.

Quinoa Taco Bowls

6 Servings | Prep Time: 10 mins. | Cook Time: 1 min. | Total Time: 31 mins.

Ingredients

1 cup Quinoa, rinsed

1 1/4 cup Water

1 cup Salsa

2 Tbsp Fresh Lime Juice, 1/2 a lime)

1 tsp Garlic Powder

1 tsp Oregano

1 tsp Cumin

1 tsp Chili Powder

1 tsp Kosher Salt (1/2 tsp table salt)

1/4 tsp Pepper

1 (15 oz) can Black Beans, drained & rinsed

1 (15 oz) can Corn, drained

Garnish

Cilantro

Avocado

Sour Cream

Jalapeño

Shredded Cheese

Instructions

1. Add all ingredients to the pressure cooker in order listed and place the lid on. Set the steam release knob to the Sealing position.

2. Press the Pressure Cook/Manual button, then the +/- button to select 1 minute. High Pressure.

3. When the cook time has finished, turn off the pot and let it sit undisturbed for 15 minute natural release. Then manually release any remaining pressure by turning the steam release knob to the Venting position.

4. Fluff with a fork and serve with any garnishes you like.

For Meal Prep

1. Package the garnishes/toppings in separate containers. Then divide the quinoa evenly between 5 meal prep containers. Keep refrigerated.

2. To reheat, microwave for 1 to 2 minutes, stirring halfway through. Add the garnishes after reheating.

Red Curry Vegetables

6 Servings | Prep Time: 15 mins. | Cook Time: 5 mins. | Total Time: 25 mins.

Ingredients

1 sm Sweet Onion, diced

2 1/2 cups Chopped Cauliflower Florets

2 1/2 cups Cubed Sweet Potato (or Butternut Squash)

1/2 cup *Red Lentils, rinsed

1 (13 oz) can Coconut Milk

1 (14 oz) can Diced Tomatoes, with juice

SAUCE

3 Tbsp Red Curry Paste (less if you have a spicy one)

1 cup Water, divided in half

3-4 lg cloves Garlic, pressed or grated

1 Tbsp Grated Fresh Ginger (or 1 1/4 tsp Ginger Powder)

2 tsp Soy Sauce, low sodium

1 tsp Turmeric

TO FINISH

2 tsp Brown Sugar (optional)

1 bunch Kale (optional) leafy part only

GARNISH

Lime juice, Fresh Cilantro Leaves

Instructions

1. Add onion, cauliflower, sweet potato, red lentils, 1/2 cup of the water, coconut milk, and diced tomatoes to the pot. Do not stir.

2. In a bowl, mix together the red curry paste, remaining 1/2 cup of water, garlic, ginger, soy sauce, and turmeric. Pour it over the vegetables in the pot. Do not stir.

3. Close the lid and set the steam release knob to the Sealing position.

4. Press the Pressure Cook/Manual button, then the +/- button to select 5 minutes. High Pressure. The pot will take several minutes to come to pressure.

5. When the cook cycle has finished, immediately turn the steam release knob to the Venting position to Quick Release the steam/pressure.

6. When the pin in the lid drops back down, open the lid.

7. Stir the curry and taste. Add optional brown sugar if desired.

8. Add the kale, if using, and stir it in. Let the pot sit for a few minutes while the kale wilts (the curry will thicken as it cools).

9. Serve alone or over rice or potatoes, with a squeeze of fresh lime juice and cilantro leaves.

Recipe Note
*Be sure to use Red Lentils. The other varieties won't cook in the short amount of time. The red lentils will break down and make this curry have a stew-like consistency.

Veggie Tortilla Pie

4-5 Servings | Prep Time: 15 mins. | Cook Time: 20 mins. | Total Time: 50 mins.

Ingredients

1 cup Water (for pressure cooker)

TORTILLA FILLING

5 (6") Corn Tortillas

1 cup Shredded Cheese, Mexican blend or cheddar, Monterey Jack

1 cup Grated Zucchini

1 cup Black Beans, canned, drained & rinsed

1 cup Frozen Corn Kernels

1 cup Salsa (not too wet)

SPICE MIX

(mix these together)

2 tsp Cumin

1/2 tsp Salt

1 tsp Garlic Powder

Instructions

1. Place 2 corn tortillas in the bottom of the 6" pan (just stack them together).
2. Sprinkle on about 2 Tbsp of the cheese.
3. Add 1/3 of the zucchini, then sprinkle on 1/3 of the spice mixture.
4. Then add 1/3 of the black beans, 1/3 of the corn kernels, and 1/3 of the Salsa.
5. Place a corn tortilla on top and gently press down.
6. Repeat steps 3-4.
7. Sprinkle 1/3 of remaining cheese, then place another corn tortilla on top and gently press down.
8. Repeat steps 3-4.
9. Sprinkle 1/2 of the remaining cheese (reserve the remaining cheese for the end).
10. Then add the remaining corn tortilla on top and gently press down. It's okay if it is slightly above the rim of the pan.
11. Cover the pan with foil and crimp it on tightly so moisture doesn't get in.
12. Add the water to the pressure cooker inner liner. Set the pan on the trivet and place in the pot.
13. Close the lid and set the steam release knob to the Sealing position.
14. Press the Pressure Cook/Manual button, then the +/- button to select 20 minutes. High Pressure.
15. When the cook cycle is finished, turn off the pot and let sit undisturbed for 10 minute natural release. Then turn the steam release knob to Venting to release the remaining pressure.
16. When the pin in the lid drops back down, open the lid.
17. Carefully remove the pan from the pressure cooker, using the handles of the trivet. Set in on a heat safe surface (still on the trivet).

18. Carefully open the foil and sprinkle the remaining cheese on top. Then close the foil and let it sit for 5-10 minutes so the cheese can melt a little, and the tortilla pie can set up.

19. When ready to serve, set a can on a plate. Then place the push pan on top of the can and gently push down to remove the tortilla pie from the pan. The plate will catch any juices.

20. Slice and serve with desired garnishes.

Recipe Note
If you don't have a push pan, just use a pan that is closest to the size of a 6" corn tortilla.

Dessert
sweets for the sweet

Rice Pudding

Ingredients

1 1/2 cups Arborio Rice (don't rinse)

2 1/4 cups Water

1/4 tsp Salt

3 cups Half and Half

3/4 cup Sugar

3 Eggs

1 tsp Vanilla

1/2 tsp Cinnamon (optional)

3/4 cup Raisins (optional)

Instructions

1. Add the rice, water, and salt to the pot. Place the lid on and set to Sealing.

2. Pressure cook on High for 3 minutes. When done, let sit undisturbed for 10 minutes (10 minute natural release).

3. Meanwhile, whisk together the milk, eggs, and vanilla. Set aside.

4. Release any remaining pressure and then open the lid.

5. Stir in the half and half mixture and the sugar & cinnamon, if using.

6. Turn on the Sauté setting and bring to a simmer, stirring constantly, then turn off the pot and remove the inner pot to a heat safe surface.

7. Stir in the raisins.

8. The rice pudding will thicken as it cools.

9. Serve warm or cold, with cream or whipped cream.

Chocolate Lava Cakes

4 Servings | Prep Time: 30 mins. | Cook Time: 7 mins. | Total Time: 42 mins.

Ingredients

MELT, MIX, SET ASIDE

4 oz Bittersweet Chocolate Chips, or Chocolate Bar, broken up (62% to 70% dark)

1/2 cup Unsalted Butter (room temp)

1/2 tsp Instant Espresso Powder (optional)

MIX TOGETHER

2 Eggs (room temp)

2 Egg Yolks (room temp)

3 Tbsp Flour

1 cup Powdered Sugar

1/4 tsp Salt

1 tsp Vanilla Extract

Tools Needed
- Trivet/Rack
- Electric Hand Mixer
- Mixing Bowls (1 microwave safe)
- 4 (6 oz) Ramekins (oven safe)
- Spatula, Measuring Cups/ Spoons

Instructions

1. Add 1 1/2 cups of water to a 6 qt or 8 qt pressure cooker. Set the trivet/rack in the bottom.

2. Spray the inside of the ramekins with cooking spray and set aside. Make sure you are using the 6 oz size ramekins.

3. In a microwave safe bowl, add the chocolate chips/chunks and the butter. Heat in microwave for 30 seconds. Then remove from microwave and slowly stir to combine. Heat again for 20 seconds and stir some more. Repeat again for 10 seconds if necessary. Stir until smooth and combined. Then stir in the espresso powder, if using. Set aside.

4. In a mixing bowl, add the eggs, yolks, flour, powdered sugar, salt, and vanilla. Use a hand mixer, mix on low speed until well combined.

5. Pour the chocolate mixture into the batter and mix on low speed to combine.

6. Pour the batter into the sprayed ramekins and distribute evenly between the four. The batter will be a bit thick.

7. Place the ramekins in the pot on the trivet/rack. 3 on the bottom, and 1 sitting on top of the 3. No need to cover them.

8. Close the lid, setting the steam release knob to Sealing, then press the Pressure Cook/Manual button, then the +/- button to select 7 minutes. High pressure.

9. When the cooking cycle is finished, turn the steam release knob to the venting position to do a Quick Release of the steam/pressure.

10. When the pin in the lid drops down you can open it. The cakes will be a little puffed up, but they will settle down.

11. Please use extreme caution as you remove the ramekins, they will be very hot, and very slippery. Use oven mitts and a small towel.

12. As soon as you are able to do so safely, invert the ramekins on individual small plates (or serve in the ramekin). Dust with powdered sugar, or garnish with ice cream, whipped cream, or fresh berries and, serve immediately.

Applesauce

Ingredients

6-8 Apples (any variety, peeled, cored, chopped)

1/4 cup Water*

Juice of 1/2 of a Lemon

1/2 tsp Cinnamon

OPTIONAL

2 Tbsp Brown Sugar

1 Tbsp Butter**

Instructions

1. Put the prepared apples in the pot with the other ingredients.

2. Close the lid and set the steam release knob to the Sealing position.

3. Press the Pressure Cook (or Manual) button, and then the +/- button to choose 4 minutes.

4. When the cooking cycle ends, let the pressure cooker sit undisturbed until the pin in the lid drops down (naturally release all of the pressure).

5. **If you are using butter, you can do a Controlled Quick Release, but do so gradually, to be sure no sauce spews out with the steam!

6. When the pin in the lid drops back down, open the lid.

7. Use a potato masher to mash the apples to the texture that you like. Or use an immersion blender to make really smooth.

8. If the applesauce is too watery for you, press the Sauté button and cook it down as much as you like, stirring constantly.

Recipe Notes
*You don't need much water to bring the pot to pressure with apples as they contain a lot of water.
**Butter is optional, but it does help reduce the foaming of the apples. If you choose not to use the butter, let the Instant Pot naturally release the pressure when it's done cooking. That will help ensure you don't get applesauce spewing from the steam release valve.

Baked Apples

Ingredients

1 1/2 cups Water (for the pressure cooker)

4 Apples (about 7-8 oz ea)

1/2 cup Butter, softened

1/4 tsp Vanilla

1 Tbsp Cinnamon

2 Tbsp Brown Sugar

1/3 cup Chopped Pecans (optional)

Instructions

1. Add 1 1/2 cups of water and a trivet/rack into the inner liner of the pressure cooker.

2. Wash and core the apples, leaving some of the bottom intact to hold the filling in. Use a melon baller or similar spoon-type utensil to scoop out a bit of the flesh. Not too much!

3. Mix the butter, vanilla, cinnamon, brown sugar, and pecans together and fill the apples with the mixture.

4. Put the apples in a pan* that is 7" in diameter and set on the trivet/rack and put it in the pressure cooker.

5. Put the lid on the pot and set the steam release knob to the Sealing position.

6. Press the Pressure Cook or Manual button, then the +/- button to select 11 minutes (9 minutes for a firmer result, 13 minutes for a softer result). Size and type of apple makes a difference. High Pressure.

7. When the cook cycle is finished, let the pot sit undisturbed for 5 minutes (5 minute natural release). Then turn the steam release knob to the Venting position to manually release the remaining steam/pressure.

8. When the pin in the lid drops down, open the lid and use tongs to carefully remove the apples.

9. Serve with some vanilla ice cream, or whipped cream for a decadent dessert!

Recipe Note

*Use a 6" diameter pan for a 3 qt pot, and a 7" or 8" diameter pan for an 8 qt pot.

Apple Crisp

6-8 Servings | Prep Time: 15 mins. | Cook Time: 1 mins. |Total Time: 28 mins.

Ingredients

7 med Apples (about 9 cups peeled/chopped)

Juice of 1/2 Small Lemon

3 tsp Cinnamon

1/4 tsp Nutmeg

1/8 tsp Ground Cloves

1/4 cup Sugar

1/2 tsp Vanilla Extract

3/4 cup Apple Juice, or cider

Crisp Topping

1/2 cup Butter, softened

1/2 cup Flour

1/2 tsp Salt

1/2 cup Brown Sugar, packed

1 1/4 cups Old Fashioned Oats

Instructions

1. Wash, peel, and cut the apples into large chunks (about 1 1/2"). Add them to the pot.

2. Add the lemon juice and toss the apples in it.

3. Sprinkle the cinnamon, nutmeg, cloves, and sugar over the apples. Toss together.

4. Add the vanilla and apple juice. Stir.

5. Add the butter, flour, salt, brown sugar, and oats to a mixing bowl. Use a pastry cutter, or your hands to mix together until combined, with small clumps that hold together.

6. Add the topping mixture to the pot, loosely, covering the apples. Don't stir.

7. Place the lid on the pot and set the steam release knob to the Sealing position.

8. Press the Pressure Cook/Manual button, then the +/- button to select 1 minute. High pressure.

9. When the cook time is finished, turn the steam release knob to the Venting position to do a Quick Release of the pressure.

10. When the pin in the lid drops back down, you can open the lid.

11. Use oven mitts to remove the inner pot to a heat safe surface. Let the apple crisp stand for a few minutes to cool a bit and thicken a little more. Serve warm with vanilla ice cream or whipped cream.

12. If you want to crisp up the topping, dish servings into oven safe dishes and broil on 450° for a few minutes. Alternatively you can transfer the entire pot of apple crisp to a baking dish and broil for a few minutes to crisp up the topping.

Banana Bread Bites

Yields 21 Bites | **Prep Time: 20 mins.** | **Cook Time: 13 mins.** | **Total Time: 34 mins.**

Ingredients

1/2 cup Butter, softened

1/2 cup Brown Sugar

1/2 cup White Sugar

2 Eggs, beaten

1 tsp Vanilla

3 Ripe Bananas, mashed

1/4 cup Buttermilk (or Sour Cream)

2 cups All Purpose Flour, sifted

1 tsp Baking Soda

1 tsp Baking Powder

1/2 tsp Cinnamon

1/2 tsp Salt

Instructions

1. Add 1 1/2 cups of water to the inner liner of the pressure cooker (2 cups if using the 8 qt).
2. Spray the bites molds with baking spray and set aside.
3. In a mixing bowl, use a hand mixer to cream the butter and sugars together.
4. Add the beaten eggs and vanilla to the creamed butter/sugar mixture. Use a spoon to mix.
5. In another mixing bowl, mash the ripe bananas using a fork.
6. Stir the bananas and buttermilk (or sour cream) into the butter/sugar mixture and mix well.
7. In another mixing bowl, sift together the flour, baking soda, baking powder, cinnamon, salt.
8. Add dry ingredients to wet ingredients and gently stir by hand, until just moistened. Don't over mix!
9. Spoon the batter into prepared bites mold*, fill openings half full (or use 2 oz ice cream scoop). Cover with foil, leaving some room for the bites to rise a little. Crimp the edges.
10. Set the trivet on the counter, and put the mold on it. Stack a second filled mold on top of that and carefully place it in the pot using the handles (*the third mold is done in a second batch*).
11. Close the lid and set the steam release knob to the Sealing position.
12. Press the Pressure Cook/Manual button, then the +/- button to select 14 minutes. High pressure.
13. After the cook time is finished, turn the steam release knob to Venting to quick release the pressure.
14. After all of the pressure is out and the pin in the lid drops down, open it and use silicone mitts or pot holders to very carefully remove the trivet, using the handles.
15. Carefully remove the foil. Release the bites from mold to a plate.
16. Serve the banana bread bites warm, slathered in butter, or let it cool and eat them as you like.

Tools You'll Need

- 6 or 8 qt Electric Pressure Cooker
- Trivet with long handles
- 3 Mixing Bowls
- Hand Mixer
- 2-3 Egg Bites Silicone Molds
- Baking Spray · Foil

Bread Pudding

Ingredients

1 1/2 cups Water, for pressure cooker

2 Tbsp Dark Rum*

1/2 cup Raisins

7 cups Day Old Brioche or Challah, Bread, cut or torn into cubes

1/2 cup Pecans, chopped

2 Eggs

1/4 cup Sugar

3/4 tsp Vanilla

3/4 tsp Cinnamon

1 Pinch of Salt

1/8 tsp Nutmeg

1 1/4 cups Half and Half, or milk

2 Tbsps Butter, melted

Bread Pudding Rum Sauce

4 Tbsps Butter

1/4 cup Sugar

1/3 cup Heavy Cream

1 Tbsp Dark Rum*

1/8 tsp Vanilla

Instructions

1. Soak the raisins in the rum for 15-30 minutes (Do not discard rum. Set aside). Or use hot water or hot apple juice to soak them.
2. Spray or butter a 1.5 to 2 quart oven safe dish. Set aside (I use a 7"x3" stainless pan).
3. Place the bread cubes and pecans in a mixing bowl. Toss to mix. Set aside.
4. In a separate bowl, whisk eggs and sugar until well combined.
5. Add vanilla, cinnamon, salt, nutmeg, and half and half. Whisk together well.
6. Drizzle in the melted butter as you whisk. Keep whisking until well combined.
7. Take the raisins from the rum (save the rum). Add the raisins to the bread cubes, tossing to mix.
8. Pour the custard mixture over the bread and lightly mix to coat all of the bread cubes. Then transfer to the prepared pan. Gently press down on the bread to help it absorb the custard. Cover the pan tightly with sprayed foil.

Cook the Bread Pudding

9. Put 1 1/2 cups of water into the inner liner of the pressure cooker.
10. Using a sling, or the handles of the rack, carefully lower the pan into the pressure cooker pot. It will need to sit on the rack, not directly on the bottom of the pot.
11. Place the lid on the pot and set the Steam Release Knob to Sealing.
12. Press the Manual (or Pressure Cook) Button. Set time to 30 minutes using the +/- button.
13. When cook cycle ends, let pot naturally release pressure for 15 minutes. Then manually release the remaining pressure by turning the knob to Venting.

14. When the pin in the lid drops open the lid and carefully remove the pan, using sling or the rack's handles (I wear my Silicone Mitts for this). Careful!

15. Let sit covered for a few minutes and prepare the sauce.

Make the Bread Pudding Sauce

16. In a small saucepan, melt the butter and sugar together over medium heat.

17. Whisk in the cream, rum (or rum flavoring), and vanilla.

18. Let mixture come to a low boil, stirring frequently, then reduce the mixture to a low simmer and let cook for 5 to 7 minutes, stirring frequently.

19. Take off heat and transfer to a small pitcher for serving.

20. Serve Bread Pudding with sauce or without.

Recipe Note
*You can omit the rum and soak the raisins in warm water or apple juice. For the sauce you can substitute 1/4 to 1/2 tsp Rum Flavoring Start with the smaller amount

Dulce de Leche Caramel

Ingredients

1 (14 oz) can Sweetened
Condensed Milk (SCM)

5 cups Water (for the
pressure cooker)

Tools You'll Need

Trivet (rack) (to go inside the
pressure cooker)

4 (4 oz) Canning Jars w/Lids
(or two 8 oz)

Spatula (to get all of the SCM
out of the can)

Instructions

1. Put the trivet in the inner pot of the pressure cooker. Pour 5 cups of water into the pot. If you are using a larger or smaller pressure cooker, you will need to increase or decrease the amount of water. You will want the water to come up most of the way, to just under the metal ring of the lid on the jars.

2. Open the can of sweetened condensed milk (SCM) using a can opener. Pour the SCM into the jars, dividing equally.

3. Put the lids on the jars, and twist to close just "finger tight." You don't want to tighten the lids too much at this point in the process.

4. Put the jars in the pot, setting them on the trivet/rack, not touching each other or the pot. Make sure the water level comes to just below the lid rings.

5. Close the lid and set to Sealing. Press the Pressure Cook/Manual button, then the +/- button to select 25 minutes (35-40 minutes for a darker result). Set to High Pressure.

6. After cooking time has ended, turn off the pot so it doesn't switch to the warm setting. Unplug it if necessary.

7. Let the pot do a full Natural Release, and do not disturb the jars until they (and the water) have cooled completely. This helps reduce the possibility of any jars breaking. It can happen, as it might in actual canning.

8. After the jars have cooled completely, remove from the pot to a towel to dry the jar.

9. Open one up and sample the goodness! If the texture is not as creamy as you'd like, just stir it with a fork really well or whisk it.

10. Keep in the fridge for up to a few weeks,

Recipe Note
Excellent to dip apples in!

Banana Bread

Ingredients

3 Ripe Bananas, mashed

1/2 cup Butter, softened

1/2 cup Brown Sugar

1/2 cup White Sugar

2 Eggs, beaten

1 tsp Vanilla

1/4 cup Buttermilk (or Sour Cream)

2 cups All Purpose Flour, sifted

1 tsp Baking Soda

1 tsp Baking Powder

1/4 tsp Cinnamon

1/2 tsp Salt

Instructions

1. Add 1 1/2 cups of water to the inner liner of the pressure cooker (2 cups if using the 8 qt).

2. Spray the 7" cake pan with baking spray and set aside.

3. In a mixing bowl, mash the ripe bananas using a fork.

4. In another mixing bowl, use a hand mixer to cream the butter and sugars together.

5. Add the beaten eggs and vanilla to the creamed butter/sugar mixture. Use a spoon to mix.

6. Stir the bananas and sour cream/buttermilk into the butter/sugar mixture and mix well.

7. In another mixing bowl, sift together the flour, baking soda, baking powder, cinnamon, salt.

8. Add the dry ingredients to the wet ingredients and gently stir by hand, until just moistened.

9. Spoon the batter into prepared cake/bundt pan and cover with foil, leaving some room for the bread to rise a little. Gently crimp the edges.

10. Set the trivet on the counter, and put the cake/bundt pan on it. Carefully lift it in the pot using the handles. Close the lid and set the steam release knob to Sealing.

11. Press the Pressure Cook/Manual button or dial, then the +/- button or dial to select 50 minutes for a bundt style pan, and 55 minutes for a regular 7" pan. High pressure.

12. After the cook time is finished, let the pot sit undisturbed for 15 minute natural release. Then turn the steam release knob to the Venting position to release the remaining pressure.

13. When the pin in the lid drops down, open it and use silicone mitts or pot holders to carefully remove the pan from the pressure cooker, using the trivet handles helps.

14. Carefully remove the foil, and let the banana bread sit for 10-15 minutes to cool a bit. If it needs to cook more, put it back in and cook a few minutes longer.

15. Serve the banana bread warm, slathered in butter.

New York Cheesecake

7 Servings | Prep Time: 30 mins. | Cook Time: 48 mins. | Total Time: 1 hr.

Ingredients

CRUST

1 cup Graham Cracker Crumbs (about 10 graham crackers)

1 Tbsp Sugar

3 Tbsp Butter melted

CHEESECAKE FILLING

2 (8 oz) pkgs Cream Cheese (room temp)

1/2 cup plus 2 Tbsp Sugar

1 1/2 tsp Vanilla

3 Tbsp Heavy Cream (room temp)

1 Tbsp Corn Starch

1/2 tsp Lemon Zest (optional)

2 Eggs (room temp)

SOUR CREAM LAYER

1 cup Sour Cream

2 Tbsp Sugar

1/4 tsp Vanilla

Instructions

Prepare the Pan

1. Use a 6 or 7"x 3" cheesecake pan (I use a 7" Push Pan, but you can use a springform pan as well. Whatever will fit comfortably in your pressure cooker).

2. Spray the pan with baking spray. If you have parchment paper, cut a piece to fit the bottom of your pan and spray that too. When using the 6" pan, you can line the sides with parchment to make a retaining wall as the filling will rise up a bit. Just cover the pan a little looser than you would with the 7".

Prepare the Pressure Cooker

3. Put 1 1/2 cups of cold water and the trivet in the inner liner of the pressure cooker.

Prepare the Crust

4. Place the graham crackers and sugar in a food processor. Pulse several times until the cookies turn into fine crumbs.

5. Add the melted butter and pulse several times to combine and soften the crumbs. You may need to scrape the bowl of the food processor and pulse a few more times.

6. Pour crust mixture into your prepared pan and use your fingers or the bottom of a small glass to press the mixture into place. Cover the entire bottom of the pan and come up the sides a little. You do not have to come all the way up the sides. You want the crust to be about 1/4" thick or so.

7. Put the pan in the freezer to chill and firm up while you prepare the cheesecake filling.

Prepare the Cheesecake Filling

8. Clean the crust residue out of the food processor.

9. Add the room temperature cream cheese and sugar. Process until smooth and creamy.

10. Add the vanilla, heavy cream, corn starch, and lemon zest, if using. Pulse several times until well combined and creamy.

11. Add the room temperature eggs last. Pulse a few short bursts until just combined. If you whip the eggs too much the cheesecake will puff up and won't have the right consistency.

12. Take the crust from the freezer and pour the filling into the pan.

13. Place the pan on a trivet/rack with handles and put it in the pot.

Cook the Cheesecake

14. Close the lid of the pressure cooker and set the steam release knob to Sealing.

15. Press the Manual (or Pressure Cook) button then the +/- button to choose 27 minutes, High pressure (Cook 5 minutes longer when using the 6" pan).

16. When cook cycle ends, let the cooker naturally release pressure for 15 minutes. Then manually release any remaining pressure.

17. When the pin in the lid drops, open the lid. VERY carefully lift the cheesecake pan out of the cooker and onto a cooling rack.

18. Cheesecake is done when it jiggles just a little (mostly in the center) when the pan is shook. It will firm up in the fridge. If it looks to liquid, put it back in and cook for another 5 minutes, and let naturally release for 10 minutes.

19. Let cool for an hour, then put the sour cream layer on.

Make the Sour Cream Layer

20. In a bowl, mix together the sour cream, sugar, and vanilla. Mix well.

21. Spread the sour cream layer on while the cheesecake is still warm, but not hot.

22. Put the cheesecake, still in the pan, into the fridge to set-up and chill for at least 4 hours before serving.

23. Serve as is, which is delicious, or top with berries, Blueberry Compote, Caramel Sauce, Lemon Curd, etc.

Dreamy Orange Cheesecake

6-8 Servings | **Prep Time: 20 mins.** | **Cook Time: 51 mins.** | **Total Time: 1 hr. 11 mins.**

Ingredients

CHOCOLATE CRUST

20 Chocolate Sandwich Cookies, filling scraped out

1 Tbsp Sugar

3 Tbsp Unsalted Butter, melted

CHEESECAKE FILLING

2 (8 oz) Pkgs Cream Cheese, room temp

1/2 cup Sugar

2 1/2 tsp Orange Zest

2 Tbsp Orange Juice

1 tsp Lemon Juice

2 tsp Vanilla

1/2 cup Sour Cream

1/2 cup Heavy Cream

2 Eggs, room temperature

Instructions

Prepare the Pan

1. Use a 7"x3" inch cheesecake pan (I use a 7" push pan. You can also use a springform pan).

2. Spray the pan with baking spray. If you have parchment paper, cut a piece to fit the bottom of your pan and spray that too.

Prepare the Pressure Cooker

3. Put 1 1/2 cups of water in the inner liner of the pressure cooker. Put the trivet in the pot as well.

Prepare a Sling

4. Usually made with aluminum foil, used to get the cheesecake in and out of the pot easily.

5. Fold a 28" length of foil along the long end 3 times. You will end up with a sling that is 28"x 3"

Prepare the Crust

6. Scrape the filling out of the cookies and place them in a food processor. Discard the filling.

7. Add 1 Tbsp sugar.

8. Pulse several times until the cookies turn into crumbs.

9. Add the melted butter and pulse several times to combine and soften the crumbs. You may need to scrape the bowl of the food processor and pulse a few more times.

10. Pour crust mixture into your prepared pan and use your fingers or the bottom of a small glass to press the mixture into place. Cover the entire bottom of the pan and come up the sides a little. You do not have to come all the way up the sides. You want the crust to be about 1/4" thick or so.

11. Put the pan in the freezer to chill and firm up while you prepare the cheesecake filling.

Recipe Continued on Next Page

Dreamy Orange Cheesecake

Prepare the Cheesecake Filling

12. Clean the crust residue out of the food processor.

13. Add the cream cheese and sugar and process until smooth and creamy.

14. Add the orange zest, orange juice, lemon juice, vanilla, sour cream, and heavy cream.

15. Pulse a several times until well combined.

16. Add the eggs last. Pulse just until combined. If you whip the eggs too much the cheesecake will puff up and won't have the right consistency.

17. Take the crust from the freezer and pour the filling into the pan.

18. Cover the pan with a paper towel, then with a piece of foil. Crimp the edges around the pan so it stays taut and secure.

19. Lay the sling out and set the pan on it, centered. Gather up the two ends and very carefully lift the pan and set it in the pressure cooker, leaving the sling with it. Just fold over the two ends of the sling on top of the pan.

Cook the Cheesecake

20. Close the lid of the pressure cooker and set the steam vent to the Sealing position.

21. Press the Manual (or Pressure Cook) button and then the + or - button to choose 36 minutes.

22. When cook cycle ends, let the cooker naturally release pressure for 15 minutes. Then turn the steam release knob to Venting and manually release the remaining pressure.

23. When the pin drops down, open the lid.

24. Gather up the two ends of the sling and VERY carefully lift the cheesecake pan out of the cooker and onto a cooling rack.

25. Leave covered for 10 minutes, then carefully peel off the foil/paper towel.

26. Test the doneness: The cheesecake should be a little jiggly when you shake the pan. It will firm up in the fridge. You don't want it super jiggly, and if it is, put the foil/paper towel back on and cook it for 5 more minutes, with a 10 minute Natural Release.

27. Let cool for 1 hour, then put the pan in the fridge to chill for at least 4 hours before serving. I prefer to make my cheesecake in the evening and let it cool overnight.

28. Remove from pan and serve as is, or with whipped cream.

Fun Stuff

in the form of dips, sauces, condiments, treats

Spinach Artichoke Dip

Yields about 2 cups | Prep Time: 10 mins. | Cook Time: 4 mins. | Total Time: 29 mins.

Ingredients

1/2 cup Water

4 cloves Garlic, pressed or very finely minced

1 (13.75 oz) can Artichoke Hearts, drained & roughly chopped

1/2 sm Onion, diced fine

1 (10 oz) pkg Frozen Chopped Spinach, partially thawed

3/4 cup Sour Cream (or plain Greek yogurt)

1/3 cup Mayonnaise

1/4 - 1/2 tsp Red Chile Flakes

8 oz Cream Cheese, cubed

1/4 tsp Salt

1/4 tsp Pepper

TO FINISH

1 1/2 cups Parmesan Cheese, shredded

1 cup Mozzarella Cheese, shredded

1/2 cup Monterey Jack Cheese, shredded

Instructions

1. Add all ingredients except Parmesan, Mozzarella, and Monterey Jack cheeses to the pot in the order listed. Break up the spinach a little. *Do not stir*.

2. Close the lid and set the steam release knob to the Sealing position.

3. Press the Pressure Cook/Manual button, then the +/- button to select 4 minutes. High Pressure.

4. When the cook cycle has finished, turn off the pot and let it sit undisturbed for 5 minutes. Then turn the steam release knob to the Venting position to release the remaining pressure.

5. When the pin in the lid drops back down, open the lid.

6. Stir in the parmesan, mozzarella, and Monterey jack cheeses. Let melt.

7. Transfer to a serving bowl and enjoy warm with bread, chips, or veggies.

8. You could also keep it in the pressure cooker and turn on the Warm setting so it stays warm.

9. Or, transfer to a small slow cooker and keep it on the Warm setting.

Recipe Note
You can freeze this dip. It reheats well.

Hummus

Ingredients

1 lb Dry Chickpeas, rinsed

1/2 tsp Baking Soda

8 cups Water

1/3 cup Fresh Lemon Juice

5 cloves Garlic

1/2 cup Sesame Tahini

1 1/2 tsp Cumin

1 tsp Kosher Salt

1/4 tsp Pepper

1/4 tsp Sweet Paprika

1/8 - 1/4 tsp Cayenne Pepper (optional)

2 Tbsp Warm Water

1 Tbsp Olive Oil

GARNISH

Drizzle of Olive Oil

1/2 tsp Sweet Paprika

2-3 Tbsp Pumpkin Seeds (Pepitas) roasted/salted

Instructions

1. Add the rinsed chickpeas, baking soda, and water to the pot. Stir.

2. Close the lid and set the steam release knob to the Sealing position.

3. Press the Pressure Cook/Manual button, then the +/- button to select 35 minutes. High Pressure.

4. When the cook time has ended, turn off the pot and let it do a full Natural Release (leaving the pot undisturbed until the pin in the lid drops back down).

5. Open the lid and carefully strain the cooked chickpeas. Rinse well with cool water. Set aside.

6. Add the lemon juice and garlic to a food processor. Pulse several times until garlic is minced.

7. *Optional Step:* Push the garlic into the lemon juice to submerge it. Let sit for a few minutes. This helps take some of the sharp taste from the garlic. The longer it sits in the lemon juice, the milder.

8. Add the chickpeas to the food processor and pulse a few times.

9. Add the tahini, cumin, salt, pepper, paprika, and cayenne. Pulse several times, then process for about 10 seconds. Start drizzling in the warm water and the mixture will start to loosen up.

10. Turn on the processor again and drizzle in the olive oil. Then taste the hummus and adjust salt, or any of the other seasonings to your taste.

11. Transfer hummus to a serving dish and drizzle with a little more olive oil. Add a few shakes of paprika, and sprinkle on the pumpkin seeds.

12. Serve with pita bread, chips, carrot sticks, or other vegetables. Spread on wraps/sandwiches.

Lemon Curd

Yield 3-4 cups | **Prep Time: 25 mins.** | **Cook Time: 9 mins.** | **Total Time: 34 mins.**

Ingredients

2 tsp Lemon Zest

1 cup Lemon Juice (about 4-5 lemons)

1 1/4 cups Sugar (reduce to 1 cup if you like it tart)

5 Tbsp Butter, softened

3 Eggs

2 Egg Yolks

Instructions

1. Pour 2 cups of water into the inner liner stainless pot. Place the trivet/rack in the pot.

2. In a mixing bowl, add the Zest of the lemons (careful not to get any of the white pith, you just want the yellow part).

3. Juice as many of the lemons as you need to get 1 cup of lemon juice. Set juice aside.

4. Add the sugar and butter to the mixing bowl with the zest, and cream together, using a hand mixer, until light and fluffy.

5. Add the eggs, egg yolks, and lemon juice to the butter mixture and mix on low speed until combined (it will be lumpy from the butter).

6. Pour into 1 cup or pint mason canning jars and put the lids on finger tight. Don't fill more than 3/4 full as the mixture will "rise" as it cooks (it does come back down when you stir it).

7. Place the jars on the trivet in the pot. Close the lid and set the steam release knob to sealing. Press the Pressure Cook/Manual button, then the +/- button to select 9 minutes.

8. After the cook time has finished, let the pot sit undisturbed for 10 minute natural release. Then turn the steam release knob to Venting and release any remaining pressure.

9. When the pin in the lid drops down, open the lid and **very carefully** remove the hot jars of curd. Use an oven mitt, or a canning jar retriever. Set the jars on a towel lined surface that can withstand the heat.

10. Carefully open one of the jars and stir the lemon curd with a fork or very small whisk until it comes together and is creamy. Repeat with remaining jars of lemon curd.

11. If there are any small lumps that you don't want in there, you can strain it into a bowl and refill the jars, or transfer to a container of your choice. Let cool for about 15 more minutes, then put in the fridge for a few hours to chill and firm up.

12. If you are going to use this lemon curd as a cake filling, add 1 1/2 Tbsp of corn starch to the mixture when you add the eggs. This will help it stay on the cake layer.

Apple Butter

Ingredients

5 lbs Apples (any variety, I use a mix) peeled, cored, chopped (about 10 apples)

2 Tbsp Fresh Lemon Juice

1/4 cup Apple Cider

1/4 tsp Ginger, powdered

1/4 tsp Nutmeg

1/4 tsp Allspice

1 1/2 tsp Cinnamon

1/8 tsp Ground Cloves

1 1/4 cups Sugar

1/4 tsp Kosher Salt (1/8 tsp table salt)

Instructions

1. Add all ingredients to the pot and place the lid on. Set the steam release knob to Sealing.

2. Press the Pressure Cook/Manual button, then the +/- button to select 7 minutes.

3. After the cook time ends, let the pot sit undisturbed for 10 minutes (10 minute Natural Release), then turn the steam release knob to the Venting position to Quick Release the remaining steam/pressure. Then turn off the pot.

4. When the pin in the lid drops down, open and use a potato masher to mash the apples.

5. Press the Slow Cook button, then the Adjust button until you have selected "More" (your model may vary. You want the highest heat setting for the Slow Cook Function). Adjust the time using the +/- button to select 5 hours. If your model gets as hot as an actual slow cooker, then use the Low heat. On Instant Pot® brand use "More."

6. Put the glass lid, or a silicone lid on the pot, but leave it ajar quite a bit so the apples can cook off their extra water and turn into apple butter. Stir once or twice throughout the slow cooking.

7. When the time is up, turn off the pot and use an immersion blender to blend the apple butter until it is smooth and glossy. If you don't have an immersion blender, let the mixture cool first, then use a regular blender.

Storage

8. Store in mason jars with lids, or other airtight container, in the fridge.

9. Once it has cooled, you can freeze apple butter in freezer bags, or in freezable canning jars (leave 1/2 inch head space).

Strawberry Jam

Yields 1 Pint | Prep Time: 10 mins. | Cook Time: 1 min. | Total Time: 11 mins.

Ingredients

4 cups Strawberries* diced
(~ 1 1/2 lbs)

1/2 cup Sugar (more for
sweeter)

2 Tbsp Lemon Juice, fresh

Optional - Slurry to Thicken
(mix together)

3 tsp Corn Starch

3 tsp Cold Water

Instructions

1. Wash the strawberries and pat dry with a paper towel. Then remove the stems/leaves.

2. Dice the strawberries and add them to the pot.

3. Add the sugar and lemon juice.

4. Close the lid and set the steam release knob to the Sealing position.

5. Press the Pressure Cook/Manual button, then the +/- button to select 1 minute. High Pressure.

6. When the cook cycle has finished, *turn off the pot* and let it sit undisturbed for 15 minute natural release. Then turn the steam release knob to Venting to release remaining pressure.

7. When the pin in the lid drops back down, open the lid.

8. Turn on the Sauté setting. Choose the Less/Low heat setting.

9. Let the mixture simmer for about 5 minutes, stirring frequently, until the jam thickens.

10. **Optional:** You can mix together the corn starch and water and stir it into the simmering jam to thicken it. This yields a thicker jam.

11. Transfer the jam to clean canning style jars with lids and keep in the refrigerator for up to 2 weeks.

12. If you want to can this, please refer to the canning jar manufacturer's guidelines for safe canning, Check the pressure cooker manufacturer's guide/information if wanting to pressure can. Many models do not can.

Recipe Note
*You can also use frozen berries.
Be sure to get the unsweetened kind.
There may be more water in them, so either cook
the water out at the end using Sauté, or use the
corn starch slurry to thicken.

Blueberry Jam

Yields ~ 1 Pint | Prep Time: 10 mins. | Cook Time: 7 mins. | Total Time: 32 mins.

Ingredients

1 1/2 - 2 lbs Fresh Blueberries

3/4 cup Sugar* (or 1/2 cup Honey) or to taste

2 Tbsp Fresh Lemon Juice

2 1/2 Tbsp Corn Starch (use 3 Tbsp if using Honey)

2 Tbsp Water (use 1 1/2 Tbsp if using Honey)

Instructions

1. Put the blueberries, sugar, and lemon juice in the pressure cooker inner pot. Close lid and set the steam release knob to the Sealing position.

2. Press the Pressure Cook/Manual button, then the +/- button to select 2 minutes. High pressure.

3. When the cook time is finished, let the pot sit undisturbed for 10 minute Natural Release. Then turn the steam release knob to Venting and release the remaining pressure.

4. Turn the pot's Sauté setting on to the **LOW** temperature.

5. In a small cup, mix the corn starch and water together until smooth. Set aside.

6. When the contents starts to simmer, stir and cook for 5 minutes to reduce it a little.

7. Add the corn starch slurry into the jam and stir. Cook a couple more minutes until thickened.

8. Turn off the pressure cooker and use silicone mitts, or a good set of pot holders to remove the inner pot to a cooling rack. Then give the jam another stir and leave it to cool.

9. When cooled, transfer to small mason jars with lids, and keep in the fridge up to 2 weeks.

Recipe Note
*If you want to use honey instead of sugar:
1. Pour the honey into the pot first. Set the Sauté setting to the LOW heat. Gently warm up the honey so it becomes thinner.
2. Then add the berries and continue with the recipe as written. I have noted the changes in amounts of other ingredients when using honey.
3. Much of that is because honey increases the liquid, so you will want to decrease the water for the slurry a little, and increase the corn starch a little.

Cranberry Sauce

Ingredients

1 (12 oz - 16 oz) pkg
Cranberries*, fresh or frozen

1/2 tsp Orange Zest (grated)

1/8 tsp Cinnamon (optional)

1/3 cup Orange Juice (fresh
squeezed is best) or water

1 cup Sugar** (If you like
it more tart, back off the
sugar by 1/4 cup)

Instructions

1. Add the cranberries, zest, cinnamon, and juice. Then pour the cup of sugar over the berries, but *do not stir*.

2. Close the lid and set steam release knob to the Sealing position.

3. Press the Pressure Cook/Manual button, and the +/- button to select 2 minutes (High pressure). When the cooking cycle finishes, turn the pot all the way off.

4. The berry mixture is a bit foamy at this point, so let the pressure naturally release for at least 5 minutes so the foam can subside.

5. Manually release the remaining pressure/steam in short bursts, until you are sure none of the sauce is going to spew out with the steam.

6. When all of the pressure is out of the pot and the pin in the lid drops, open and stir the cranberry sauce very well. Taste the cranberry sauce after it has finished cooking, and if you like it sweeter, add more sugar, 1 Tbsp at a time, stirring well.

7. Transfer to a serving dish and chill. It will thicken as it cools.

Recipe Notes
*This recipe can be doubled. Keep the cook time the same.
**Taste the cranberry sauce after it has finished cooking, and if you like it sweeter, add more sugar, 1 Tbsp at a time, stirring well.
If you like it more tart, back off the sugar by 1/4 cup before cooking.

Marinara Fresh Tomato Sauce

Yield 10 cups | Prep Time: 20 mins. | Cook Time: 40 mins. | Total Time: 1 hr. 20 mins.

Ingredients

4 Tbsp Olive Oil

1 small Onion, chopped

5 cloves Garlic, minced

5 lbs Tomatoes, unpeeled, chopped, about 9 1/2 cups (any variety or mix)

1/2 cup Red Wine

1/2 cup Water** (optional) see Notes

3 tsp Kosher Salt

1/2 tsp Pepper

1 Tbsp Cocoa Powder, unsweetened (cuts acidity and adds complexity. You won't notice it). But don't use dark!

2 tsp Basil, dried

2 1/2 Tbsp Italian Seasoning

1/4 - 1/2 tsp Red Pepper Flakes

2 tsp Oregano, dried

2 Tbsp Parsley Flakes, dried

3-4 (6 oz) cans Tomato Paste

Add Only if the Sauce is too Acidic (after pressure cooking)

2 tsp Sugar (if needed)

1/4 - 1/2 tsp Baking Soda (if needed)

Instructions

1. Before you begin the cooking process, have all of your veggies chopped & ingredients measured and ready to go.

2. Turn on the Sauté setting. When the pot is Hot, add the olive oil. Don't add the oil to a cold pot. Then add the onion and cook, stirring occasionally, until turning translucent.

3. Add the minced garlic and cook, stirring constantly, for about 30 seconds.

4. Add the tomatoes and stir. If your tomatoes aren't very juicy, add 1/2 cup of water.

5. Add the red wine, salt, pepper, cocoa powder, basil, Italian seasoning, red pepper flakes, oregano, and parsley flakes. Stir well to combine.

6. Add the tomato paste, but do not stir it in. Leave it sitting on top. If you stir it in it will be too thick and the pot may scorch and not come to pressure

7. Also, you will not have to add any additional liquid as the red wine and juice from the tomatoes is plenty to get the pot to pressure.

8. Close the lid and set the steam release knob to Sealing. Press the Pressure Cook/Manual button, then the +/- button to select 25 minutes.

9. After the cook cycle is finished, turn the pot off so it doesn't go to the Warm setting. Then leave it to Naturally Release the pressure until the pin in the lid drops down. Then open the lid and give the sauce a stir. Careful of the hot sauce splattering, so stir slowly!

10. Taste, and if the sauce is too acidic, either add the sugar, or add the baking soda. Stir it in and let it sit a while. Then taste and adjust as necessary.

11. Let the sauce cool, then use an immersion blender, food processor, or blender to puree it nice and smooth. It is best to do this when the sauce has cooled.

12. Transfer the sauce to jars with lids. Keep in the fridge for up to 5 days. You can freeze it as well.

Elderberry Syrup & Gummies

Ingredients

1 cup Elderberries, dried organic or non irradiated

4 cups Filtered Water

2 inch knob Ginger, chopped, fresh

Peel of 1 Lemon (try not to get any of the white pith)

2 Cinnamon Sticks, organic

OPTIONAL INGREDIENTS (add with the elderberries)

8-12 Cloves, whole

2 Tbsp Rose Hips, dried

Add After Pressure Cooking and Cooling

3/4 - 1 cup Raw Honey

Juice of 1 Lemon

FOR THE GUMMIES

1 cup Elderberry Syrup, divided

1/4 cup Gelatin (or 4 Knox packets, or 4 Tbsp)

2/3 cup plus 1 Tbsp Hot Water (not boiling)

Instructions

Syrup

1. Add all ingredients except honey and lemon juice to the inner liner of the pressure cooker.

2. Place lid on and set the steam release knob to the Sealing position.

3. Press the Pressure Cook (or Manual) button and then the +/- button and select 15 minutes. When the cook cycle finishes, turn off the pot so it doesn't go to the Warming setting. Let it fully Naturally Release the pressure.

4. Open the lid and take out the inner pot and strain the liquid into a glass bowl to cool.

5. Optional Step: Turn on the Sauté setting to the LOW temperature. Let the syrup simmer and reduce for 5 to 15 minutes, stirring occasionally, until desired thickness is achieved (I personally do not reduce mine).

6. When cool, about room temp, add the honey and whisk until fully incorporated (if you add the honey to hot syrup, it will kill off the good properties of the raw honey).

7. Add the juice of 1 lemon and whisk. Taste and add more honey if you like it sweeter, or more lemon if you like it tart.

8. Transfer the elderberry syrup to a bottle or mason jar with a lid and refrigerate for up to 2 months.

Elderberry Syrup Serving*:

For intensive use: Adults: 2 teaspoons 4 times daily, Children: 1 teaspoon 4 times daily.

For daily maintenance: Adults: 2 teaspoons daily , Children: 1 teaspoon daily.

Gummies

1. Place the silicone gummy molds on a baking sheet or large platter to support them.
2. In a small bowl, add 1/4 cup of the cooled elderberry syrup, and then whisk in the gelatin well to dissolve.
3. Add in the hot water and stir well until thoroughly dissolved.
4. Stir in the remaining elderberry syrup.
5. Carefully pour the mixture into each mold, filling to the top. A miniature baster/dropper works well for this.
6. Put the baking sheet with the molds on it into the refrigerator and chill about 1 hour, or until they become firm.
7. Pop the gummies out of the molds and place into a glass airtight container with a lid. Store in the refrigerator for up to 2 months.
8. Dosage can be from 1 to 3 gummies a day for kids 2 and over, depending on the size mold you use (check with pediatrician to be sure of dosage, and if these are right for your kids/situation).

Recipe Note
*As I'm not a medical professional, and am not intending to give any kind of medical advice, please check with your doctor before using and check for any drug interactions, etc. Do some research, and use at your own risk.

Vanilla Extract

Yields about 1 qt | Prep Time: 20 mins. | Cook Time: 30 mins. | Total Time: 1 hr. 40 mins.

Ingredients

24 Vanilla Beans (grade "B")

4 cups Vodka (cheapest kind) or use Vegetable Glycerin

TOOLS

Metal trivet/rack

2 (16 oz) Canning Jars, (w/lids)

8 (4 oz) Glass Bottles

5 oz hot sauce bottles also work

Recipe Notes

1. **Be Safe! Don't make vanilla near open flames (because of the alcohol).**

2. **Always let the pot Naturally Release FULLY, then let the jars cool.**

3. **Vanilla is best left in the jars with the beans, and only transferred to the gift bottles just before gifting as it will be stronger from sitting longer with the beans.**

4. **When you fill the gift bottles, put some of the beans in each one.**

5. **Shake the jars a few times a week after you first make the vanilla. Agitation helps the extraction continue.**

(make at your own risk)

Instructions

1. Cut all of the vanilla beans in half cross-ways, then split lengthwise 3/4 of the way, leaving attached (kind of like a banana peel).

2. Put 12 vanilla beans into each pint jar (that's 24 halves each). If you are using smaller or larger jars, adjust accordingly.

3. Pour the vodka into each jar, filling to the bottom lid thread.

4. Put the lids on the jars finger-tight (that's just tightened, and not as tight as when you store them).

5. Put 1 1/2 cups (3 in 8 qt) of water into the stainless inner pot of the pressure cooker. Then put the metal trivet/rack in. Set the jars on the metal rack, not touching each other of the side of the pot.

6. Put the lid on the pot and set the steam release knob to the Sealing position.

7. Press the Pressure Cook (or Manual) button then the +/- button to select 30 minutes.

8. After the cook is finished, turn off the pot so it doesn't go to the Warm setting.

9. Let the pot do a **FULL NATURAL RELEASE** of the pressure. You can let it sit after that as long as you want. I let the jars cool down quite a bit in the pot before I move them to a cooling rack to finish cooling.

10. You can keep the vanilla in the jars with the beans and keep extracting, which it will do indefinitely, or transfer to the bottles as you like (put some beans in the bottles).

11. Since vanilla makes a nice gift, I do use the 4 oz or 5 oz bottles, and add 2 or 3 of the beans to each bottle as that will look nice, and it keeps extracting.

Hot Sauce

Yields 18-20 oz | Prep Time: 25 mins. | Cook Time: 2 mins. | Total Time: 1 hr. 15 mins.

Ingredients

RED HOT SAUCE

3/4 - 1 lb Fresno Peppers, (or Cayenne)

1/4 cup Carrot, shredded

6 Cloves of Garlic, peeled & smashed

1 Roasted Red Pepper (I use jarred)

1 cup White Vinegar

1/4 cup Apple Cider Vinegar

1/2 cup Water

1 Tbsp Smoked Sea Salt (or use Kosher)

4 (5 oz) Glass Hot Sauce Bottles

OPTIONAL ADD-INS

1 Tbsp Smoked Paprika

2 Chipotle Chiles in Adobo

GREEN HOT SAUCE

12-16 oz Green Chiles (Hatch, Jalapeño, etc)

8 Cloves of Garlic, peeled & smashed

1 Green Bell Pepper, chopped (roast it first for even more flavor!)

1 cup White Vinegar

1/4 cup Apple Cider Vinegar

1/2 cup Water

1 Tbsp Smoked Sea Salt, (or Kosher)

4 (5 oz) Glass Hot Sauce Bottles

Instructions

1. Cut the tops off of the peppers and discard. Chop the peppers in thirds. Add to the inner liner of the pot. Wear gloves and eye protection. *Clean your knife handle & cutting board after chopping peppers. Don't rub your eyes!*

2. Add in the remaining ingredients.

3. Close the lid of the pressure cooker and set the steam release knob to the Sealing position.

4. Press Manual/Pressure Cook button, then the +/- button to select 2 minutes. High Pressure.

5. When cooking cycle ends, **LET IT FULLY NATURALLY RELEASE PRESSURE**. Do not do a Quick Release or manually release the pressure. You don't want to inhale pepper fumes!

6. After all of the pressure is out of the pot, open the lid carefully, facing it away from your face. **Don't breathe in the fumes!**

7. Let the mixture cool, then transfer it to a blender and blend until smooth. You can use an immersion blender (though I find the regular blender makes it smoother). Be very careful, and wear gloves and eye protection.

8. Strain blended mixture through a strainer, and fill your hot sauce bottles! You could also leave unstrained and put in jars to enjoy a thicker hot sauce.

9. The hot sauce gets better as it ages a bit. It will keep in the fridge for several months.

Iced Tea

Ingredients

8 cups Water

3 family sized Tea Bags (or 10-12 regular sized) I use Black Tea

For Sweet Tea

1/2 - 3/4 cup Sugar (or more or less to taste)

FUN VARIATIONS

4 Lemon Wedges (optional) add after pressure cooking while still hot. Let steep.

Mint Leaves (as many as you like, after pressure cooking)

2 tsp Fresh Rosemary Leaves (put them in cheesecloth and steep in the hot tea)

1 Tbsp Peach Simple Syrup per cup, after pressure cooking

Instructions

1. Pour the water into the inner liner of the pressure cooker.

2. Add the sugar, if using, and stir (You can add the sugar after pressure cooking if you'd prefer to taste it first).

3. Add the tea bags. Close the lid and set the steam release knob to the Sealing position.

4. Press the Pressure Cook/Manual button or dial and then the +/- to select 4 minutes. It will take a few minutes to come to pressure.

5. After cook cycle has finished, turn off the pot and let the pot sit undisturbed for 20-30 minute natural release. This will keep the tea from becoming bitter (Quick Release makes the water boil, causing bitterness).

6. Manually release the remaining pressure/steam. There shouldn't be much left. When the pin in the lid drops back down, open the lid and remove the tea bags.

7. Add sugar, stir, and taste. Start with the lesser amount and add more, if desired.

8. Serve over ice and garnish as you like.

Maple Candied Pecans

Ingredients

4 cups Pecan Halves, raw

2/3 cup Real Maple Syrup

1/4 tsp Maple Extract (optional, to enhance maple flavor)

1 tsp Vanilla

2 tsp Cinnamon

1/4 tsp Nutmeg

1/4 tsp Allspice

1/2 tsp Ginger, powdered

1/4 tsp Kosher Salt (or 1/8 tsp table salt)

1/4 tsp Cayenne Pepper (optional) or more to taste

1/2 cup Water

TO FINISH (optional)

1/2 cup White Sugar

1/2 cup Brown Sugar

1 1/2 tsp Cinnamon

Instructions

1. Add pecans, maple syrup, vanilla, cinnamon, nutmeg, allspice, salt, and cayenne powder to the pot of your pressure cooker. Turn on the Sauté setting and stir well. Cook for 5-10 minutes, stirring constantly.

2. Cancel the sauté setting. Add the water and stir gently. Place the lid on the pot and turn the steam release knob to the Sealing position.

3. Press the Pressure Cook/Manual button, then the +/- button to select 8 minutes. High Pressure.

4. While nuts are cooking, preheat oven to 300° F, and line a baking sheet with parchment paper.

5. When the cooking cycle is finished, turn off the pot and turn the steam release knob to the Venting position to do a Quick Release of the steam. Remove the lid and stir the nuts.

6. Pour the nuts onto the parchment lined baking sheet and spread them out into a single layer as much as possible.

7. Bake for 10 minutes. Then remove from oven and stir, place back in oven for about 5 more minutes, but check on them during baking to make sure they don't burn.

8. Remove from oven and let cool completely before packaging so they will not stick together.

If You Want to Add the Sugar Coating

1. While nuts are pressure cooking, add sugars and cinnamon to a gallon size plastic or paper bag. Shake up to mix. Set aside.

2. When you take nuts out of the oven, cool until still warm, but not hot, and still a bit sticky.

3. Add half of the nuts to the bag and shake them to coat with the sugar mixture Be careful and close the bag before shaking. Remove nuts to a fresh sheet of parchment to continue cooling. Repeat with second half of nuts. Or, just do half of the nuts and you'll have two varieties!

4. Discard leftover sugar mixture, or save it for toast!

Spice Blends

spice is life

Cajun Spice Blend

4 oz | Prep Time: 15 mins. | Cook Time: 0 mins. | Total Time: 15 mins.

Ingredients

2 Tbsp Granulated Garlic (or garlic powder)

2 Tbsp Onion Powder

2 Tbsp Basil

2 Tbsp Oregano

1 Tbsp Thyme

1 Tbsp Black Pepper

1 Tbsp Cayenne Pepper (use 1 tsp for less spicy version)

2 Tbsp Kosher Salt

6 Tbsp Paprika

Instructions

Add all ingredients to a mason style jar, put the lid on, and shake well to mix the spices up. Store covered, in a cool, dry place.

This recipe can be doubled, tripled, etc.

Easy Taco Seasoning

~1 cup | Prep Time: 20 mins. | Cook Time: 0 mins. | Total Time: 20 mins.

Ingredients

3 Tbsp Chili Powder

1/2 tsp Garlic Powder

1/2 tsp Onion Powder

1/4 tsp Cayenne Pepper

1/2 tsp Oregano

1 tsp Paprika

3 1/2 tsp Cumin

1 tsp Salt (more or less to taste)

2 tsp Black Pepper

1 tsp Corn Starch

Instructions

Mix all ingredients together in a bowl.

Transfer to an air-tight container. I like to use mason jars.

This Easy Taco Seasoning recipe is fairly low sodium. If you want a little more salt, add 1 tsp to the recipe.

Onion Soup Mix

1 Packet | Prep Time: 15 mins. | Cook Time: 0 mins. | Total Time: 15 mins.

Ingredients

4 Tbsp Minced Dry Onion Flakes

2 Tbsp Beef Bouillon Powder, low sodium

½ tsp Onion Powder

¼ tsp Parsley Flakes

1/8 tsp Ground Celery Seeds

1/8 tsp Black Pepper

1/8 tsp Sweet Paprika

1/8 tsp Salt (optional)

Instructions

Mix all ingredients together and store in an air tight container, such as a mason jar. Store in a cool dark place, such as a cupboard or pantry.

This recipe can be doubled, tripled, etc.

Ranch Dressing Mix

~1 cup | Prep Time: 20 mins. | Cook Time: 0 mins. | Total Time: 20 mins.

Ingredients

1/3 cup Buttermilk Powder

1/3 cup Dried Parsley Flakes

1 Tbsp Dried Chives

1 Tbsp Dill Weed

1 Tbsp Onion Powder

1 Tbsp Garlic Powder

1 Tbsp Pepper

1 tsp Salt (use more or less to taste)

Instructions

Mix all of the ingredients together well. Store in an air tight container in the refrigerator for up to 3 months.

3 Tbsp. is equal to 1 ranch packet.

To Make Dressing*

Mix 1 Tbsp of Ranch Dressing Mix with 1/3 cup milk and 1/3 cup of mayo or Greek yogurt. Stir well and let stand/chill for 15 minutes before using.

To Make Dip

Mix together 1 Tbsp of Ranch Dressing Mix with 1 cup mayo or sour cream and 1 cup cottage cheese. Let stand/chill for 20 minutes before serving. Taste and add more dressing mix if desired.

Baked Chicken Spice Rub

~1/2 cup | Prep Time: 10 mins. | Cook Time: 0 mins. | Total Time: 10 mins.

Ingredients

1 1/2 Tbsp Kosher Salt (or 2 tsp table salt, or to taste)

1 Tbsp Pepper

1 1/2 tsp Onion Powder

1 1/2 Tbsp Garlic Powder

1 1/2 Tbsp Smoked Paprika

Instructions

Add all ingredients to a mason style jar, put the lid on, and shake well to mix the spices up. Store covered, in a cool, dry place.

Use 1 Tbsp of the spice rub for 2 average sized (8 oz) chicken breasts.

Ribs Spice Rub

~1/2 cup | Prep Time: 20 mins. | Cook Time: 0 mins. | Total Time: 20 mins.

Ingredients

2 Tbsp Kosher Salt

1 Tbsp Coarse Black Pepper

1 Tbsp Cumin Powder

1 Tbsp Chili Powder

2 Tbsp Smoked Paprika

1 Tbsp Sweet Paprika

1 Tbsp Garlic Powder, or granulated garlic

1 Tbsp Onion Powder

2 Tbsp Brown Sugar

1 tsp Cayenne Pepper

Instructions

Add all ingredients to a mason style jar, put the lid on, and shake well to mix the spices up. Store covered, in a cool, dry place.

I suggest doubling this recipe. It keeps very well.

Rotisserie Chicken Spice Rub

Ingredients

1 1/2 Tbsp Kosher Salt* (or 2 tsp table salt)

1 tsp White Pepper

1/2 tsp Black Pepper

1 1/2 Tbsp Garlic Powder

1 Tbsp Onion Powder

1 Tbsp Sweet paprika

1 Tbsp Smoked Paprika

1/2 tsp Cayenne Pepper

1 tsp Thyme (or Tarragon)

Instructions

Add all ingredients to a jar and place the lid on. Shake well to combine. Store in a cool, dark place.

Rub on chicken or other meat before cooking.

This recipe can be doubled, tripled, etc.

Fajita Seasoning Mix

Ingredients

2 Tbsp Chili Powder

1 tsp Cumin

1/2 tsp Garlic Powder

1/2 tsp Onion Powder

1 tsp Salt

1 tsp Coriander Powder

1 tsp Paprika

1/4 tsp Cayenne

1 tsp Sugar

1 tsp Corn Starch

1/2 tsp Tajin (optional) a Mexican seasoning w/lime

Instructions

Add all of the ingredients together and put in a 1 cup mason jar with a lid. Give it a good shake to mix it up.

Store in a cool, dark place.

Use on chicken or pork, or in ground beef for fajitas, tacos, burritos, etc.

Time Charts & More

how long do I cook it?

Pressure Cooking Time Chart - Vegetables

Cook times are approximate. Please use as a guide only.

Vegetables*	Fresh (in minutes)	Frozen (in minutes)
Artichoke**, whole, trimmed	9 – 12	11 – 13
Artichoke, hearts	4 – 5	5 – 6
Asparagus, whole or cut	0 – 2	1 – 3
Beans, green, yellow or wax, whole	1 – 2	2 – 3
Beets**, small, whole	11 – 13	13 – 15
Beets, large**, whole	20 – 25	25 – 30
Broccoli, florets	0 – 2	1 – 3
Broccoli, stalks	3 – 4	4 – 5
Brussels sprouts, whole	3 – 4	4 – 5
Cabbage, all colors, shredded	2 – 3	3 – 4
Cabbage, all colors, wedges	3 – 4	4 – 5
Carrots, sliced or shredded	1 – 2	2 – 3
Carrots, whole or chunked	2 – 3	3 – 4
Cauliflower florets	0 – 2	1 – 3
Celery, chunks	2 – 3	3 – 4
Collard Greens	4 – 5	5 – 6
Corn, kernels	1 – 2	2 – 3
Corn, on the cob	2 – 4	3 – 4
Eggplant, slices or chunks	2 – 3	3 – 4
Endive	1 – 2	2 – 3
Escarole, chopped	1 – 2	2 – 3
Green beans, whole	2 – 3	3 – 4
Greens (beet, kale, spinach, chard), chopped	3 – 6	4 – 7
Leeks	2 – 4	3 – 5
Okra	2 – 3	3 – 4

**Most vegetables require a Quick Pressure Release. Some potatoes, beets, and a few others need to NPR for ~10 minutes.

Pressure Cooking Time Chart - Vegetables

Cook times are approximate. Please use as a guide only.

Vegetables*	Fresh (in minutes)	Frozen (in minutes)
Onions, sliced	2 – 3	3 – 4
Parsnips, sliced	1 – 2	2 – 3
Parsnips, chunks	2 – 4	4 – 6
Peas, in the pod	1 – 2	2 – 3
Peas, green	1 – 2	2 – 3
Potatoes, in cubes	7 – 9	9 – 11
Potatoes**, whole, baby	10 – 12	12 – 14
Potatoes**, whole, large	12 – 15	15 – 19
Pumpkin, small slices or chunks	4 – 5	6 – 7
Pumpkin, small, whole (1-2 lbs)	12 – 15	N/A
Rutabaga, slices	3 – 5	4 – 6
Rutabaga, chunks	4 – 6	6 – 8
Spinach	1 – 2	3 – 4
Squash, acorn, slices or chunks	6 – 7	8 – 9
Squash, butternut, slices or chunks	8 – 10	10 – 12
Sweet potato, in cubes	7 – 9	9 – 11
Sweet potato**, whole, small	10 – 12	12 – 14
Sweet potato**, whole, large	12 – 15	15 – 19
Sweet pepper, slices or chunks	1 – 3	2 – 4
Tomatoes, in quarters	2 – 3	4 – 5
Tomatoes, whole	3 – 5	5 – 7
Turnip, chunks	2 – 4	4 – 6
Yam, in cubes	7 – 9	9 – 11
Yam, whole**, small	10 – 12	12 – 14
Yam, whole**, large	12 – 15	15 – 19
Zucchini, slices or chunks	2 – 3	3 – 4

Pressure Cooking Time Chart - Meat/Poultry/Fish

Meat - Poultry - Fish	Cook Time high pressure (in minutes)	Pressure Release NPR= natural release QR=quick release
Beef - Stew Pieces	25	10 min. NPR
Beef - Large Pieces	35	10 min. NPR
Beef - Ribs	35	10 min. NPR
Oxtails	50	15 min. NPR
Venison Roast	15 min. per lb	10 min. NPR
Chicken - Breasts	6 min. per lb	10 min. NPR
Chicken - Whole	7 min. per lb	10 min. NPR
Chicken - Bone Stock	120-240	25 min. NPR
Eggs - Lg	5	5 min. NPR
Lamb - Leg	15 min. per lb	10 min. NPR
Pork - Butt Roast	15 min. per lb	10 min. NPR
Pork - Baby Back Ribs	15-20 min. per lb	10 min. NPR
Pork Chops - Thin	6-8	10 min. NPR
Pork Chops - Thick	10-14	10 min. NPR
Pork Chops - Boneless	7-15	10 min. NPR
Pork - Country Style Ribs	20-24	10 min. NPR
Ham - Bone-In	3-5 min. per lb	25 min. NPR
Ham - Spiral	3-5	10 min. NPR
Pork Loin Roast	45	10 min. NPR
Pork Tenderloin	0-2	15 min. NPR
Crab Legs	3	QR
Lobster Tail	4-5	QR
Salmon	2-3	QR
Salmon - Pot-In-Pot	3-5	QR
Shrimp - Large	2-3	QR

Cook times are approximate. Please use as a guide only.

I'd like to say that cooking charts are an absolute, but when it comes to food, there are many variables.

Pressure cooker cook times are based on many things, such as thickness, density, size, temperature at the time of cooking, and even age as in the case of eggs, beans, and some grains.

Different pots will vary in temperature as well.

Once you start cooking with your electric pressure cooker you will find what works for your situation. I suggest starting with the lower amount of time since you can cook longer if necessary.

When cooking most meats in the electric pressure cooker, it is good to do a NPR - Natural Pressure Release so the meat stays moist.

Quick Releasing beef, pork, most chicken, etc., will draw the moisture out and cause it to be dry and tough.

When cooking fish, you can do a Quick Release so it doesn't overcook. You can use Low Pressure for delicate fish as well as shellfish.

The recipes in this book are all High Pressure, unless otherwise stated in the instructions.

Each recipe will tell you whether to use a NPR or a QR.

When cooking beans and legumes in the electric pressure cooker, you have the choice to soak them or cook from dry, unsoaked.

It depends on the time you have to make the recipe. The great thing about a pressure cooker is that dry beans are not a problem! Some cook pretty fast from dry.

I suggest always using a NPR - Natural Pressure Release when cooking beans and legumes, pulses, etc.

They foam up while cooking, and a Quick Release could cause the foamy bean liquid to spew out with the steam, or worse, clog the vent and the steam would not be able to escape.

Be careful not to overfill the pot when cooking these foods. 1/2 to 2/3 full is the max you should fill it.

Beans & Legumes	Unsoaked high pressure (in minutes)	Soaked high pressure (in minutes)
Adzuki Beans	20-25	10-15
Black Beans	20-25	6-8
Black-Eyed Peas	14-18	4-5
Chickpeas	35-40	10-15
Kidney Beans - Red	20-25	7-8
Kidney Beans - White	25-30	6-9
Lentils - Green	8-10	--
Lentils - Yellow	1-2	--
Lima Beans	12-14	6-10
Navy Beans	20-25	7-8
Peas	10-15	15-20
Pinto Beans	25-30	6-9
Soy Beans	35-45	18-20

Grains	Time high pressure (in minutes)	Water Ratios
Barley-Pearl	20-22	1:2.5
Congee	15-20	1:4 - 1:5
Millet	15-20	1:4 - 1:5
Oatmeal	2-3	1:2
Steel Cut Oats	9-11	2:3
Porridge	5-7	1:6 - 1:7
Quinoa	1	1:1.25
Rice - Basmati	3-4	1:1
Rice - Brown	20-22	1:1
Rice - Jasmine	3	1:1
Rice - White	3	1:1
Rice - Wild	20-25	1:2

Grains and rice can have varying cook times, based on the variety, fiber content, and even the age of the grain.

As with beans, old grains may require a longer cook time. Check the packaging of your grains or rice to find out the expiration date.

Unfortunately, you won't always know if you have old grains, as the age at the time of packaging may be unknown.

Start with the lower amount of time.

Grains and most rice should be Quick Released, except in certain situations.

My recipes tell you when to QR and when to NPR the grains or rice.

Pantry Staples for Pressure Cooking

My recipes use most of these ingredients at some point. Though you don't have to have all of these, many will last a long time in your pantry and are nice to have on hand.

LIQUIDS
Broth (veg, beef, chicken)
Apple Juice
Dr. Pepper
Dark Beer
Red Wine

DRY BEANS/LEGUMES
Pinto Beans
Black Beans
Navy Beans
Red Kidney Beans
Small Red Beans
Garbanzo Beans
15 Beans Mix
Great Northern Beans
Split Peas
Lentils (different varieties)

PASTA
Spaghetti
Cappellini
Fettuccine
Bow Tie
Penne
Ditalini
Orzo
Gnocchi
Lasagna
Ziti
Rigatoni
Shells

OILS & VINEGARS
Olive Oil
Neutral Oil (Peanut, Sunflower, Canola)
Balsamic Vinegar
Flavored Balsamics
Apple Cider Vinegar
Red Wine Vinegar
Rice Wine Vinegar

SPICES & FLAVORFUL INGREDIENTS
Kosher Salt
Onion Soup Mix
Ranch Dressing Packets
Au Jus Packets
Taco Seasoning
Cajun Seasoning
Italian Seasoning
Bouillon (veg, beef, chicken)
Garlic Powder
Onion Powder
Dehydrated Onions
Cumin
Chili Powder Curry Powder
Oregano
Thyme
Bay Leaves Pepper
Smoked Paprika
Basil
Seasoned Salt
Vanilla
Flavored Extracts

GRAINS
Quinoa
Whole Oats (Oat Groats)
Steel Cut Oats
Old Fashioned Oats
Jasmine Rice
Long Grain White Rice
Jasmine Rice
Basmati Rice
Brown Rice

VEGETABLES
Potatoes
Sweet Potatoes
Spaghetti Squash
Onions
Shallots
Scallions
Garlic
Cabbage
Carrots
Celery

CONDIMENTS
Worcestershire Sauce
Liquid Smoke
Ketchup
Yellow Mustard
Dijon Mustard
Curry Paste
BBQ Sauce
Soy Sauce
Sriracha
Hot Sauce

Pantry Staples for Pressure Cooking

CANNED GOODS
Diced Tomatoes
Stewed Tomatoes
Tomato Sauce
Chipotles in Adobo
Coconut Milk
Evaporated Milk
Sweetened Cond. Milk
Broths
"Cream of" Soups
Mushrooms
Corn
Pumpkin Puree
Jarred Spaghetti Sauce
Jarred Marinara Sauce

MEATS - Keep in Freezer
BEEF
Beef Roasts (Chuck, Rump, etc.)
Oxtails
Ground Beef
Meatballs
PORK
Pork Shoulder Roast
Pork Ribs (Baby Back & Country Style)
Ham Hocks

Cooked Ham
Bacon
Poultry
Chicken Thighs
Chicken Breasts
Chicken Wings
Chicken Legs
Ground Turkey Kielbasa
Smoked Turkey Necks
Meatballs
Whole Chickens

Kitchen Conversions

1/16 teaspoon	dash
1/8 teaspoon	a pinch
3 teaspoons	1 Tablespoon
1/8 cup	2 Tablespoons
1/4 cup	4 Tablespoons
1/3 cup	5 Tablespoons
1/2 cup	8 Tablespoons
3/4 cup	12 Tablespoons
1 cup	16 Tablespoons
1 pound	16 ounces

8 fluid oz	1 cup
1 pint	2 cups
1 quart	2 pints or 4 cups
1 gallon	4 quarts or 16 cups

High Altitude Cook Time Adjustments for Electric Pressure Cookers

Increase Cook Time 5% for every 1,000 feet Over 2,000' Elevation

Elevation	% of Increase	Multiply Cook Time By
3,000'	5%	1.05
4,000'	10%	1.10
5,000'	15%	1.15
6,000'	20%	1.20
7,000'	25%	1.25
8,000'	30%	1.30
9,000'	35%	1.35
10,000'	40%	1.40

Round to Nearest Whole Minute

Frequently Asked Questions

These are some of the questions that I get asked about using a pressure cooker, and pressure cooking in general.

Why is My Cook Time longer Than What the Recipe Says?

Traditionally, cook times are measured once the food is in the appliance/pot after warming up. For example, You preheat your oven before adding the cake, right? Well the recipe will not include that preheating time, just the amount of time it takes to cook the cake in the oven.

The difference when pressure cooking is that the food happens to be in the pot during that warming up (pressure building) phase. The cook time starts when the pot has reached full pressure.

Having said that, the food is actually cooking/thawing/warming during this preheating phase, but that is not considered part of the actual cook time.

If I Double a Recipe Do I Need to Double the Cook Time?

Not in most cases. Since pressure cooking times are calculated by size and density of the food, having more or less of the same size doesn't change how long they need to cook.

For example, a whole potato will take about 25 minutes to cook. If you have 8 potatoes of the same size in the pot, it will still only take about 25 minutes to cook them all. If some of those potatoes are much larger than the others, they will not be cooked all the way. Smaller potatoes will be overcooked.

Here is an example of when you do need to increase/decrease the cook time.

Let's say you are cooking a pot roast. If you have a 3 pound roast, it may need to cook for 80 minutes (depending on the thickness). If you double the size of your pot roast and cook a 6 pound roast, you will need to increase the cook

time (to about 110 minutes) as that will be a larger, thicker roast. It will need to cook longer for the pressure to reach all the way to the center to break down the cartilage and such to make it tender.

Now if you were to cut that 6 pound roast in half, you will end up with two 3 pound roasts that will cook in the 80 minute time frame.

If you cut the roast into 1 pound pieces, you can decrease the cook time by almost half (about 50 minutes) because those pieces are smaller and require less cook time. So whether you have three 1 pound pieces , or six 1 pound pieces, the cook time will be the same (about 50 minutes).

Why Do Some Recipes Take A Long Time To Come To Pressure?

The amount of time it takes for a pot to come to pressure is due to:

How full the pot is. A fuller pot will take longer to come to pressure because it has to heat the whole amount before steam starts being produced.

The type of food in the pot. Liquids will take less time to come to pressure than denser foods, or recipes with frozen meat in them.

Why Didn't My Pot Come To Pressure?

Usually this is because there was not enough thin liquid in the pot to create the amount of steam necessary to bring the pot to pressure (see "BURN" warning).

Another reason could be that the pot was not sealed correctly, and the steam escaped before it could build up. Check the steam release knob (turn it to Sealing), and check to make sure the silicone sealing ring is installed properly.

About the Author

Sandy Clifton is a total foodie!

She is a cook, recipe developer, instructor, and food blogger.

She is the founder of Simply Happy Foodie, a blog that has hundreds of easy and delicious recipes, and millions of followers.

Sandy grew up, and still lives in Washington State. She loves living there among the evergreen trees with her husband Paul, and Pug Gizmo.

She enjoys gardening, photography, movies, and the ballet. She has an affinity for techy gadgets and cookware!

Sandy's love of cooking grew from an early age, watching her mom and nana cook. She has always loved it. She enjoys teaching others how to cook, and to use their electric pressure cookers!

You can find her online at:

www.SimplyHappyFoodie.com

Index

Printed in Great Britain
by Amazon

25072300R00130